100 Years of Soviet and Russian Military Parades 1917-2017 ★ Volume 1

# The Red Army On Parade
### 1917 ★ 1945

*To Elizabeth & Katya, with fond memories of skating on Red Square at the dawn of the 21st Century.*

The Red Army On Parade 1917-1945
©Canfora Publishing/Grafisk Form&Förlag, 2017
Print: Printbest , Estonia

Canfora Publishing/Grafisk Form&Förlag, 2017
Upplandsgatan 96A
113 44 Stockholm, Sweden
info@canfora.se, www.canfora.se

# Contents

| | |
|---|---|
| Foreword | 4 |
| Soviet and Russian Military Parades - An Individual Perspective | 5 |
| Red Square | 7 |
| The Russian Revolution and Soviet Industrialisation | 10 |
| Introduction | 12 |
| 1. Early Russian Parades 1917-1920 | 19 |
| 2. Soviet Military Parades in the 1920s | 31 |
| 3. Soviet Military Parades in the 1930s | 55 |
| 4. Soviet Military Parades in the Pre-War 1940s | 137 |
| 5. The Wartime 7th November Military Parades | 154 |
| 6. Soviet Victory Parades in 1945 | 180 |
| 7. Red Army "Tekhnika" Displayed on Red Square 1917-1945 | 222 |
| Bibliography | 248 |
| Glossary | 250 |

**Уважаемые друзья!**

Перед Вами уникальная книга об истории военных парадов на Красной площади.

Она многое расскажет об истории нашей страны – России, самоотверженности ее народа, героических традициях Армии и Флота.

Примечательно, что автор книги – иностранец, который, живя в России, по его признанию, полюбил и понял нашу страну.

Это по-настоящему приятно.

Несмотря на то, что книга охватывает столетний период времени, история военных парадов в России, безусловно, глубже.

В судьбах нашего Отечества парады имеют особый, можно сказать, священный смысл. Все они посвящались важнейшим событиям жизни государства, победам русской армии в великих сражениях на суше и на море.

Первый из них состоялся в эпоху Петра Великого, когда Москва встречала русское воинство, одержавшее победу над шведскими войсками у крепости Нотебург в 1702 году.

Самый главный парад в истории нашей страны проведен на Красной площади летом 1945-го. Это был парад Великой Победы нашей страны в Великой Отечественной войне.

Сегодня военные парады, проходящие во многих российских городах, – воплощение нашей благодарности поколениям, защитившим и отстоявшим независимость Отечества, и – напоминание, что нет такой силы, которая смогла бы покорить наш народ.

Грандиозность, торжественность и зрелищность военных парадов в России по достоинству оценена не только у нас в стране, но и за рубежом. Об этом свидетельствует живой интерес к ним иностранных политиков, журналистов и военных специалистов.

В России помнят свою героическую историю и свято чтят традиции. Поэтому уверен, что книга об истории военных парадов будет иметь продолжение.

**Министр обороны Российской Федерации**
**Герой Российской Федерации**
**генерал армии**

Сергей ШОЙГУ

### Dear reader!

This is a rather rare and unique book about history of military parades on the Red Square.

It will tell you a lot about history of Russia, selflessness of its people, and heroic traditions of the Russian Armed Forces.

The book is unique for the fact that it is written by a foreigner, who fell in love with this country as he admits and got an insight about it while living here.

It is truly pleasant.

The book covers a century of military parades in Russia. However, this history certainly stretches back further.

Military parades have a special, even sacred significance in history of our Fatherland. They have been devoted to most important events in this country, Russian victories in great battles at sea and on land.

The first parade took place in times of Peter the Great, when Moscow was saluting the Russian troops that had defeated Swedish army at the Noteburg fortress in 1702.

The main parade in our history was held on the Red Square in summer 1945, marking the Great Victory in the Great Patriotic War.

Modern parades that take place countrywide serve as gratitude to generations that had defended this country and upheld its independence, and as a reminder that there is no force on earth that could conquer our people.

The Russian military parades are highly appreciated for their grandeur, solemnity and attractiveness not only in this country but also abroad. This is reflected in keen interest of foreign politicians, journalists and military experts in this subject.

The Russian people do remember its heroic history and honor the traditions. Therefore, I am completely convinced that we will see more books about history of military parades in the future.

**Minister of Defence of the Russian Federation**
**Hero of the Russian Federation**
**General of the Army**

**Sergei SHOIGU**

# Soviet and Russian Military Parades – An Individual Perspective

The annual Soviet military parades held on Moscow's Red Square were for the majority of the 20th Century the Soviet Union's military showcase for the world; annual demonstrations of military technology and projected military might. Growing up in Great Britain during the 1970s, the Soviet era Red Square military parades were for the author a television event viewed at a distance, an annual public viewing of the Soviet War Machine. As fate would have it the author would subsequently live and work in the Russian Federation for nearly three decades, and would witness many of the post-Soviet parades on a first hand basis. From the break-up of the Soviet Union until 2008 there were no military parades involving heavy equipment held on Red Square; though parades were held in other cities of the Russian Federation and the newly independent republics of the former Soviet Union. Tanks were however deployed in Moscow in 1991 and 1993, but in both cases to put down attempted coup d'état's rather than for ceremonial purposes.

The banners of the 10 Russian fronts at the end of World War Two are paraded on Red Square during the 70th anniversary of Victory in Europe, 9th May 2015. (Russian Ministry of Defence)

To witness such events is to understand the thin veneer that separates civilization from anarchy in any country.

Military parades involving military equipment or "tekhnika" made their return to Red Square in 2008, now as annual victory parades held on 9th May in commemoration of victory in World War Two. The 2008 parade was originally expected to be a one-off, however there was a repeat parade the following year and again for the 65th Anniversary of VE Day in Europe in 2010. The Red Square military parades had again become a standard feature of the Moscow calendar and, in what would have been the 100th year anniversary of the 1917 Great October Socialist Revolution, the Russian Federation staged a military parade on 9th May 2017 in the old tradition of demonstrating military might on Red Square.

The author, whose individual role should the Cold War have ever turned hot was to sit tight at a map location near Braunschweig in Germany and report on the unit composition of Soviet armoured spearheads rolling across the German plains to an undefined ultimate target location, understood perfectly well, as did most that have served in the military, that a direct conflict between the superpowers was in reality an unlikely prospect. If for no other reason than that experienced and pragmatic politicians held sway on both sides of the divide. Further, it was understood that conventional warfare would quickly turn nuclear as the only defence option after a matter of days of rear-guard action by NATO forces in Europe. That was then. Today, the Russian leader Vladimir Putin has proven more pragmatic and diplomatic than might reasonably be expected of him in the circumstances of the pressures that the Russian Federation has been put under in recent years from American and European sanctions related to the 2014 fighting in Crimea and Ukraine. While achieving nothing positive, the sanctions have destroyed much international business with Russia, and led directly to company failures and unemployment in Europe and the United States. Political relationships between the Russian Federation and the former Cold War Western powers have simultaneously been set back two decades, and all the positive developments in relations since 1991 nullified. Meantime the Crimea is at peace and expanding economically, while emigration from Ukraine continues, with many Ukrainian nationals continuing to move to the Russian Federation for work and stability as they have always done since the break-up of the Soviet Union in 1991.

With regard to the fundamental purpose of the Soviet, and now Russian military parades on Red Square, they have always, beyond being an obvious show of might intended for international consumption, also been an important element in binding the population of what was for most of the 20th Century a highly militarised nation. The parades were primarily a show of strength for external audiences, but were also a patriotic showpiece which had a genuine impact in uniting the domestic population, something that the current 9th May Victory parades continue to do. By comparison with today's realities, the Soviet era parades were perhaps more "honest propaganda" as a show of national deterrent than many of the proxy wars now being fought in selected countries. Nobody ever died as a result of these parades and at a global level the Cold War superpowers were in a permanent status of check and balance.

The Red Square Parades as they are now re-constituted in the 21st Century are a showpiece of military might in a very different era to that under which they were conceived. Or perhaps not. Just as in 1917, the Russian Federation is today a relatively fledgling post-Soviet independent state, as are all the former states of the Soviet Union. Western foreign countries are actively involved in trying to trade with the Russian Federation and access its (primarily mineral) resources, while in recent years simultaneously acting against it politically and economically, most recently by means of direct sanctions. In this context, the background political situation is not so very different from when the inaugural 7th November 1918 parade was organized on the first anniversary of the Russian Revolution. After the dissolution of the Soviet Union in 1991, the popular narrative in Western countries became that the United States and Europe had "won" the Cold War. The majority of former Warsaw Pact states defected to join the European Union and NATO. Many Russians moved abroad, now having the opportunity to do so under the freedoms that the new and less autocratic Russian system allowed. Many Russian citizens having spent time abroad also decided to return home to their country of origin where the Russian soul and a feeling of national entity remains an important binding factor among all the inhabitants of the country, both local and foreign.

This book is intended as a neutral account of the armoured vehicles and weapons systems that have been demonstrated on Red Square in the past century, which were in context the showpiece weapons of their time. It is also however a nostalgic recounting of a time when ordinary people, regardless of their preferred bloc or political viewpoint, felt that their governments were in the aggregate acting in the interests of their core citizens, and their respective indigenous populations. A time when, irrespective of whether Soviet or Western, ordinary people felt they belonged to and were part of their own society and that the society concerned was a stable entity with a future mirroring its past.

The weapons displayed on Red Square over the last 100 years have often been formidable. Major wars are not however won or lost exclusively by armies and military technology, but ultimately by national resolve, as the United States learned for-instance during the Vietnam War and both Cold War adversaries have since learned in Afghanistan.

At the time of writing, the world, in particularly Europe, is overall less stable than during the Cold War. The Russian Federation has meantime been reverted by the United States and some European countries to its traditional Soviet era adversarial "enemy" role, despite its citizens sharing the same core values as their European neighbours. Some politicians in Europe have in recent months tried to ensure that the Russian Federation remains the target of public focus and concern. Much of the population of Europe is however well educated, well travelled, and worldly, as are many Russians today, and such political statements are consequently understood in context. In many countries of Europe today, there are greater concerns than the rather unlikely event of Russian military action that have a more direct impact on the current status quo.

The modern day Russian military parades on Red Square continue to make a statement that goes far beyond a demonstration of military might. They are also a statement of national integrity and preparedness, and unity in the face of external adversity, a national specific not contained to official ceremonial events on Red Square.

The current Red Square parades continue to commemorate the ever declining number of living veterans, and those who served and died in the defence of the country in World War Two, in which the Soviet Union suffered disproportionately in terms of both military and civilian casualties. The parades held on Red Square in recent years first and foremost commemorate the many millions of Russian and Soviet national souls, military and civilian, that died for their country in order to secure its future.

*James Kinnear, November 2017*

# Red Square

The name "Red Square" as it is known in the English language comes from the Old Russian word "Krasny", which can mean "Red" but is actually formed from the Russian word "Krasivy", meaning beautiful. The square is thereby actually "Beautiful Square", though over the years the name "Red Square" has become the predominant term as understood by foreigners.

Red Square was originally established as a market and fairground between the walls of the Kremlin and the region of "Kitai Gorod" - another translational conundrum, in that the area and its namesake metro station is in turn known to foreigners as "China Town". "Kitai" can however mean both "China" and "stick", and it is the latter reference that refers to the region to the east of Red Square, the "stick town" of peasant housing outside the protection of the original Kremlin walls. By the beginning of the 20th Century, "Beautiful Square" was a well-established meeting place and market; the closest the population could get to the formidable walls of the Kremlin itself. The square was latterly covered in cobbles and became centre stage for all manner of events and celebrations. The use of what became ingrained in foreign parlance, as "Red Square" as a setting for military parades is very much a Soviet phenomenon. From the first anniversary of the 1917 "Great October Socialist Revolution" to the present day, "Red Square" has served for exactly a century as the central stage for annual displays of Russian, Soviet, and now again Russian, military might.

Red Square is set in the heart of Moscow, hemmed in between the walls of the Kremlin on one side and the frontage onto Red Square of "GUM" - the Gosudarstvenny Universalny Magazin (State Universal Store) on the other, with the Historical Museum at the entrance and St. Basil's Cathedral at the "spusk" or exit, providing an ideal parade square setting, though access and egress has always required consummate precision on the part of the armoured columns passing through the square.

In the immediate aftermath of the Russian Revolution, a handful of armoured vehicles began to join the crowds on Red Square, with the armoured elements of these gatherings being for-

Marching columns at the start of the Victory Day commemorative parade on Red Square, 9th May 2017. (Russian Ministry of Defence)

malised at the beginning of the 1920s. With the death of Lenin on 21st January 1924, the requirement to entomb the founder of the Soviet state for posterity led to the building of the centrepiece of all future Soviet, and latterly Russian, military parades, the Lenin Mausoleum. Within days of Lenin's death, a wooden mausoleum designed by the architect Aleksey Shchusev had been constructed allowing mourners to pass through and pay their respects to the founder of the new Soviet state. In August 1924, an enlarged, but still wooden, tomb replaced the original tomb. The third and definitive tomb, constructed of concrete with marble and granite facing was completed in 1930, and it was from this monolith block structure that generations of Soviet military and political leadership would henceforth review the passing parades of Soviet military might.

Although international attention during the 20th Century was always focused on the Soviet era military parades held on Red Square annually in May and November, military parades were also held in many other Russian cities and those of the former Soviet Union. This series of books concentrates on the globally renowned Red Square parades but includes some illustrations from parades held in some other Soviet and latterly Russian cities, including Leningrad (St.Petersburg), Kuibyshev (Samara), Sverdlovsk (Ekaterinburg) and Khabarovsk.

Red Square as it appeared in 1872. Though now neatly cobbled, the square looks little different today.

The original Lenin Mausoleum was a wooden structure, replaced by the current concrete and stone building in 1930.

T-34-85 tanks cross Red Square during the 7th November 2012 commemorative parade (Andrey Aksenov)

A Second World War veteran receives flowers after the 7th November 2013 commemorative parade (Andrey Aksenov)

# The Russian Revolution and Soviet Industrialisation

The Russian Revolution was a defining moment in European history. Before the outbreak of World War One, a set of relatively small European countries with large and powerful empires, including Austro-Hungary, Italy, France, Germany, Great Britain, Holland, Portugal, Russia and Ottoman Turkey dominated the world stage. The 1914-18 war financially bankrupted most of these former colonial powers however, and Great Britain, formerly the world's largest creditor, was in the immediate aftermath of the war transformed into the world's largest debtor as a direct result of the huge financial outlays involved in the war years.

Post 1918, the European colonial powers would gradually all begin to lose their foreign empires, having neither the political nor financial resources to continue running them. The war had resulted in the deaths of some 10 million people in direct combat, perhaps another 5 million from famine and disease. The new world order that emerged from 1918 was very different from the colonial rivalries of the pre-war period, with the economies and industrial might of all the European participants having been decimated by the war endured on European soil.

France was financially ruined, as was Germany, with the United States becoming the world's predominant financial powerhouse in the years that followed the war, until that credit-based financial system also collapsed in the Great Depression that followed the Wall Street Crash of 1929, the effects of which were felt around the world, not least in Europe.

The country that underwent the most significant change as a result of World War One was Imperial Russia. In the years immediately prior to the outbreak of war, Russia had been making significant political and trade inroads into countries which the old world colonial powers regarded as their direct sphere of influence, with Asia and the Far East being areas of particular contention. World War One temporarily postponed this colonial rivalry, but Russia would re-emerge after the war as a very different country to the one that had entered that war, and would in consequence be seen as a significant threat to the established order.

The stresses of Russian participation in the First World War brought the economic and political maladies that had resulted in the original 1905 Russian Revolution back to boiling point. The Russian Revolutions of February and October 1917 swept Tsar Nicholas II from power and ended the monarchy as a ruling system. The new Bolshevik government immediately sued for peace with Germany, which was clearly not in the interests of the old European colonial powers still fighting Germany on the Western Front. Pre-war Imperial Russia, led by a monarchy, relatively integrated into the European political system and even speaking French as the language of diplomacy, was replaced by a Bolshevik government in 1917, now driving a very different political system, based at least theoretically on worker's rights and freedoms. Russia took its own very different path from the rest of Europe and the outside world after October 1917, with the formation of a Worker's Socialist society led by Vladimir Ilyich Ulyanov, better known historically as Lenin. The fledgling Russian RSFSR state would rapidly encompass neighbouring European and Asian countries to become the Soviet Union, formed on 28th December 1922.

The history of the Russian Revolution and the

formation of the Soviet Union is beyond the scope of this study, but the Russian Revolution, the birth of Soviet Russia and the economic and industrial growth of the Soviet Union was a direct result of the same war in Europe which had decimated the old world order, particularly in Europe and its former colonies, and given scope for the Russian Revolution and ultimately the rise of the Soviet Union as a new economic and military power to rival the pre-war colonial European powers. The crippling reparation terms dealt out to Germany after the war would in that country lead to economic hardships for ordinary citizens, and the inevitable rise of nationalism as a result, and would directly lay the grounds for the Second World War.

The effects of World War One and the Russian Revolution resulted in the rise of a new world order. The pre-war "superpowers" (particularly France, Great Britain, Japan and the United States) attempted to return Russia to its pre-revolutionary status by direct military intervention during the Russian Civil War that ensued after the Russian Revolution. All the foreign powers failed in their respective military endeavours, and would ultimately accept the new regime in Russia, having no option but to cooperate with the de-facto rise of the Soviet Union as a new world power.

Meantime, as the fledgling Russian state emerged from the effects of World War One, the Russian Revolution and the following Civil War, the country developed a strategy through a series of Five Year Plans to develop the economy, the industrial and ultimately the military capacity of the new state. Not being bound by previous conventions, the Soviet Union sought out technical and commercial relationships around the world, and in order to develop its military industrial capacity imported military technology designs and ideas from several countries, including Germany, Great Britain, Italy and the United States. It was aided in this effort by foreign entrepreneurial engineers such as the tank designer Walter J. Christie in the United States and the former submarine turned tank designer Edward Grote in Germany, and by American companies such as Autocar, Moreland and Wright. The single biggest contribution to the development of the Soviet motor industry came from the multinational American Ford Motor Company, which was contracted by the Soviet government to transfer vehicle production technology to the Soviet Union, resulting in the building of the colossal GAZ vehicle plant in the city of Gorky. There were however many other similar technology transfer contracts between the Soviet Union and the United States, with the STZ plant in Stalingrad being built with the assistance of the U.S. Caterpillar company.

The Soviet Union was formally recognized by the United States of America only in 1933, long after the Ford and other technology transfer deals with the country had been concluded, and series production of modified Soviet variants of the original Ford designs had already commenced at the GAZ plant.

The Russian Revolution was the crucible from which a new world power would be forged, with the Soviet Union becoming directly involved in world politics as it worked to spread the Soviet form of socialism beyond its immediate borders. From the end of the Russian Civil War and the formation of the Soviet Union in 1922 until the late 1930s the Soviet Union took its place among the other "troublesome" countries of the world including Germany, Italy and Spain where the existing order was being challenged as a result of economic hardships and characterful leadership. At the end of the 1930s the Soviet Union made attempts at alliances with other European states to bolster defence against an increasingly aggressive Germany, but was rejected, leading to Soviet participation in an interim alliance of necessity with Germany which would ultimately result in the partitioning of Poland by both countries. The German invasion of Poland on 1st September 1939 prompted the start of World War Two in Europe. The Soviet invasion of Poland from the east on 17th September prompted no direct response against the Soviet Union, and as alliances changed, the Soviet Union went from pariah state to staunch ally in 1941, and for all the historical bias that has been introduced in schools since that time, the fact remains that 90% of German forces were pre-occupied on the Eastern Front from the beginning of the war against the Soviet Union in 1941 until 1944, the start of that onslaught being at a time when the majority of mainland Europe had surrendered within days or weeks of invasion and Great Britain stood virtually alone protected by its island geography. Without Soviet participation in World War Two, Europe would today without doubt look very different. However, as victory approached in May 1945, the Allies were already planning for defence mechanisms against a Soviet Union which by 1945 was a honed and combat hardened country which had lost 27 million souls in a fight to the death against Nazism, and was not about to accept second tier political status in the post-war order.

For nearly half a century from the end of World War Two until the abolition of the Soviet Union in 1991, there were essentially two power blocks in the world, the United States and its European former colonial allies (with the political and military status of the latter being a fraction of their 19th Century influence - and their colonial status continuing to erode as the 20th Century progressed) which formed into NATO in 1949, and the Soviet Union, joined in 1955 by the countries that formed the Warsaw Pact.

One of the consistent windows on the Soviet Union for Western countries was the annual display of Russian military might on Moscow's Red Square, the military parades being threaded seamlessly through all the decades of the Soviet Union's existence. To observe who was standing on the review stand on the Lenin Mausoleum and their exact location relative to the "Vozhd" (leader) was to understand the domestic order of the Soviet Union and predict the next iteration of political leadership. To review the military equipment on display (which was a primary source of Western intelligence reporting on Soviet military technology during the Cold War) was to take note of what the Soviet Union had chosen to display for public consumption, or, as in the case of the non-appearance of the T-34 and the KV in the final pre-war parades, that which the country had chosen to conceal in order to mask ongoing preparations for total war. The "schum" (background noise) of military displays on Red Square was usually also intermixed with elements of "maskirovka" (disguise), such that while some weapons were openly displayed as soon as they entered service, the more secretive vehicles, such as the wartime T-34 medium and KV heavy tanks were as noted not displayed until war broke out, while in the post-war era tanks such as the T-64 were displayed only many years after they had entered service, and some like the T-10 heavy tank were displayed only once. In the 1960s strategic weapons such as the RT-20P mobile ICBM system and the GR-1 rocket were displayed as current service technology though they would never actually enter service. Overall, the Red Square parades were always, and remain today, a spectacle of Soviet and now Russian military might to be reviewed exactly as intended. A statement to the world that the Soviet Union, and today the Russian Federation is, as in the past, ready to defend itself by military means and has the capability to do so.

..........................................................

### Note on the Julian and Gregorian calendar.

The Bolshevik "Velikaya Oktyabrskaya Revolutsiya" or "Great October Revolution" took place on 25th October 1917 in accordance with the Julian calendar. By the time of the first anniversary of the revolution in 1918, the country had moved from the Julian to the Gregorian calendar, a 13 day difference, hence from 1918 until the collapse of the Soviet Union in 1991 the anniversary celebrations for the "Dien Velikoi Oktyabrskoi Sotsialisticheskoi Revolutsii" or "Day of the Great October Socialist Revolution" were held annually on 7th November.

> *"The Russian Army is a wall which, however far it may retreat, you will always find in front of you"*
>
> General Antoine Henri Jomini - Crimea Campaign 1854-56*

*Antoine Henri Jomini was a Swiss national who served in the French Army under Napoleon. He was able to decline participation in the 1812 attack on Russia due to his nationality, and later served as a military advisor to both Russian Tsar Nicholas I and Tsar Alexander II. The above quote was made before the Crimean War of 1854-56 during which the British Light Brigade infamously charged directly into Russian artillery fire at the Battle of Balaclava. The quote, based on Napoleon's experience in Russia in 1812, would subsequently hold true for the foreign interventions during the Russian Civil War that followed the Russian Revolution, and again for the Wehrmacht in 1941-45, as it would without doubt also hold true today.
Those who have not travelled widely in Russia cannot hope to understand the scale of the country, where the geography, the weather and "national specifics" with regard to both tenacity and mentality are all factors most foreigners simply cannot begin to comprehend.

# Introduction

Although best known for its Soviet era annual military parades, the history of military parades and march pasts in the region of Red Square outside the Kremlin walls goes back to the days when Red Square was an open market area near the Kremlin walls. During the reign of Tsar Aleksei Mikhailovich (who reigned from 1645-1676) troops returning after the siege of Smolensk and its recapture from the Polish army were led through Red Square by Tsar Aleksei Mikhailovich carrying his own child in hands. The first "official" military parade in the region of Red Square took place on 11th October 1702 after the Noteburg fortress was captured from the Swedish by the army of Tsar Peter I. The parade was actually held not on the market square itself, but on Myasnitskaya, which was covered with red cloth for the occasion. Columns of troops followed the Tsar's gold painted horse-drawn carriage to which were attached captured Swedish army banners. In the years that followed, military parades were held within the Kremlin and in the surrounding streets for a variety of reasons including military victories, royal birthdays, and for religious and social occasions. Tsar Nicholas II was the last Russian Tsar to hold a military parade within the Kremlin walls, subsequent to which the Russian monarchy was swept aside by the Russian Revolution in 1917 and the era of Red Army military parades on Red Square began.

From the time of their introduction in 1918 immediately following the Russian Revolution until the end of the Soviet Union in 1991, the military parades held on Moscow's Red Square were the default annual demonstration of Red Army and latterly Soviet Army military might. As formal diplomatic relationships began to be re-established from the early 1920s, the annual parades also became the highlight of the year for foreign military observers of the Red Army and much later the post-War Soviet Army.

The regular annual tradition of military parades on Red Square and in other large cities in the Soviet Union with military connections and suitable parade squares began with the first post-Revolutionary parade held on 1st May 1918 at Lenin's initiative, with representation from fledgling elements of the Red Army, the Air Fleet and the Navy (the names of all of which changed over the decades) to be latterly joined in the post-war era by the VDV airborne forces and later by RVSN Strategic Rocket Forces.

In May 1918 at the time of the first Red Army military parade (actually held at Khodynka field in the north-west of Moscow rather than Red Square), the Russian Soviet Federative Socialist Republic (RSFSR) was at the beginning of the Russian Civil War (1918-21), with some 300,000 Red Army troops fighting approximately 700,000 White Russian and interventionist forces from 17 nations including France, Great Britain, Japan and the United States.

In most years from 1918 until 1941 parades with a military element were held annually on 1st May, celebrating the Workers and Peasant's May Day holiday, and 7th November celebrating the annual anniversary of the Great October Socialist Revolution. The pre-war pattern of 1st May and 7th November parades was continued after the war; the last "May Day" parade with a military element being held on 1st May 1968. The 1st May parades thereafter reverted to purely civilian demonstrations, with the 7th November parades remaining the default annual military parades until the collapse of the Soviet Union in 1991.

The most poignant of all Soviet military parades on Red Square was held on 7th November 1941, when Wehrmacht forces were at their closest point located at Khimki, within 16km of Red of Red Square. There were no formal parades in Moscow from 1942-44, with military parades resuming on 1st May 1945, the same day Germany presented its initial conditional surrender terms to the Red Army in Berlin. The World War Two in Europe (VE Day) Victory Parade was held on Red Square on 24th June 1945, with subsequent VE Day parades in celebration of the victory over Axis forces in World War Two being held on the 20th anniversary of victory on 9th May 1965, the 40th anniversary on 9th May 1985, with the last Soviet era Victory Parade being the 45th anniversary on 9th May 1990. In the post-Soviet Russian Federation there was a Victory Parade for the 50th anniversary on 9th May 1995, and since 2008 these parades have been held annually on 9th May. Less well known are the Victory against Japan (VJ Day) parades held in the Soviet Far East in several locations during September 1945.

The military parades originally held on Moscow's Red Square, and latterly extended to many regional cities of the fledgling Russian RSFSR and the republics of the Soviet Union, were originally intended as a public display of military might intended for internal as much as external consumption. Though the Moscow Red Square parades were always the ones covered by the Western press and attended by embassy military attachés, and therefore the most widely known, in fact military parades were held on the same dates in many other Soviet cities, including Leningrad (now St. Petersburg), Kuibyshev (now Samara), Sverdlovsk (now Ekaterinburg), and further flung cities such as Sevastopol and Vladivostock. Most republics also held annual military parades, with major displays in Minsk in Belorussia and Kiev and Kharkov in Ukraine.

From the break-up of the Soviet Union in 1991 until 2008 there were no military parades involving heavy equipment held on Red Square. On 9th May 1995, a single parade was held celebrating the 50th Anniversary of Victory over Germany (VE Day), but with the armoured columns moving along Kutuzovsky Prospect, a long avenue located to the west of the city centre. Red Square was during the 1990s restricted to more limited parades of infantry and veterans. While the 1990s were devoid of parades involving military equipment or "tekhnika" as described in Russian on Moscow's Red Square, military parades were nevertheless held during this period in other Russian regional cities, and in the major cities of several now independent sates of the former Soviet Union.

Full-scale military parades including "tekhnika" made their return to Red Square on 9th May 2008, now re-inaugurated as Victory Parades, commemorating the Allied Victory in Europe in World War Two as held in 1945, 1965, 1985, 1990 and 1995. At the time, the 2008 Victory Parade was expected to be a one-off, however the following year there was a parade on 9th May 2009, and again for the 65th Anniversary of VE Day in Europe in 2010. The Red Square military parades have since become an annual feature of the Moscow calendar and the focal point of 9th May commemoration in the Russian Federation.

The modern Russian Federation did not in 2017 formally celebrate the 100th Anniversary of the 1917 Russian Revolution. The Russian RSFSR, born out of the Revolution and civil war, became the founding state of the four republics that formed the Soviet Union in 1922 and ultimately during the 1930s and 1940s incorporated 15 republics under the Soviet banner. The fledgling state survived civil war in 1919-22, famine and political repression in the 1930s, and German invasion in 1941, resulting in total Soviet victory in 1945. Four decades of isolation followed during the Cold War, during which a large percentage of the nation's national budget was spent on defence and military technology. Ultimately the United States and its NATO allies had the financial wherewithal to survive the Cold War era, that for the Soviet Union became an increasingly major financial burden on the State, which was formally dissolved in 1991.

For two decades the relationship between the post-Soviet Russian Federation and its former

Western adversaries changed to that of business and trading, with major foreign investment in the Russian Federation, major business in return, a normalisation of relations and the Russian Federation taking its place on the world stage as a partner rather than an adversary, real or perceived. During that time many Russians took advantage of their new freedom to travel and in many cases emigrate, and many citizens of the now independent former republics chose in turn to move to the Russian Federation for work, advancement and in many cases to live in stability and safety in contrast with the instability in their own home republics.

Meantime, independence in all of the former Soviet republics brought with it ethnic tensions and inevitable conflicts between factions that had been held in check by the Soviet Union for the majority of the 20th Century. Major fighting broke out in some former republics at the end of the 1980s, with armed conflict breaking out in Nagorno Karabakh in 1988 and in Transnistria in 1989. In the early 1990s a long but largely undocumented civil war in Tajikistan was followed by the first of two wars in Chechnya and fighting in Dagestan. Some of the former republics of the Soviet Union did not adjust well to the new political and economic realities of being separated from what had effectively been the political controller and financial paymaster of the entire region for most of the 20th Century.

Many former republics struggled politically and economically with their newly granted independence, and many citizens from Azerbaijan, Georgia, Tajikistan, Uzbekistan and Ukraine moved to Russia for work, a future, and often for the basic necessity of family safety. Many citizens of the now independent former republics that often denigrate the Russian Federation, while often living there, in fact owe their education, their upbringing and their personal development to the basics of life that the Soviet Union provided its citizens.

The dawn of the 21st Century did not auger well for the Russian Federation. The first decade of the 21st century began with the Second Chechen War, followed by a short but brutal conflict with Georgia over Southern Ossetia in 2008, and open conflict in the formerly sleepy towns and villages of Eastern Ukraine in 2014. At the time of writing an uneasy peace holds in Eastern Ukraine, while several million Ukrainians continue to live and work in the Russian Federation. For the most part however, the majority of the populations of the Russian Federation and all the former Soviet republics have in the 21st Century lived in peace and relative prosperity.

Today, in 2017, the Russian Federation finds itself effectively in the same position as that of the fledgling Bolshevik state exactly a Century before. While the Russian Federation is criticised by the Western press, the reality remains that the citizens of the former Soviet Union share a long if often troubled history, and the populations of the Russian Federation and the former Soviet republics share many common values, which unite people in times of national threat. The political differences between the Russian Federation and Ukraine are for-instance highlighted in the Western press, while omitting the fact that extremely large numbers of Russians and Ukrainians are actually married to each other and work in each other's countries.

Soviet and modern Russian military parades are "what it says on the tin" – a display of military might for the benefit of the target audience. But behind the displays there is however a sense of unity between different Russian nationals with differing religions and backgrounds, with a shared identity and sense of nationhood. That unity is as powerful as any military technology, and not necessarily universally shared around the modern world.

A Garford-Putilov armoured car being used as a platform for speeches during a meeting on Red Square, 1st May 1918. (Mikhail Baryatinsky)

# Early Russian Parades
# 1917-1920

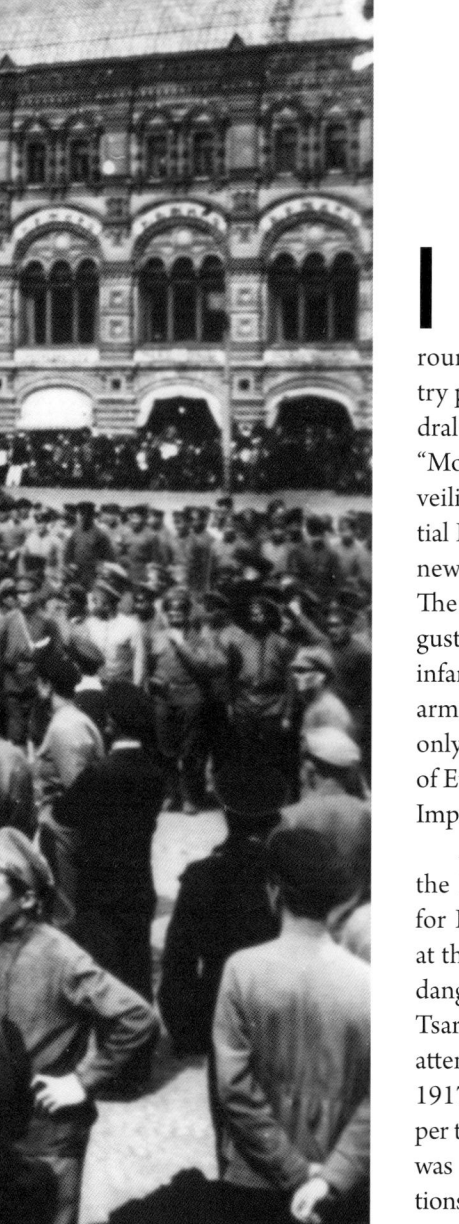

In the final years of Imperial Tsarist Russia, there were occasional military celebrations within the Kremlin walls and the streets surrounding the Kremlin. On 30th May 1912, infantry paraded before the Christ the Saviour Cathedral located along the embankment of the River "Moskva" from the Kremlin at the time of the unveiling of a statue to Alexander III. The Presidential Regiment of Imperial Russia paraded past the new statue, in the presence of Tsar Nicholas II. The last pre-revolutionary parade was on 8th August 1914, when Tsar Nicholas II presided over an infantry parade outside the walls of the Kremlin armoury. World War One had begun in Europe only days before, and by the end of the war much of Europe had been inexorably changed, not least Imperial Russia.

As with all the countries that participated in the First World War, the war was a major drain for Imperial Russia, with major losses in troops at the front and severe depravations at home, the dangers of which were not entirely apparent to Tsar Nicholas II even with the hindsight of the attempted revolution of 1905. The country in 1917 again turned to revolution, and on 2nd (15th per the new calendar) March 1917 Tsar Nicholas II was forced to abdicate after the first of two revolutions that year that would introduce a new form of government which was to last almost 75 years.

On 4th March 1917 (17th per new calendar), only two days after the formal abdication of Tsar Nicholas II, and with Russia still engaged in the war but a new Provisional Government in place, the first post-Imperial military parade was held on Moscow's Red Square rather than the former Tsarist capital in the north of the country. The troops were met with great enthusiasm by crowds of local citizens. Colonel Gruzinov, the commander of the Moscow Garrison reviewed a parade of infantry and cavalry belonging to the new "Revolutionary Army", which included a flypast by a variety of aircraft. The second and decisive revolution in October 1917 led to the Bolsheviks sweeping to power under the leadership of a certain Vladimir Ilyich Ulyanov, better known as Lenin. The headquarters of the new government was on 12th March 1918 formally moved to Moscow, which city would henceforth become the outside world's window on the new Communist state.

The Red Army was formed on 28th January 1918, with the Council of People's Commissars as the supreme command authority. Operational control of the army was the responsibility of the Narkomvoenmor - the Commissariat for Military Affairs, with Nikolai Krylenko appointed as the first commander, Aleksandr Myasnikyan as his deputy and Nikolai Podvoisky as Commissar for War. In January 1918 the fledgling Red Army also established a command structure for its inherited armoured forces, the "Soviet of Armoured Units", later re-designated the Central Armoured Directorate, and later again as the Chief Armoured Directorate (GBTU).

On the morning of 23rd February 1918 Germany presented an ultimatum to the new Bolshevik government. In response, an appeal by the Council of People's Commissars and headed "Socialist Fatherland in danger!" was published in local newspapers, and volunteers started to join the new Red Army in mass numbers as a direct result. Some time later, on 27th January 1922, an official holiday was established in the Russian Soviet Federative Socialist Republic (RSFSR) as the Day of the Red Army and Fleet, to be celebrated on 23rd February annually. It was renamed as the Day of the Soviet Army and Navy in 1946. The traditional holiday, ostensibly for the male population of the country has continued to the present day under its various descriptions, with women having their own holiday on 8th March, International Women's Day. In 2002, the day was renamed again, as the more neutral "Dien Zashitnika Otechestva" or defender of the Fatherland day.

# 1st May 1918 - The First Bolshevik Military Parade

One of the Bolshevik government's main priorities on seizing power was to stop the war with Germany, the economic hardships of which for the Russian population had led directly to the overthrow of Tsar Nicholas II. To continue the war would inevitably lead to the Bolshevik government enduring a similar fate, so after frenzied negotiations the Bolsheviks in March 1918 signed the Treaty of Brest-Litovsk with Germany, effectively ending the fledgling country's participation in the war. This move by Russia was much to the chagrin of other European powers which had relied on a high percentage of German forces being distracted on the First World War "Russian Front".

With Russia nominally now at peace and free to get on with building communism and a new society fit for the proudly proclaimed "Workers and Peasants" to reside in, the country now had to develop a Red Army to protect the new Bolshevik Russian state; and furthermore required to ensure all concerned knew of its capability. Accordingly, on 1st May 1918 the Bolsheviks held the first ever formal post "Great October Revolution" parade as a demonstration to the world that the emerging Soviet Union had the capability to defend itself. At the time of this first Red Square military parade, Russia was at the beginning of the Russian Civil War (1918-21), during which as many as 300,000 Red Army troops were engaged in combat with approximately 700,000 White Russian and interventionist forces from France, Great Britain, Japan, the United States and several other countries. The Bolshevik parades, which began in May 1918 as a demonstration to the world that the emerging Soviet Union had the capability to defend itself, would become an annual event. Lenin had not himself originally been in favour of a full time standing Red Army, preferring that the "narod" (the people) all be armed for defence as required. After the Treaty of Brest-Litovsk, it was Lev Trotsky who finally persuaded Lenin that a standing army was required.

The first post-revolutionary parade with a military element was held on Red Square on 1st May 1918, followed immediately thereafter by a combined military ground forces and air show at the Khodynka airfield, with the first demonstrations of Red Army military might being split between the two locations.

The 1st May 1918 morning military assembly was held on Red Square in conjunction with the civilian demonstrations. This was followed by an afternoon joint land and air force parade held at 16:30 at Khodynskoye Pole (Khodynka Field) in north-west Moscow. The morning Red Square parade was ostensibly held as a May Day holiday pa-

A column of armoured cars passes through Red Square on 1st May 1918. The vehicle in the foreground is a Garford-Putilov, armoured at the Putilovsky plant on an imported Garford chassis. (Mikhail Baryatinsky)

rade for Soviet workers, but with units of the Moscow Garrison of the Red Army marching ahead of the civilian workers procession. The military elements then moved directly up Tverskaya and Petrogradskoe Shosse* to Khodynka field, where the first post-revolutionary full scale Red Army military parade was held, led by the same Moscow Garrison which had marched on Red Square earlier that day, accompanied by additional elements of artillery and engineering forces and an air display by the first inklings of what would become the Red Army Air Force.

In May 1918 at the time of the first formal Red Square military parade celebrating the 1917 Revolution, the newly emerging country was exiting its participation in the First World War, but the fledgling state was also on the verge of the Russian Civil War which would rage from 1918-21.

The 1st May 1918 parade at Khodynka was a joint exercise between the Moscow Garrison of the Red Army and an aviation display by the RKKVF - The Workers and Peasants Red Air Fleet. The parade was taken by Lev Trotsky, then commissar for Army and Navy Affairs (Narkomvoenmor), with a reported 30,000 troops on parade. The parade commander was I. I. Vatsetis, commander of the Latvian (rifle) division. Vatsetis would in July 1918 become commander of the Eastern Front, and would later be promoted to Commander of the Armed Forces of the RSFSR. Overall command of the parades was under the direction of the commander of the Moscow military district (MVO) N.I. Muralov. The parade and the airshow that followed were both attended by V.I. Lenin.

The afternoon military parade began with columns of marching infantry from regiments of the 1st Moscow Rifle Division, Latvian Rifle Division, 4th Moscow Revolutionary Regiment, Warsaw Revolutionary Regiment, and International and Communist battalions. The infantry and naval forces columns were followed by cavalry, "tachanki" horse drawn machine gun carts, horse-drawn artillery, and elements of army engineer units. The mechanised part of the display included bicycles modified for all-terrain use. A small num-

---

* Tverskaya Street was so-named from the 17th century until 1932, renamed Gorky Street in 1932 and from 1990 again renamed Tverskaya. Petrogradskoe Shosse was so named from 1915 to 1924, and thereafter named Leningradsky Prospekt.

A 1st series Austin armoured car of the 5th Armoured Division, Petrograd, July 1917. (RGAKFD SPB)

ber of Garford, Izhorsky and other armoured cars were displayed both on Red Square and later in the day at Khodynka. An interesting incident during the Khodynka parade was that the Latvian Rifle Regiment, one of the strongest supporters of the communist movement during the revolution and which also served as security forces for the Bolshevik government left the parade column during the event to demonstrate their disdain for Lev Trotsky. The Red Army was in 1918 far from a homogeneous organisation.

The 1st May 1918 parade on Khodynka field was the first post-revolutionary military parade, the first Red Army military parade that would be the precursor to a tradition that has continued with a few interruptions to the present day.

The immediate post-revolutionary situation in what would in 1922 become the Soviet Union was in 1918 far from stable, with the Bolsheviks that had gained victory in the revolution being violently opposed by White forces, primarily based in the Caucasus and Ukraine, with various international elements still present in strength after the end of the war. Almost immediately following the revolution, fighting broke out between Czechoslovakian Legion units and the Red Army in what would ultimately develop into a full scale intervention by no less than 17 foreign nations, led by France, Great Britain, the Unites States, Japan and even post-war Germany, all of which dispatched expeditionary forces into the territory of Russia, with direct foreign involvement in support of the White Army against the Bolshevik Red Army.

Approximately 30% of former Russian Imperial Army officers joined the Red Army, this number including many officers of the former Imperial Army General Staff who were more than capable of planning large scale operations. Another 40% of former Russian Imperial Army officers joined the White Armies, while the remaining 30% returned to civil life, fled or disappeared into the ether. These numbers changed significantly during the years of the Civil War, and particularly after foreign intervention. The well known Russian officer General Brusilov for-instance joined the Red Army after the Polish Army entered Ukraine in 1920 and many officers followed his lead.

# Khodynskoye Pole (Khodynka Field)

Khodynskoye Pole (Khodynka Field), a large open area which is today located in the region located between the modern metro stations of "Dinamo", "Aeroport" and "Oktyabrskoye Pole" would in later years become become the Moscow Central Aerodrome named after M.V. Frunze. The Central Aerodrome was abandoned as a commercial airport with the growth of the city and the building of several new airports in the Moscow region in the latter decades of the 20th Century. Nevertheless, the Khodynskoye Pole (colloquially known as Khodynka) was until 2015 the default staging ground for final parade practices, undertaken for a period of approximately two months before each Red Square military parade.

The field remained largely intact until the late 1990s, but is today partly built over by apartment blocks. Until as late as 2016 Khodynka was nevertheless still used for final parade training and for marshalling before 21st Century Red Square military parades. The first tanks shown in Moscow after the Russian Revolution were demonstrated to the Russian political and military leadership at Khodynka before the first Red Square parades became more commonly observed. Khodynka is also the location of the "Aerostar" Hotel, one of the first modern post-Soviet hotels in Moscow.

The first Red Army military parade was held at Khodynka, in the north west of Moscow, in 1918. Parade rehearsals continued to be staged there until 2015.

THE RED ARMY ON PARADE 1917-45

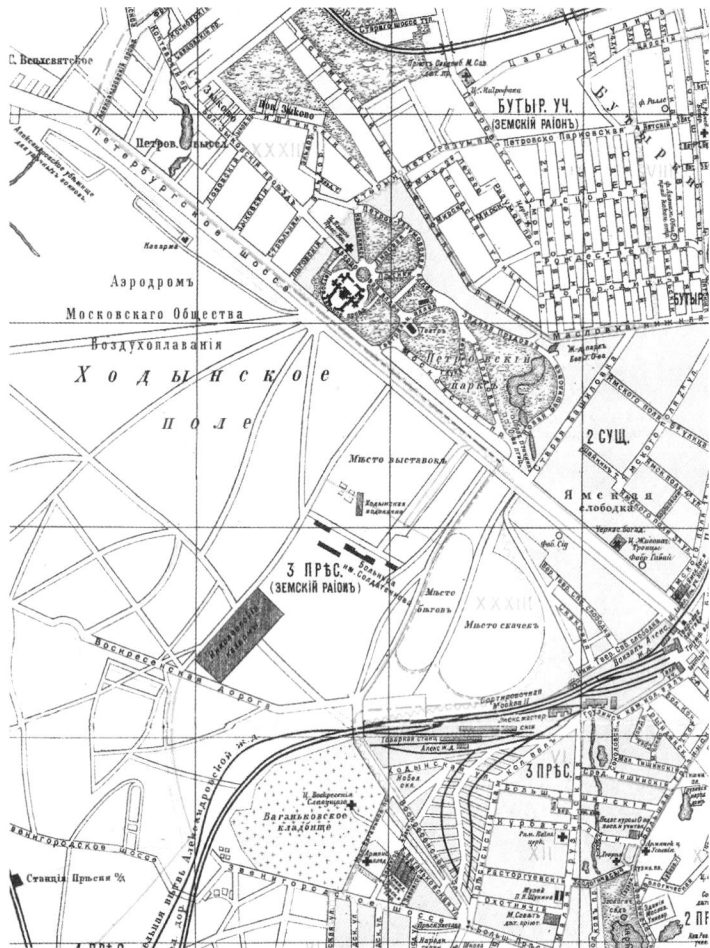

A map of Khodynka as it was in 1919. The field has a long and sometimes tragic history. During the coronation of Tsar Nicholas II in 1896, 1389 people were killed during a stampede. The region became the Soviet Union's first passenger airport in the 1930s and the original home of domestic aviation, with plants and engineering bureaus based there from the 1930s including Sukhoi and Ilyushin. Khodynka was closed as an active aviation centre in 2003, but continued to be used as a military parade staging area until 2015.

Red Army infantry march on Red Square in 1918. It was only in later years that the lamp posts were removed and the square accurately cobbled to allow large scale military parades.

# 11th August 1918

A Bolshevik Party meeting was held on Red Square on 11th August 1918, during which a Putilov-Garford armoured car, built and armoured in Leningrad on an imported U.S. Garford truck chassis was driven around the square. Although not exactly a military parade, the now regular appearance of armoured vehicles on Red Square was a precursor of things to come.

A 2nd Series Austin armoured car traverses Red Square infront of the earliest parade review stand. 11th August 1918. The banner reads "Glory to the fallen fighters of the Proletarian Revolution".

# 7th November 1918 – 1st Anniversary of the Great October Socialist Revolution

On 7th November 1918 the Bolshevik Russian state celebrated the first anniversary of the "Great October Revolution" with a parade held on Red Square, presided over by Vladimir Ilyich Ulyanov - Lenin. The parade which included military school cadets, reserve workers regiments and battalions, machine gunners, cavalry, light and heavy artillery which passed beneath a review stand from which Lenin received the parade. The Kremlin wall and some buildings around the square had been seriously damaged during fierce fighting the previous year. The wooden stand for revolutionary leaders to review parades was built at the same time the Kremlin walls were repaired. The 7th November parade concluded with a flypast by the Workers and Peasants Red Air Fleet (RKKVF).

At the time of the parade, the country had withdrawn from active participation in the "Great War" in Europe, but was now engaged in a civil war with foreign military intervention that would continue in some areas until the autumn of 1922, with sporadic fighting in some regions for several months thereafter.

# 24th November 1918

There was one final military parade in 1918, on 24th November for "officers day", with a march-past before Lenin on the review stand as on 7th November, followed by a meeting of senior officers, doubtless accompanied by a small quantity of vodka.

# 1919

As 1919 dawned, the Russian Civil War raged, with the most active period of the entire civil war being from January to November 1919. Bolshevik forces engaged the White Army under the command of General Anton I. Denikin, Commander of Armed Forces of Southern Russia (VSUR) and Admiral Aleksandr Vasilievich Kolchak in Siberia, whose efforts were aided and assisted by direct foreign intervention. The war was ultimately unsuccessful for those nations that had attacked the Bolshevik state. The foreign "colonial superpowers" were all ultimately forced to retreat, while countries such as Poland that had contingents of troops operating in Russia were in turn invaded by the Red Army as the war ebbed and flowed. By 1919 it was already clear to the world that the new Bolshevik state was a permanent reality that would need to be dealt with politically, not militarily, and the threat of communism being spread by the new state would need to be dealt with on a country by country basis, as attacking the Russian "Rodina" (Motherland) had proven ineffective.

On 7th March 1919, the Bolshevik state held the Congress of the 3rd International as part of which troops of the Moscow Garrison marched on Red Square, the infantry being followed by horse drawn artillery, cadets from military academies and various internationalist organisations. The military parade was followed by a civilian demonstration, with V.I. Lenin present during the celebrations on Red Square. The parade was held against a backdrop of civil war raging across much of the country. It would be during the next gathering on Red Square, held on 1st May, that evidence of the first major combat successes of Bolshevik forces would be seen on Red Square, and the tradition of the square being used to demonstrate armoured might, captured or indigenous, began in earnest.

# 1st May 1919

The May Day "Rabochikh i Krestyan" (workers and peasants) parade in 1919 by tradition now contained a military element. Columns of marching infantry passed before V.I. Lenin as he personally reviewed the parade of as yet far from unified, or uniformly dressed, military personnel. A single Jeffery-Poplavko armoured car also appeared on Red Square. The significant event of the military part of the May 1919 parade was however not the columns of infantry, but the first formal appearance of tanks, specifically one tank, on Red Square. As the civil war raged around the country, the Bolsheviks had begun to capture various armoured vehicles, representative samples of which duly ended up on Red Square to demonstrate the military prowess of the Bolshevik revolution in containing its internal and external detractors.

The first tank to traverse the cobbles of Red Square was paraded during the 1st May 1919 Red Square parade in the form of a war-trophy French Automitrailleuse à chenilles Renault FT modèle 1917, better known by its company designation Renault-FT-17 and known by the Russians as the "Reno" (Renault FT-17) tank. The tank was one of five French built Renault tanks captured from White Russian forces under the command of General Anton I. Denikin on 18th March 1919 during a battle near Beryozovka station on the outskirts of the Ukrainian city of Odessa. One or more of these trophy tanks were duly brought to Moscow where on 1st May 1919 an example was presented for review by Lenin, and then paraded through Red Square, giving the crowds their first viewing of enemy war trophies resulting from a

The first tank to be paraded on Red Square was a French Automitrailleuse à chenilles Renault FT modèle 1917 (Renault FT-17) captured by the Red Army near Odessa. The captured tanks were evaluated, and formed the basis of the first Russian tank, the KS.

strengthening Soviet state and its armed forces. The "Reno" paraded through Red Square was accompanied by several armoured cars which had been armoured in Russia on the basis of imported chassis, however the Renault FT-17 has the claim to fame as being the first tank demonstrated on Red Square.

The Renault FT-17 tank paraded on Red Square in May 1919 was more than the display of a captured enemy tank. In contrast with other European countries such as Great Britain, France and Germany, Imperial Russia did not have the industrial capacity to design and built tanks during the First World War, and so had concentrated on the assembly of armoured cars on imported chassis. The capture and use of foreign built tanks during the Russian Civil War gave the Red Army an opportunity to evaluate these different foreign designs however, and as the new Soviet state rapidly industrialised, provided the capability to manufacture Soviet tanks based on the best features of tanks developed by other countries, giving the country the ability to leap-frog the development timeline required for military industrialisation.

In contrast to the lumbering British Mk.V tanks, a significant number of which had also been captured during the Civil War, the Renault FT-17 displayed on Red Square in May 1919 was considered a relatively small and modern design appropriate for further development in Russia. After its Red Square parade debut, the captured Renault FT-17 was used as an "obrazets" or prototype example for the first Russian "domestic" tank design. After being paraded through Red Square the captured Renault FT-17 tank was sent to the Krasnoye Sormovo plant in Nizhny Novgorod (later Gorky) which was instructed to organize series production of indigenous Russian tanks on the basis of the sample FT-17 tank provided.

Work on developing a Russian variant of the Renault tank (the "Russky-Reno") was duly car-

British built Mk.V tanks captured from White Army forces during the civil war being paraded through Red Square. These captured tanks were paraded from 1919 until as late as 1929.

Vladimir Ilyich Ulyanov - better known as Lenin, addresses the crowds on Red Square, 25th May 1919.

ried out at the Krasnoye Sormovo plant (hence its KS designation), with local modifications to the original design to simplify production in Russia with available tooling and technology. The tank was reverse-engineered by a combined team from the Putilov and Izhorsky plants under the direction of N. Khrulev, with the assistance of the Ryabushinskiy-Kuznetsov Company, better known as the nationalized AMO plant (later ZiS/ZiL) in Moscow, which managed to procure a quantity of FIAT engines from Italy before the embargo imposed by Western nations took effect. Series production of the new design was to be undertaken at the Sormovo (Krasnoye Sormovo) plant in Nizhny Novgorod, with the hull and turret armour set provided by the Izhorsky plant near Petrograd (later Leningrad, today St. Petersburg).

The first prototype of the new tank was completed on 31st August 1920, with the tank thereafter undergoing three months of plant trials. The French origin 37mm "Hotchkiss" armament, obtained from the Obukhov plant was installed on the original prototype on 1st December 1920.

The first indigenous Russian tank design to enter production was accepted into service with the Red Army bearing the name KS, named after its place of assembly, Krasnoye Sormovo. In service the KS tank was also known as the "Russky-Reno" (Russian Renault, sometimes reversed), the Legky Tank "M" or Maly Tank "M" (light and small tank M respectively), but most often as the Legky Tank "KS" (Light Tank KS - Krasnoye Sormovo). A total of only 15 KS tanks were built or modified in 1920-21, including the original prototype. The KS tank was in Red Army service from 1920 until 1930, during which time it is not believed to have seen active combat. The fifteen KS tanks assembled in the Sormovo plant formed the 7th Tank Brigade that participated in subsequent Red Square parades.

It should be noted that although Soviet sources claim that KS series production consisted of the first Renault prototype and fourteen additional tanks, subsequent post-Soviet era research indicates that some of these tanks were rebuilt from existing Renault FT-17 tanks captured from White Russian forces. The KS was nevertheless the first Russian tank to enter "series" production, and the beginning of a tank production industry that would become the most expansive in the world.

The first Red Army military parade was held at Khodynka, north west of Moscow city centre on 1st May 1919.

Infantry of the 36th Rifle Division at Khodynka, 1st May 1919. Subsequently, all main parades were held on Red Square, however the huge field (later Moscow's first airport) remained a training ground for Red Square parades until as late as 2015.

## 25th May 1919 – First Red Army Parade on Red Square

The first formal parade dedicated to the newly formed "Raboche-Krestyanskaya Krasnaya Armiya (RKKA) the Workers and Peasant's Red Army held on Red Square rather than at Khodynka was held on a warm, balmy day in the early summer of 1919. The assembled marching troops, cavalry and infantry riding bicycles were reviewed by V.I. Lenin, who formally reviewed the parade, with Lev Trotsky* and other members of the Bolshevik Party standing alongside. The parade included workers regiments, communist battalions, and cadets from military schools. The Red Army was meantime engaged in combat with General Denikin's White Army forces on several fronts. Despite the international support, military opposition to the Bolshevik revolution was gradually waning, and in October 1919, after a series of successes as he pushed north from the Caucasus, General Denikin's White Army forces were categorically defeated by Bolshevik forces at Orel and pushed back to Novorossysk. The tide had decisively turned in favour of the Red Army as the second anniversary of the Great October Revolution approached.

## 7th November 1919 – 2nd Anniversary of the Great October Socialist Revolution

After the first historic anniversary of the Great October Revolution in 1918, the second and subsequent parades were broadly similar in nature for several years thereafter. The 7th November 1919 military parade was primarily an infantry parade, with a small display of horse drawn artillery; however a small number of armoured cars and a handful of captured tanks were also present. The second anniversary parade of the Great October Revolution was undertaken against the backdrop of a country still in the middle of a protracted civil war, which would continue to rage as the country entered the second decade of the 20th Century.

* Lev Trotsky was the head of the head of the Revolutionary Military Council of the RSFSR from 6th September 1918 to 26th January 1925. He attended the parades alongside Lenin in this capacity.

Mk.V "Rikardo" tanks captured from White Russian forces during the civil war on parade in Moscow, 1st May 1925. Mk. A "Taylor", original Renault FT-17 and Soviet built KS tanks are waiting to enter the square. (O. Baranov)

THE RED ARMY ON PARADE 1917-45

# Soviet Military Parades in the
# 1920s

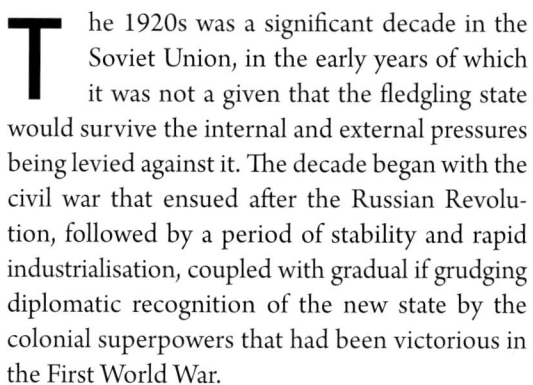

The 1920s was a significant decade in the Soviet Union, in the early years of which it was not a given that the fledgling state would survive the internal and external pressures being levied against it. The decade began with the civil war that ensued after the Russian Revolution, followed by a period of stability and rapid industrialisation, coupled with gradual if grudging diplomatic recognition of the new state by the colonial superpowers that had been victorious in the First World War.

By the beginning of 1920 the civil war was however turning decisively in favour of the Bolsheviks. After a series of battlefield defeats in the summer and autumn of 1919, Admiral Kolchak on 4th January 1920 relinquished supreme command of the anti-Bolshevik White forces to General Denikin. He subsequently turned himself over to Czech forces and asked for allied protection, but was handed over to the Mensheviks in Irkutsk - who in turn handed him over to the Bolsheviks. He was executed on 7th January 1920. In March 1920, Denikin's forces, already pushed back to Novorossysk, were then forced to evacuate to Crimea as a final refuge and in April Denikin turned over his command to General Piotr N. Wrangel, and fled, first to Constantinople, then Great Britain, and eventually to Hungary.

In 1922, the Russian Soviet Federative Socialist Republic (RSFSR) joined with Belorussia, the Transcaucasian Federation (split in 1936 into Azerbaijan, Armenia and Georgia) and Ukraine to form the Union of Soviet Socialist Republics – the USSR or Soviet Union, which would ultimately encompass 15 republics within its borders. The Soviet Union was the first country in the world to have a government based on Marxist socialist principles, which sent shock waves around the world, particularly within Europe and the United States.

As stability ensued after the hardship years of World War One, the Russian Revolution and the ensuing international backed civil war, the fledgling Soviet Union began to rapidly industrialise. The Bolshevik army, soon to become the Red Army, had inherited a collection of various First World War era armoured cars and transport vehicles. Vehicles captured by the Bolsheviks during the Civil War were later added to this mix, including 83 tanks of British and French origin. Captured British tanks, examples of which were displayed on Red Square during the 1920s included 12 British Mk.A "Whippet" tanks (designated "Taylor" in Russian service from their engine nameplates) and a few Mk.V tanks (designated "Rikardo" in Russian service) which were used by the Red Army until the very beginning of the 1930s.

Soviet military parades in the 1920s began with a mix of these foreign "trophy" tanks and armoured vehicles, including the British Mk.V and Renault FT-17 tanks and various imported armoured cars. While these war trophy exhibits were being demonstrated at military parades in the first half of the 1920s, the country was meantime rapidly industrialising, and the indigenous Russian KS tank would be joined by the MS-1 (T-18) as the Red Army began to receive locally produced tanks to replace the captured tanks of World War One vintage.

By 1924, the Soviet Union had produced its first miliary aircraft, and by the following year had also begun domestic mass production of infantry rifles. Later in the decade, the Soviet Union demonstrated its first fully fledged indigenous ar-

31

moured vehicle designs, the BA-27 armoured car and the aforementioned MS-1 (T-18) tank. Based purely on the public displays of military might alone, it was evident to those countries that maintained foreign embassy staff in the new socialist state, and thereby had a direct point of observation, that a step-change was occuring in the Soviet Union. From a western European standpoint, the country had transitioned within a single decade from being a useful second front to wear down German imperial ambitions during World War One, via temporary useful status as a pariah revolutionary state, to major industrial and military power in its own right by the end of the second decade of the 20th Century. The Soviet State that emerged from revolution in 1917 was by the end of the 1920s re-engaged with most of its former adversaries, but on very different terms to those that had existed with Imperial Russia before the outbreak of World War One. By the end of the 1920s, Soviet state industrialisation was exponential, and by the end of the decade the Red Army was receiving small arms, armoured cars, tanks and aircraft of indigenous origin. More disturbingly for the weakening colonial powers of western Europe, the now not-so-fledlging Soviet state was developing its military industrial complex, including technology transfers and military training, in cooperation with the very state that the victorious powers had ensured received all of the blame for World War One - Germany.

# 1920

With the country in a state of civil war, there was no military parade held on 1st May 1920, instead of which there was held an "All Russia Communist Subbotnik". This in 1920 involved the restoration of industrial buildings, railroad facilities and equipment destroyed or abandoned during the civil war, but in latter years became a Soviet tradition whereby citizens would clean-up of streets, parks and public areas. The tradition of a "subbotnik" day for cleaning up public areas continued through until the final days of the Soviet Union and even beyond. On 12th May there was a small parade by graduates of a machine-gun training course held within the Kremlin walls and attended by V.I.Lenin, but Red Square was quiet. An exhibition was however organised within the corridors of the GUM department store and the periphery of Red Square in the early summer of 1920 entitled "Zhizn Krasnoy Armii i Flota" (Life of the Red Army and Navy) which included equipment captured in battle from the two split White Armies and international forces during the civil war. The displays included larger equipment including armoured cars, tanks and artillery.

Several Renault French Automitrailleuse à chenilles Renault FT modèle 1917 (Renault FT) tanks captured near Odessa during the civil war were from 1919 paraded through Red Square. The tank was used as the basis for the Soviet KS which was almost identical but had a distinctive turret. These particular tanks are being shown in at Blagoveshchensk in the Amur region in 1920 after capture from American forces.

Captured British Mk.V "Rikardo" tanks parade through Red Square after the death of Lenin in 1924. Note the "nuisance" lamp posts which would later be removed to allow multiple columns of armoured vehicles to pass the Lenin Mausoleum, under construction at the time of this photograph.

# 27th June 1920 – Parade devoted to the 2nd Komintern International Congress

Although the 27th June parade devoted to the 2nd Komintern International Congress was primarily a civilian parade, there was one nuance in that the infantry involved paraded past a wooden review stand mounted atop an earth embankment directly under the Kremlin walls. The reasoning behind this was to make the parade more "military" and less ceremonial in appearance. There was also no military parade on 7th November 1920.

While the parades were underway during 1920, the first two examples of the KS or Reno-Russky tank were completed at the Krasnoye Sormovo plant in Nizhny Novgorod* (Gorky from 1932). The Soviet tank industry had taken its first steps towards becoming the most powerful tank production enterprise in the world.

# 17th June 1921

There was no military element to the May Day celebrations in 1921, however there was as a military parade during the 3rd Komintern International Congress on 17th June 1921. There was also no military parade on 7th November 1921.

Meanwhile, in Nizhny Novgorod the small batch of "series production" Reno-Russkiy (KS) tanks were completed at the Krasnoye Sormovo plant, which would soon make their debut on Red Square.

---

*Nizhny Novgorod was renamed Gorky on 7th October 1932. After the demise of the Soviet Union the city reverted to the name Nizhny Novgorod.

THE RED ARMY ON PARADE 1917-45

A column of Austin-Putilov "Kegresse" half-track armoured cars passes through Red Square, 1st May 1922. Note the rough surface of the parade square.

One of three Prombron-1 military command car prototypes being demonstrated on Red Square in 1922. The former Russo-Balt company was nationalised after the revolution, becoming the Armour Repair and Auto Plant (BTAZ) №1 within the PromBron holding. The Prombron-1 was based on the pre-war Russo-Balt S24-40 XVIII series.

# May 1st 1922

The gradual militarisation of the May Day parades continued in 1922. The 1st May 1922 "Workers and Peasants" parade was again reviewed by Lev Trotsky in his position as Commander of the Soviet Military Council, who in contrast with earlier years stood at ground level rather than on the temporary parade review stand. The parade was largely civilian in nature but is significant in that it culminated with a display of infantry and navy forces led by a military band. It was the first time that a military element had been introduced into the May Day parades. It was also the first time a military orchestra had taken part in such a parade.

In August 1922, an agreement was signed between the Soviet Union and Germany that would have a profound effect on the development of modern weapons and tactics in both countries. The two countries which had suffered most at the hands of the victors of World War One, namely Germany as a result of the harsh terms of the Versailles Treaty and the Soviet Union as established in 1922 after several years of civil war and foreign intervention after the Russian Revolution of 1917, on that date signed an agreement on military cooperation between their respective pariah states.

The treaty, signed on 11th August 1922 between the German Reichswehr and the Red Army allowed for military cooperation on military technology. This specifically included armour, aviation and chemical warfare, and for the establishment of German military training centres on Soviet soil allowing such joint developments to be carried out far from prying eyes. Critically, the treaty also had provisions regarding the development of armoured and combined arms strategy and tactics, the beginnings of the art of "Blitzkrieg" as developed by Germany and the Soviet Union while the old world order concentrated on the development of tanks for infantry support as they had been utilized in the First World War. In return for providing training grounds deep in the Soviet hinterland, Germany agreed to allow the Red Army to conduct military exercises alongside the Reichswehr and to share industrial and military technology developments. The Reichswehr had established an office in Moscow by 1924 and cooperation was conducted in secret, albeit with some press speculation in 1926 in European papers. Armoured warfare technology and operational training was developed and practiced in Kazan, and aviation warfare and pilot training carried out at Lipetsk near Voronezh. There were even plans to build

A display of military equipment captured from the White army during the civil war. In the foreground is a Bullock-Lombard half-track tractor. Red Square, Moscow, summer 1920.

German Junkers aircraft, at the former BTAZ №1 armour repair plant at Fili in the suburbs of Moscow, and 100 aircraft were in fact built in collaboration with Junkers from 1923-1927.

The German "Kama" Panzerschule was meantime established in Kazan in 1926, with the first nine German tanks arriving there in 1929, three light tanks with 37mm armament and six medium tanks with 75mm armament. Three British Carden-Loyd light tanks procured by the Soviet Union were delivered to the Reichswehr in return. One of the German training officers who visited Kazan during these years (in the summer of 1932) was Heinz Guderian, while "graduates" of the joint training exercises in the Soviet Union and the small officer training school established in Moscow included the famous panzer commanders Keitel, Mannstein and Model*.

The cooperation began to dissolve in 1932 as politics changed in Germany, and with the rise to power of Hitler, all such cooperation came to an abrupt halt. The Soviet Union formally asked the Reichswehr to close all facilities and depart the Soviet Union in August of 1933, and by September of that year all German staff had departed the country. The period of cooperation had been borne out of necessity as the pariah states of Germany and the Soviet Union combined their efforts to build their respective armed forces with the minimum of outside interference. The results were both positive and negative for the Soviet Union. The country had learned much of German "Blitzkrieg" armoured warfare thinking in the late 1920s and very early 1930s - which could explain the Soviet preoccupation with tank and anti-tank gun developments. But Germany had gained immense capability from the covert training cooperation, and had begun to craft the art of Blitzkrieg while on Soviet soil. By the time the Germans departed the Soviet Union in 1933, the collaborative aviation efforts at Lipetsk had meantime included early design work on the German Ju-87 later developed in Germany from 1934-37, and had resulted in the training of over 120 pilots for the Luftwaffe. Never more so was the phrase a double-edged sword more appropriate than when describing the Soviet German period of military cooperation in 1924-33.

---

* In the summer of 1940, Wilhelm Keitel, now a Field Marshal and head of German Army General Staff (OKW) sent a memorandum to Hitler, warning of the dangers of considering war with the Soviet Union, and simultaneously asking for retirement, which was refused. It was Keitel who would ultimately sign the German capitulation in May 1945. He was executed for war crimes in 1946.

# 7th November 1922 – 5th Anniversary of the Great October Socialist Revolution

The 7th November 1922 military parade celebrating the 5th anniversary of the Great October Socialist Revolution marked a new era for the fledgling state. By October 1922 the civil war had petered out in most of the country, though sporadic fighting continued for several months thereafter. The 7th November 1922 parade was thereby the first "peacetime" parade in the new state, which would be formally known as the Soviet Union from 28th December 1922. In the years following the end of the Russian civil war the new country was officially recognized by its former civil war era major adversaries, beginning with Great Britain, followed by France, Germany and Japan, with the USA belatedly providing the Soviet Union with full diplomatic recognition only in 1933. As the civil war came to its inevitable conclusion, with foreign intervention forces in particular having learned hard lessons as to the extent of Russian geography, distances and weather extremes, the battle hardened Red Army had in service aproximately 300 armoured cars of 22 different types. It also inherited the aforementioned 83 captured tanks, primarily of French and British origin.

The 1922 November parade was reviewed as in previous years by the Commander of the Revvoensovet, the Revolutionary Military Council (RVS), Lev Trotsky, now looking on from a newly built review stand on the square under the Kremlin walls, which location in differing forms would become the default observation platform for the Soviet hierarchy from that day until the end of the Soviet Union. Infantry units from the founder members of the Union of Soviet Socialist Republics (abbreviated to USSR or the Soviet Union), namely Russia, Ukraine, Belorussia and the Transcaucasian Federation (split in 1936 into Azerbaijan, Armenia and Georgia) marched through Red Square followed by cavalry, horse drawn artillery, various captured trucks and significantly large columns of Austin-Kegresse half-track armoured cars, followed by tractors and towed artillery. All of which manoeuvred over the slightly less than even ground of Red Square, avoiding the tramlines and lamp posts, which would in the years ahead be cleared to allow larger parades of massed armour and military equipment.

The year 1922 was significant for two other reasons. Firstly, it was the first year that both May and November were used for military parades, a tradition that would continue until the mid years of the post-war Cold War period. Secondly, and more fundamentally important, another element was added to the structure and format of Soviet military parades in 1922, in that for the first time observers from foreign diplomatic missions were invited to the parades. Their presence ensured that the message related to the growing military strength of the Soviet Union would be adequately broadcast to the world at large. As such, 1922 might be regarded as the year in which the focus of the parades became as much about delivering a message for foreign consumption as being purely a domestic display for domestic audiences.

FIAT-15ter trucks, each armed with two 7.62mm PM-1910 "Maxim" machine guns and what appears to be a Lewis machine gun, parade through Red Square. (Viktor Kulikov)

# 1923

The outcome of the civil war following the Russian Revolution did not provide the desired result that the colonial power victors of World War One would have liked. Having expended considerable military efforts in the southern, far northern and far eastern regions of the Soviet Union to no ultimate avail, Great Britain, France, Japan and the United States in particular were now forced to accept that the emerging communist state was not about to disappear, and may well have expansionist colonial ambitions of its own. Great Britain saw the situation as a return to the "Great Game" of the previous century, not least as the newly developing Soviet Union encompassed states straddling the Silk Roads that were central to trade between the Middle East and Asia, and of course in the south within striking distance of Great Britain's crown jewel, India. Viewing the potential trade with the new Soviet Union while at the same time cognisant of the military threat this new "colonial" power could pose, Great Britain resigned itself to diplomatic recognition of the new state, followed in due course by the other major European powers.

Diplomatic acceptance was not however an indication that relations with the Soviet Union's former adversaries were necessarily warming. Great Britain was concerned in particular with regard to Soviet commercial and diplomatic agents making inroads into regions of southern Asia, which Great Britain saw as a direct threat to its interests there. Great Britain had however been far from successful in its own military incursions into the newly formed state, so was clearly not in a position to take a military stance on the subject. Due specifically to this "Soviet Interference" in India, diplomatic relations with Great Britain remained complex, deteriorating to the point whereby on 8th May 1923 Lord Curzon sent a letter to Moscow indicating that unless the Soviet Union removed all its agents from Asia within ten days then trade sanctions would follow, a diplomatic position that almost exactly 100 years later remains remarkably familiar. Prior to World War One such a declaration would have been regarded by the British government as a prelude to war; however that option had already been attempted by a combination of foreign powers during the Russian Civil War and had ultimately failed. Realistically, there was no British will to enter another conflict on the same territory with the same "enemy" and doubtless with the same inevitable outcome. As American and Japanese forces had discovered when making military inroads from the Pacific side of the fledging state during the Civil War, the Soviet Union was geographically vast and thereby militarily not the best target for military endeavours. Diplomacy thereby remained the only option available. Full diplomatic relations were gradually re-established between the Western Powers and the Soviet Union in the 1920s, starting with Great Britain, which was the first large European state to recognize the Soviet State in February 1924, having been preceded in this by Germany, Finland, Latvia and Poland.

On 1st May 1923, a military parade was held on Red Square as part of the overall May Day workers celebrations, with the event being filmed from the air for the first time.

# 7th November 1923 – 6th Anniversary of the Great October Socialist Revolution

On 7th November 1923 the Soviet Union celebrated the 6th Anniversary of the "Great October Socialist Revolution" with a military parade. The parade was taken by the Commissar of Military Affairs Nikolai Podvoisky, who had held differing posts during the civil war but was in 1923 both head of SportinterN (Sport International) and head of High Council of Physical Culture. The parade was commanded by the commander of the Moscow Military District (MVO), Nikolai Muralov. The commander of the armed forces of the republics, Kamenev, was also in attendance.

The parade commenced with infantry now in new Red Army uniforms, followed by cavalry and massed formations of troops on bicycles, accompanied by the first elements of mechanisation, with the armoured cars on display now followed by small tracked "Bolshevik" tractors towing field artillery. It was an early start, but the mechanisation of the Red Army would increase exponentially in the years ahead.

As Lenin was at the time seriously ill, he was not present at the parade, and was represented by a temporary plaster statue painted white for the occasion.

The Renault FT-17 became the prototype for the first Soviet tank, the KS. Although only a very small number of KS tanks were built at the Krasnoye Sormovo plant (hence KS) the tank represented the birth of tank production in the Soviet Union. (Mikhail Svirin)

# 1924

1924 would prove to be another monumental year in the history of the Soviet Union. The year started with the death of the nation's founder, Vladimir Ilyich Ulyanov (Lenin) who died on 21st January 1924. He died only days before Great Britain on 1st February 1924 became the first major international power to recognize the fledgling Soviet Union, one lasting consequence of which is that to this day cars registered to the British Embassy and British companies have a number plate starting "001". Almost a decade later, in 1933, the United States would be the fourth major international power to recognize the Soviet Union, with American registered cars to this day in consequence having the prefix "004". Somewhat prophetically, Germany was one of the first countries to diplomatically recognise the Soviet Union, on 23rd July 1923, several months before Great Britain.

Further to the diplomatic intrigues in India alluded to previously, and despite the apparent softening of relations with Great Britain and formal diplomatic recognition of the new state, relationships with Great Britain deteriorated sharply in 1924 as a result of a scandal known in Great Britain as the "Zinoviev letter". The letter, purportedly from the head of the Komintern, demanded that British Communists set up infiltration in the British armed forces and, further, prepare for Civil War in Great Britain. The authenticity of the letter and the surrounding scandal are not immediately relevant here, but suffice to note that relations between the Soviet Union and countries in Europe continued to be less than cordial in the mid 1920s even as diplomatic relations between the Soviet Union and the outer world were becoming normalised.

# 1st May 1924

By the time of the 1st May parade on Red Square, an earth embankment had been erected near the Kremlin walls on which a temporary Lenin memorial and review stand had been erected, such that the 1st May 1924 parade was the first military parade reviewed from a formal, albeit temporary structure.

The 1st May parade included infantry, some marching with gas masks, and as in previous years a single column of World War One era captured armoured cars and trucks.

The small temporary wooden mausoleum built on Red Square immediately after the death of Lenin in January 1924 was replaced later in May by a larger, more permanent, but still wooden building, from the raised podium of which parades would be reviewed until the new and final concrete and marble iteration of the Lenin Mausoleum as it is known to all today was built in 1929-30.

Austin, FIAT-Izhorsky, Garford-Putilov and other World War One era armoured cars were parded through Red Square in the early 1920s before Soviet domestic armoured car production started in 1927.

# 7th November 1924 – 7th Anniversary of the Great October Socialist Revolution

The 7th November 1924 military parade was the first anniversary parade to be held after the death of Lenin. As had seemed inevitable after the initial throws of revolutionary success, the year had been symbolised by infighting within the Bolshevik Party as central committee members vied for power in the Soviet high command infrastructure.

The Parade of the Troops of the Moscow Garrison devoted to the 7th Anniversary of the Revolution was unremarkable other than that the ongoing industrialisation of the state and the consequential mechanisation of the Red Army was apparent from the new vehicles displayed on Red Square.

The parade commander in November 1924 was G.D. Bazilevich, the Deputy Commander of the Moscow Military District (MVO), with the parade review held in the presence of the chairman of Central Executive Committee of the Soviet Union (TsIK SSSR), M.I. Kalinin. The parade was however taken by the representative of the "Revvoensovet" (Revolutionary Military Council - RVS) Lev Trotsky, with other members of the RVS on the review stand including M.V. Frunze, S.M. Budenny, and the MVO commander K.E. Voroshilov. It would be the first and last time Trotsky would review the now traditional 7th November parade, as he was relieved of his position as People's Commissar of Army and Navy affairs (Narkomvoenflot) some weeks later, to be replaced at the parades by the Civil War hero, Mikhail V. Frunze.

While the Soviet Union was adjusting to a future without its founding leader, in Germany a disgruntled World War One veteran and former art-historian turned political activist was completing a book on his vision for the future of that nation, which was in hindsight an almost mirror image of the Soviet Union's rise from pariah status to new found industrial and military strength.

Entitled "Mein Kampf" (My Struggle), the German title suggested that given the rise to power of his NSDAP National Socialist Party, then in accordance with his view of the new world order Germany would amongst other things renounce the Versailles Treaty, build up the country's armed forces, and restore national pride. This was a theoretical moot point in 1924, but a decade later it would become for Europe a very grim reality.

The November 1924 parade on Red Square began with a marching parade by Red Army (RKKA) military academy staff, students and officer cadets, followed by infantry, OGPU internal security, border troops, and specialists including engineering troops. Horse drawn "tachanki" machine gun carts and artillery followed. The 1924 parade was however notable due primarily to the parade debut of new and indigenously designed and built military vehicles, specifically the first series production truck. The AMO-F-15 was based on the Italian FIAT-15ter design already in service with the Red Army. The Kommunar tracked artillery tractor, as also displayed, was built at the Kharkov Steam Locomotive Plant (KhPZ) from 1924 until 1931, based on a German Hanomag design.

The Renault FT-17 (foreground) became the prototype for the first Soviet tank, the KS (right). Although only a very small number of KS tanks were built at Krasnoye Sormovo plant (hence KS) the tank represented the birth of tank production in the Soviet Union.

The new AMO-F-15 4x2 truck which had its parade debut on 7th November 1924 had only just entered series production. The first prototype was completed on 1st November, with the first pre-production batch of 10 vehicles completed on 6th November, all of which were duly displayed on Red Square the following day. The AMO-F-15 entered series production later in that year as a Soviet modification of the FIAT-15ter, the first of which had been assembled at AMO and displayed on Red Square in 1918-19. The AMO-F-15 was the result of a technology transfer agreement with the Italian company and was built under licence at the AMO (later ZiS) plant in Moscow. The 1.5 tonne payload 4x2 AMO F-15 was a significant vehicle in the mechanisation of the Red Army in that it represented the first series production military transport vehicle. It was paraded on 7th November in standard general service, anti-aircraft (mounting tandem 7.62mm PM-1910 anti-aircraft machine guns), searchlight and "ZT" sound locator versions.

The 1924 parade also included the first appearance of the Kommunar tracked artillery tractor which continued to be paraded on Red Square during the mid 1920s, towing the 76.2mm M-1915-28 anti-aircraft gun and other artillery. The Kommunar was in of itself not a remarkable vehicle; however the deployment of tracked artillery tractors in the Red Army in the mid 1920s was an indication of the rapid mechanisation of the Red Army at a time when other European powers - often later defined as having highly mechanised armies - were almost exclusively reliant on horse drawn artillery.

# 23rd February 1925

In 1925, a new national holiday was introduced in the Soviet Union on the 7th anniversary of the foundation of the Red Army - "Day of the Red Army and Fleet", based on the events of 23rd February 1918 and the decision made in 1922 to establish a professional holiday for the armed forces. The new holiday was intended primarily for serving members of the Red Army and other military forces, however the celebration has over the years been extended more generically to the male population of the country. In recognition of the new holiday, a military parade was held on 23rd February 1925. The parade included military cadets, sappers and NKVD forces, but no armoured vehicles or tanks. The parade by the Moscow Garrison was taken by the People's Commissar of the Army and Navy Mikhail Frunze, mounted on horseback. The date would thereafter become a national holiday, and is celebrated to the present day in the Russian Federation.

# 1st May 1925 - Parade of Troops of the Moscow Garrison

The 1st May 1925 parade by the Moscow Garrison was reviewed by Mikhail V. Frunze on horseback, with the parade commander being K.E.Voroshilov, then Commander of the Moscow Garrison, also on horseback. Voroshilov would soon thereafter take up the position of Minister responsible for the Army and Navy. In the background, also watching the parade from the review stand was a man whose later career would literally influence the lives and deaths of millions - Iosif Stalin.

The military part of the May Day parade began with officer cadets, infantry, and naval troops of the Baltic Fleet and even the higher school of military "maskirovka" (disguise), followed by infantry on bicycles, motorcycles armed with machine guns, cavalry and a single row of armoured cars which had recently seen service in the Civil War, including "FIAT" and "Garford" vehicles.

There followed a column of tanks, British "Taylor" (Whippet) and no less than nine "Ricardo" (Mk. V - of mixed type) tanks captured during the Civil War, one of which only just made it across the square before subsequently breaking down. A mix of Renault FT-17 and Soviet "KS" tanks were also paraded through the square.

The parade was the first mass demonstration of armour on Red Square, albeit primarily a collection of Civil War era trophies rather than indigenous tanks, and which were paraded through Red Square in May rather than November. It was overall also the first major demonstration of Soviet mechanized might, with the vehicles on the ground accompanied by a fly-past of 88 aircraft.

There was no 7th November parade in 1925 due to the death of Mikhail Frunze on 31st October 1925 while undergoing an operation

A FIAT-Izhorsky armoured car on Red Square, 1st May 1925. Note the wooden Lenin Mausoleum which was replaced in 1929-1930 by the final concrete and marble iteration which (in slightly modified form) can still be seen today. The Izhorsky Plant received 50 FIAT chassis in the summer of 1917, and by April 1918 had built 47 armoured cars of this type on the chassis.

THE RED ARMY ON PARADE 1917-45

The Renault FT-17 was chosen for domestic development in the RSFSR (Russia before the formation of the Soviet Union) on the basis that it was light, manoeuverable and well armed.

The AMO F-15 entered series production in 1924 and the first production batch was displayed on Red Square on 7th November that year, literally days after they were assembled. These AMO F-15 trucks are taking part in the All-Russia Automobile Expedition of 1925 (Gruzovik Press)

that he did not feel was required, but which senior party officials, including Stalin, had insisted he undergo. Another of the founding members of the revolution was dead, but on the international diplomatic front the Soviet Union was gaining ground. The year 1925 closed with China, Japan and several countries in South America joining Great Britain in diplomatically recognizing the Soviet Union as a nation state, with the country beginning to be accomodated around the worlds as a necessary trade partner.

# 1st May 1926

On 1st May 1926 there was a parade of troops of the Moscow Garrison. Although there were no new revelations on Red Square, the first two MS-1 (T-18) tanks were completed in 1926, and these would soon appear on Red Square together with the first series production indigenous Russian armoured car design.

# 7th November 1926 - 9th Anniversary of the Great October Socialist Revolution

On 7th November the traditional parade of Troops of the Moscow Garrison was held. The parade was reviewed by K.E.Voroshilov, with the parade commander being the new MVO commander - G.D.Basilevich.

# 1927

By the spring of 1927, relations between the Soviet Union and Europe, and in particular Great Britain were at their lowest ebb since the Allied Intervention following the Russian Revolution of 1917. The latter was primarily due to British concerns over Soviet expansion into formerly British spheres of influence in Asia and Asia Pacific rather than anything directly related to the spread of communism. Great Britain would break off diplomatic relations with the Soviet Union in 1927, only to restore them again in 1929. The Soviet Union was meanwhile in a period of rapid industrialisation, and by 1927 had begun to master series production of the first generation of indigenous armoured cars and tanks in addition to military transport vehicles and other military technology as disparate as infantry rifles and aerosans. Although this mechanisation was alluded to during the Red Square parades attended by foreign military attaches, the development of mechanised warfare tactics was meantime being carried out far from the public gaze in military centres including Kazan and Lipetsk in cooperation with the other pariah nation of Europe, Germany.

# 1st May 1927

Having mastered the ability to develop and series manufacture a variety of indigenous military equipment, the mid to late 1920s was a time of technical modernisation within the Red Army, both in terms of equipment supplied and operational training in its use. The Soviet Union had by 1924 begun a major programme of aircraft development and construction. By 1925, indigenously designed rifles were beginning to be produced for the Red Army, and from 1927 the Red Army began to receive its first domestically designed and produced armoured cars (the BA-27) and tanks (the MS-1) in addition to the AMO F-15 truck which had entered series production in 1924.

Many of the tanks, armoured cars and transport vehicles paraded on Red Square in the 1920s were of foreign origin having been captured during the Russian Civil War. These Berleit searchlight vehicles are on parade on 1st May 1927.

The May 1927 parade was as for the previous November parade reviewed by K.E. Voroshilov, with the parade commander being again the MVO commander G.D. Basilevich. Red Square was as usual traversed by cadets of military academies, infantry, naval infantry, cavalry, artillery batteries, armoured cars and tanks. The parade concluded with a military flypast which was becoming a traditional feature of Red Square military parades.

By 1927 the Soviet Union was well advanced in the production of various types of domestically developed weapons and equipment, and 1927 was a fundamental year in the roll-out of some of the heavier equipment types. The MS-1 had in 1927 entered "series" production, with 23 being completed in 1927. Simultaneously with the provision of new equipment types, the Red Army had also begun a period of rapid mechanisation.

# 7th November 1927 – 10th Anniversary of the Great October Socialist Revolution

By 1927, the now Soviet state had since the 1917 Russian Revolution survived its first full decade in existence, despite four years of bitter civil war involving significant foreign intervention by European nations, the United States and Japan and other European based forces including Polish and Czech legions.

The 7th November parade was a major anniversary; however as the country celebrated, the founding Bolshevik Party and government was mired in bitter internal conflicts and recriminations. Trotsky, the most famous of the revolutionaries, was himself falling out of favour within the government, and at the time of the 7th November parade had been recently ejected from the Central Committee. However, his United Opposition faction within government had popular support among the general population, and ordinary citizens were beginning to take to the streets in his support. It was therefore not unconceivable that the country would in 1927 again slide towards a coup d'état and civil war just at the time of the 10th anniversary celebrations. This concern was reflected in the 7th November 1927 parade organization, in that the parade was taken by the chairman of the Central Executive Committee of the USSR, Mikhail I. Kalinin, a civilian, with the parade commander being chairman of the Revvoensovet (Revolutionary Military Council - RVS) K.E. Voroshilov. Stalin was again present on the podium, and as before was for the moment still very much in the background. While the formal parade was underway the "United Opposition", led by Trotsky and Kamenev in Moscow and Zinoviev in Leningrad attempted to hold their own 10th Anniversary demonstrations in central Moscow and Leningrad. These were primarily against State policy that after the revolution had allowed the return and growth of minimal private enterprise, to which these "superbolsheviks" were opposed as it went against the spirit of the revolution. These demonstrations were violently broken up by mounted militia, also described in some Russian sources as horsemen from the Northern- Caucasus that both just "happened" to be located in Moscow at the time. Students meantime protested both for and against the protesters in the streets surrounding Red Square. The 7th November 10th Anniversary parade on Red Square was conducted in the eye of a storm, with the official demonstrations on Red Square being in sharp contrast to the unauthorised demonstrations in the surrounding streets which were simultaneously being broken up by the aforementioned militia horsemen.

The 10th Anniversary parade consisted of the now usual mix of cadets from military schools, infantry, sailors and marines from the Baltic and Black sea fleets, troops from other military districts and units of the OGPU, a combination of police and the secret police - the latter in time becomming the NKVD. The Soviet government wanted to demonstrate to the domestic population and the outside world that all their people, young and old, students and workers, were behind the Red Army in being ready to defend their country. A significant nuance to this particular parade was that only a small number of the marching infantry were armed with rifles, primarily the OGPU secret police troops, which might be considered a curious omission but for the fact that there were also no armoured cars or tanks present during this important anniversary parade. The parade was however joined by units of cavalry from the Northern Caucasus, presumably those not actively engaged in breaking up demonstrations nearby. The lack of weapons, and also the arrival of "Cossack" cavalry from the "Severo-Kavkazky Kavalerlsky Polk" - the Northern Caucasus Cavalry Regiment - were apparently both ordained on Stalin's advice, there being real fear that massed armed forces gathered for a Red Square parade might just be used by an individual such as Trotsky to stage a military coup d'état. Due to poor weather, the planned aviation display over Red Square was also cancelled, which

Mk. V "Rikardo" tanks pass the Lenin Mausoleum, 1st May 1928 (Mikhail Baryatinsky)

considering the background tensions may not have been an entirely weather related issue.

Only days after the parade, on 12th November, Lev Trotsky was arrested and thrown out of the Bolshevik Party for subversion, as was Zinoviev. Elsewhere in Europe in 1927 the developing social unrest as a result of the tumultuous economic problems that followed the First World War continued to gather momentum in mainland Europe, not least in Germany, where National Socialism had within a short timescale gone from obscurity and derision to being seen as a panacea for the nation's ills. Meantime in Italy, the young Benito Mussolini, democratically elected as Prime Minister in October 1922, had in the years 1925-27 consolidated his position to that of dictator by means mirroring those that were second nature to the rising leadership of Germany and the Soviet Union.

# 1st May 1928

With the political tensions of late 1927 over, K.E. Voroshilov took the military parade for the 1st May national holiday celebrations on Red Square. The parade was commanded by the MVO commander B.M. Shaposhnikov. The captured British Mk. V "Ricardo" tanks reappeared on Red Square and passed the wooden Lenin Mausoleum, followed by various artillery and anti-aircraft and searchlight vehicles on the AMO F-15 chassis.

# 7th November 1928 - 11th Anniversary of the Great October Socialist Revolution

The 7th November 1928 parade was again back to being reviewed by M. I. Kalinin with the parade commanded by the acting commander of the Moscow Garrison, N. V. Kuibyshev. K. E. Voroshilov and B. M. Shaposhnikov*, stood on the review tribunal watching the parade, which included one of the final appearances of the original Renault FT-17, accompanied by a single FIAT-3000 passing through Red Square alongside the Soviet Reno-Russky or KS, as the last of the captured (and in the case of the FIAT, purchased) revolutionary era tanks were replaced by indigenous Soviet types. The KS was being rapidly replaced by the MS-1 (T-18) of which 28 were completed in 1928 as series production of the first truly mass production tank slowly ramped up.

---

Boris Shaposhnikov was a former Imperial Russian Army colonel who joined the Red Army and masterminded the Russian Civil War campaigns of 1919-20. In later years (1937-1942) he was promoted to head of the Red Army General Staff, and thereafter became People's Commissar of Defence. He died of natural causes two weeks before the end of the Second World War in Europe.

THE RED ARMY ON PARADE 1917-45

A contemporary photograph of the Spasskaya Tower. Designed by the Italian architect Pietro Antonio Solari and completed in 1491, the tower is the main government entrance to the Kremlin from Red Square. Soviet and modern Russian parades have always started when the 7 metre diameter clock face reads 10:00 precisely. The only exception was on 7th November 1941 when the parade started at 08:00 in the early winter dawn to avoid potential air attack from the German Luftwaffe. (Russian Ministry of Defence)

This rear view of captured Mk.V tanks parading through Red Square was judging by the double column also most likely taken on 1st May 1928.

Renault FT-17 (right) and FIAT-3000 (left) tanks parade through Red Square on 7th November 1928. The FIAT-3000 is named "F. Dzerzinsky", after the founder of what latterly became the KGB, today known as the FSB. (Mikhail Svirin)

# 1929

1929 would prove to be a momentous historical year in world history. The events which unfolded were far from the Soviet Union, but the domino effect of the single occurrence on another continent would in time prove catastrophic for both Europe and the Soviet Union. All was not well domestically in the Soviet Union of 1929, with shortages of food and clothing throughout the country, and grain harvest failures in several republics, most notably Ukraine. The now established tradition of military parades nevertheless continued in Moscow and other cities as the early clouds of a gathering storm in Europe appeared on the distant horizon. The year 1929 witnessed the combat debut of the Soviet "Red Army" and also the combat debut of the MS-1 tank, nine of which were involved in battles with the Chinese on the Kitaisko-Vostochnaya Zheleznaya Doroga (KhZhD) - the Chinese Eastern Railroad running between Chita and Vladivostok/Port Arthur. The Red Army readily defeated the Chinese, which was duly noted internationally.

# 1st May 1929

The 1st May 1929 May day parade was reviewed by K.E.Voroshilov, with the parade commanded by the MVO commander I. P. Uborevich. The parade line-up, and the appearance of new indigenous Russian production vehicles reflected a more stable political environment as compared to 1927, and the Soviet Union was by 1929 considerably more stable domestically than many other countries around the world.

In 1929 there was an exponential increase in the number and types of military equipment on display; however Red Square was in a poor state of repair, with potholes and ruts, with the cobbles being covered in sand for the duration of the parade. The wooden Lenin Mausoleum was in need of repair or replacement, and the original lamp posts were still in place, causing considerable difficulties for infantry and vehicles in maintaining straight columns as they traversed the square.

The May 1929 parade included horse-drawn "tachanki" carriages armed with twin 7.62mm PM-1910 "Maxim" machine guns, a large number of motorcycles, and the diminutive "Bolshevik" tracked artillery tractors towing 76.2mm M-1915/28 anti-aircraft guns.

The 1.5 tonne AMO-F-15 which had entered series production in 1924 was evident in quantity at the 1st May 1929 parade. The AMO-F-15 was displayed in several variants including open-cab vehicles with two 7.62mm PM-1910 "Maxim" machine guns in the cargo area, the motorised equivalent of the "Tachanki" horse-drawn machine gun carriages of the previous generation, together with anti-aircraft machine gun and searchlight vehicles. The parade also saw the public debut of the first Soviet indigenous armoured car, the BA-27, which was based on a modified AMO-F-15 chassis. The BA-27s were fitted with mock-up main turret armament for parade purposes during their May parade debut. Soviet designed and produced MS-1 (Maliy Soprovozhdeniya - small infantry support) tanks followed, also fitted with mock-up turret main armament.

The AMO-F-15 trucks mounting anti-aircraft machine guns, searchlights and sound locators were followed by the debut of the new and indige-

The BA-27 was the first series production Soviet armoured car. Based on a strengthened AMO F-15 chassis, it was accepted for service with the Red Army in 1927 and paraded on Red Square from 1929.

The BA-27 armoured car and the MS-1 (T-18) tank both had their Red Square public debut in 1929, representing the start of Soviet armoured car and tank "series" production respectively. (Tank Museum: TM3202/D4)

By the end of the 1920s all manner of specialised military vehicles began to appear during Red Square parades. These AMO F-15 "ZT-4" anti-aircraft sound locator vehicles (used to detect incoming aircraft engine noise) are shown on parade in 1929.

nously designed BA-27 armoured car. Tracked artillery tractors towing wheeled artillery followed. Then came the turn of the light, "manoeuvre" tanks, presumably MS-1, followed by what was described by commentators at the time as "huge heavy tanks", the captured British Mk. V "Rikardo" tanks which were a standard parade participant throghout the 1920s. An Antonov ANT-9 aircraft was on 1st May also statically displayed on Red Square near St. Basil's Cathedral.

# 7th November 1929 – 12th Anniversary of the Great October Socialist Revolution

In the months between the Soviet military parades of May and November 1929 a singular event had occurred, far from the Soviet Union. The consequences of this single event would have a major effect on the economies of much of the world, and the economic fallout would lead to social disorder in Europe and further precipitate the makings of World War Two. The event occurred on Wall Street, New York, beginning on 24th October and culminating on 29th October 1929. The final day went down in history as the "Wall Street Crash", the day the American stockmarket crashed and with it the American dream of a capital and credit based democracy. The economic fallout for the average citizen in the United States was disastrous, with the resulting devastation in the farming states such as Oklahoma never better documented than in the American author John Steinbeck's classic book "The Grapes of Wrath". The fallout was not contained to the United States, and as in more recent years manifested itself round the world, causing financial and social devastation, particularly in Europe. The average citizen in Germany, still unrecovered from the financial implications of the Versailles Treaty, was now faced with the same issues of lack of employment and prospects as in the United States, added to the pre-existing burden of hyper-inflation which was already ravaging Germany in the late 1920s. Germany suffered perhaps disproportionately more than most European countries as the result of the American-centric "Great Depression" not least because it already had a less than robust industrial economy, as a direct result of Allied retribution after World War One, and also in part because the United States after the crash prematurely recalled the loans it had made to Germany over the years 1924-29. The outlook in Germany in 1929 had already looked bleak before the Wall Street Crash, and the shockwaves from a stock market crash on another continent quickly took effect. German unemployment in September 1929 stood at 1.3 million. A year after the Wall Street Crash it had more than doubled to 3.0 million, and by 1933 it would double again, reaching 6.1 million. A solution was however at hand, and the failed Austrian art historian noted previously was in 1929 well advanced with his plans to restore German national pride. He had already written a popular book about his plans which he had published in July 1925, the aforementioned "Mein Kampf".

Meanwhile, back in the Socialist Utopia of the Soviet Union, the country was largely oblivious to the economic crisis occuring in the outside world, particularly in the United States and Europe. While the Soviet Union had its own domestic issues to contend with, not least dealing with the aftermath of recently failing grain harvests and food distribution problems which would be manifested in the early years of the next decade, the Soviet Union at the end of the 1920s seemed, relative to the chaos in the outside world, to be an oasis of calm and order.

The 7th November 1929 parade on Red Square, celebrating the 12th anniversary of the "Great October Revolution" was reviewed by K.E.Voroshilov with the parade commander again being I. P. Uborevich. The parade was significant in that it highlighted the rapidly increasing military industrial capacability of the Soviet Union. The Red Army was rapidly mechanising, and in November 1929 the military parade included massed columns of motorcycles, GAZ-A command cars, the indigenous AMO-F-15, the Soviet Union's first indigenous series production armoured car (the BA-27) and tank (the MS-1), while the parades themselves continued to grow in scale. The BA-27 armoured car and MS-1 tank had both had their public debut in May, but for their second appearance in November 1929 they were fitted with their standard armament. T-18 production increased exponentially to 317 tanks assembled in 1929. The tank was modified even as it entered series production, and the T-18 M-1930 version (with a turet bustle and other changes) was paraded at the very end of the decade.

Concluding a decade long tradition, nine Mk.V "Ricardo" tanks traversed Red Square in November 1929 alongside the new Soviet indigenous design armoured vehicles, albeit with one of the "Ricardo" tanks barely making it to the end of Red Square before breaking down. The Renault and Vickers trophy tanks had served their purpose, and were replaced by indigenous tank designs in the following decade, with the T-34 medium and KV heavy tanks entering series production less than ten years after the Mk.V was last paraded on Red Square. Meantime, in the autumn of 1929, in an obscure incident on the "Kitaiskaya Vostochnaya Zheleznaya Doroga" (KVZhD), the China Eastern Railroad, nine of the ten MS-1 (T-18) tanks delivered to the Eastern Siberian city of Chita by rail were used in combat against Chinese troops of the Mukden Army. Far from Moscow and obscure to this day, the incident was the first operational use of a Soviet built tank in combat.

An early prototype MS-1 (T-18) tank, with an AMO F-15 truck in the background, on Red Square during the parade for the 12th anniversary of the "Great October Revolution" on 7th November 1929. The MS-1 has the turret inscription "Our answer to Chamberlain", referring to British Foreign Minister Chamberlain's criticism of Soviet policy towards China.

A column of MS-1 (T-18) tanks at the same 12th anniversary parade on 7th November 1929. Note that one side of the square is closed off during construction of the definitive concrete and marble version of the Lenin Mausoleum.

THE RED ARMY ON PARADE 1917-45

The T-20 Komsomolets light tracked artillery tractor was a regular Red Square parade participant during the late 1930s. These Komsomolets tractors are towing 76.2mm M-1927 Regimental guns during the 7th November 1938 military parade in Moscow.

# Soviet Military Parades in the 1930s

As the 1930s dawned, the Soviet Union after a slow but steady start in the mid 1920s began to exponentially industrialise, aided in no small part by US multinational companies such as Ford, which assisted the Soviet Union with mass production technology, including the building of a giant new vehicle plant at Nizhny Novgorod, to assemble Soviet versions of Ford designs in numbers that would become highly impressive even by the standards of the American Ford Motor Company.

As the Soviet Union industrialised, and the Red Army continued to mechanise, elsewhere in the world the inevitable conclusion of severe austerity and the need for basic mineral resources required by militarising powers became ever more apparent as the 1930s progressed. The world witnessed the spectacular rise to power of Hitler and the National-Socialist NSDAP (Nazi) Party during the mid 1930s, which was the main focus of political concern in Europe at the time, but this was predated by the remorseless advance into Chinese territory of the Japanese army. In Europe the inevitable clash of political systems that would culminate in World War Two had begun by the middle of the decade, with the Spanish Civil War being the first proxy-war in Europe where the future combattants in a European wide war tested tactics, equipment and political resolve in equal measure. As conflicts began to escalate in Europe and elsewhere, the size of Red Square parades also increased exponentially, latterly joined by military parades in Germany as the Third Reich brought its covert militarisation into the open in the latter years of the decade.

In the Soviet Union, the 1930s witnessed the combined results of rapid national industrialisation and the concurrent mechanisation of the Red Army. The country entered the decade with the MS-1 (T-18) which was the first Soviet truly indigenous tank design. Tank development was however so dramatic in the early 1930s that the MS-1 was rendered obsolescent almost as soon as it entered service due to the dramatically quick introduction of new tank types in all weight classes, the result of embracing the most progressive of foreign designs and adapting them for the Red Army. The British Vickers 6 ton light tank was adapted in the Soviet Union as the T-26, while the American Walter J. Christie's M-1928/M-1931 cruiser tank was adapted as the BT series, which would at the end of the decade via the A-20 and A-32 morph into the T-34 medium tank. The 1930s was the decade in which the Soviet Union best demonstrated its massed armoured might, with displays of T-26 light tanks being later supplemented as the decade unfolded by everything from small amphibious tanks such as the T-37 and T-38, and BT "fast" (cruiser) tanks to multi-turreted monsters such as the T-28 medium and T-35 heavy tanks.

The new displays of armoured military might were impresssive, and in the case of tanks such as the T-35 were deliberately designed to be so. However the rapid mechanisation of the Red Army was of more significance as the threat of war edged ever closer. The 1930s saw the exponential growth in both domestic vehicle types and production numbers available to the Red Army, with new generations of Soviet domestic vehicle and military truck production including designs from production centres in Moscow (ZiS), Gorky (GAZ) and

Yaroslavl (YaG), with tracked tractor production in Chelyabinsk (ChTZ) and Kharkov (KhTZ), and tank production in Kharkov (KhPZ), Leningrad (LKZ) and several other cities.

The exponential growth in military vehicle production was significantly aided by the foreign contracts entered into at the beginning of the decade. The contract with Ford to build and equip the GAZ plant in Gorky to produce the GAZ-A, GAZ-AA and later GAZ-AAA introduced mass vehicle production to the Soviet Union, on a scale that rapidly dwarfed that of some of the countries which provided the original technology. Other foreign companies such as the US company "Autocar" had their designs modified in the Soviet Union, in the case of Autocar the vehicle becoming via the AMO series the mass production ZiS-5, the standard 3 tonne load carrier of World War Two. Other manufacturers such as Caterpillar would also see their designs and technology being used in the Soviet Union on a production scale that would have been entirely inconceivable in the previous decade.

The 1930s also witnessed the Soviet Union displaying the country's massed armoured might, with displays of everything from the T-26 light tank to the multi-turreted monsters, the T-28 medium and T-35 "Land Battleship" designs, as also for some time favoured in Great Britain and Germany. Mechanisation of the Red Army resulted in the widespread replacement of horse drawn with mechanised and towed artillery, with the GAZ-AA and ZiS-5 4x2 trucks appearing in 1932-33, joined by a range of dedicated light, medium and heavy artillery tractors.

Not all tanks displayed on Red Square in the 1930s entered service with the Red Army. Some tanks and vehicles were paraded only on a single occasion, such as the OGPU design bureau developed PT-1 prototype which paraded through Red Square only once, at high speed, and the BAD and BAD-2 armoured cars paraded only on Uritsky Square in Leningrad.

Artillery was increasingly mechanised during the 1930s, with the early "Kommunar" artillery tractors being replaced as the decade unfolded by specialised designs such as the "Komintern" and the "Voroshilovets" which would serve the Red Army in large numbers. Throughout the 1930s the Red Army was in a phase of rapid mechanisation. The first Soviet mechanised brigade was formed in 1930, with a tank regiment of 110 tanks, a mechanised infantry brigade, and reconnaissance and artillery battalions.

# 1st May 1930

The 1st May 1930 parade was reviewed by K.E. Voroshilov, with the parade commander being the MVO deputy commander N.D.Kashirin. The 1st May 1930 May Day parade was unusual, in that due to building of the new concrete and marble Lenin Mausoleum and the gardens under the Kremlin wall, the right side of the square was closed off and the parade was thereby required to filter through the remaining half of the square. The parade began with marching columns from the Central Military Command, followed by columns from the military academy of the Red Army, the "Vystrel" school, and the "Voenno-Vozdushnaya Akademiya" (the Air Force Academy), chemical warfare troops, military cadets, cavalry of the VTsIK school, columns of Red Army infantry, border forces, and troops of the "Dzerzhinsky" division, cavalry and horse drawn artillery, communications and communications troops, medical services and others.

The parade itself was on a larger scale than in previous years, and according to Soviet archives left a definite impression on those in attendance. The MS-1 tank was no longer accompanied by the captured British Mk.V tanks which had been displayed on Red Square throughout the 1920s alongside indigenous Soviet designed tanks.

The 1st May 1930 Red Square parade included a display of 9 BA-27 armoured cars which were individually named after the party leadership. The AMO-F-15 based air defence machine gun, searchlight and sound locator vehicles were joined by purpose designed Kommunar tracked artillery tractors towing various medium and heavy artillery, heralding the ongoing and rapid mechanisation of the Red Army.

The Bolshevik tracked tractor was one the first indigenous Soviet tracked artillery tractors to be paraded through Red Square. These dimunitive looking tractors are towing World War One era 76.2mm M-1915 anti-aircraft guns on Red Square during the 1st May 1930 parade. The Bolshevik was based on the Holt 5 ton tractor, and was built in the "Bolshevik" plant in Petrograd (later Leningrad) in 1923-24 (O.Baronov)

The first results of the industrialisation partnerships with foreign companies began to be seen in 1930, with an early GAZ-A light passenger car making its first appearance on Red square as a command car. The GAZ-A was being prepared for mass production at GAZ (actually designated NAZ at the time as the plant was located in Nizhny Novgorod (hence the "N") the name of the city being changed in 1932 to Gorky, after the writer Maxim Gorky, hence the "G" (GAZ) replacing the original "N" (NAZ).

The May Day 1930 celebrations were accompanied by a flypast by various aircraft including the Tupolev TB-1 bomber.

The MS-1 (T-18) infantry support tank quickly replaced the KS as the first mass production indigenous Soviet tank design. These tanks were paraded through Red Square in the very late 1920s and very early 1930s. Shown here are the later variant of the T-18, sometimes designated T-18 M-1930, with revisions including the addition of a turret bustle. (Mikhail Baryatinsky)

Although the Moscow Red Square parades always had the media attention, other cities, particularly Leningrad, also staged large annual military parades. These early MS-1 (T-18) tanks are parading through Leningrad's Uritsky Square (formerly Palace Square) in front of the Hermitage buildings on 1st May 1930. (O. Baronov)

# 7th November 1930 – 13th Anniversary of the Great October Socialist Revolution

By 7th November 1930, the new marble-faced Lenin Mausoleum was complete, and the remodelling of Red Square was also finished, with the old lamp standards removed and the cobbles renewed to provide a parade square now cleared for ever larger military parades. 1930 was a watershed year in the presentation of Red Square parades, in that the year saw the introduction of a much wider range of military vehicles beginning to enter series production, and now displayed on a greatly improved Red Square.

The 7th November 1930 parade was reviewed by K.E.Voroshilov, with the parade commander being MVO commander A.I.Kork. Stalin stood impasively in the background on the Lenin Mausoleum as the troops, armoured vehicles and artillery rumbled across the newly laid cobbles of Red Square.

The marching infantry were followed by massed motorcycles, including solo and sidecar combination motorcycles with machine gun armament, and even the cameo appearance of a motorcycle combination with armoured shielding for the driver and a 7.62mm DT machine gun in the sidecar. Several GAZ-As were now on parade as column lead cars, followed by already obsolescent AMO-F-15s with infantry in the rear cargo areas, AMO-F-15s with an early form of quadruple 7.62mm PM-1910 "Maxim" anti-aircraft machine gun (later standardized as the "4M"), new Ya-4 and AMO-4, YaG-5 with 122mm howitzers and their gun crews in the rear cargo area. The MS-1 tanks paraded on Red Square were now the modified T-18 M-1930, fitted with a turret bustle among other changes.

Red Square was not always the uniformly cobbled parade square as it is now known, as seen in this photograph. The original wooden Lenin Mausoleum was replaced by a new concrete and marble mausoleum and parade tribunal in 1930. The surface of Red Square was upgraded with new cobbles, the lamp posts removed, an entrance arch demolished and monuments moved at Stalin's instruction to accommodate ever larger military parades in the 1930s.

The 1930 parades were significantly larger than earlier, and the range of new vehicles also growing as the Soviet Union began an era of exponential industrialisation. Although the square had been remodelled to allow larger parades, not least by the removal of the old lamp standards in the way of infantry and vehicles alike, the main obstruction to larger parades remained, in that the Voskresensky Gate (a tandem archway structure to the left side of the Historical Museum at the entrance to Red Square) remained in place, blocking the left entrance to Red Square and hence reducing the potential "traffic flow" onto the square by half. Larger parades as were being planned for the 1930s could not be contemplated with the gate in place, which was resolved with the demolition of the gate in 1931 on the direct orders of Stalin.

MS-1 (T-18) tanks parade through Red Square, 7th November 1930. These later T-18 M-1930 production model tanks have several modifications, the most obvious of which was the addition of a turret bustle. (Mikhail Baryatinsky)

These MS-1 (T-18 M-1930) tanks assembling for a parade in early 1930s Leningrad are indicative of the generation change that occurred in Soviet tank technology over a very short period. In the background are T-26 M-1931 and T-26 M-1933 tanks which effectively replaced the MS-1 (T-18) as quickly as the T-18 had replaced the KS, all achieved in just over a decade of the first Soviet KS tank being assembled.

# 1st May 1931

Further significant changes were made to Red Square in 1931. In addition to the demolition of the twin-arched and twin towered Voskresensky Gate, now providing access to Red Square from both sides of the Historical Museum, long standing monuments were moved from their original central location to the far end of the square close to St. Basil's Cathedral, again to ensure uncluttered access for the much enlarged scale of military parades planned for the 1930s, with further demolitions following in 1936.

The 1st May 1931 parade, reviewed by K.E. Voroshilov, primarily consisted of known tanks and vehicles, but the quantities of each on display was now growing considerably. The AMO-F-15 which had entered limited series production in 1924 was in 1931 displayed in searchlight and anti-aircraft machine gun mounting guises. The AMO F-15 had served the Red Army well, but would be replaced the following year by the mass production GAZ-AA produced at the newly established GAZ plant in Gorky (formerly Nizhny Novgorod), while the AMO plant in Moscow had already started production of newer AMO chassis such as the AMO-3 and AMO-4 and would soon thereafter convert to series production of the heavier ZiS-5, the default "trekhtonka" (three tonne) general service truck which would see the Red Army through to the end of World War Two.

Although the MS-1(T-18) remained the main tank type displayed on Red Square in May of 1931, with production actually peaking at 445 tanks delivered in 1931 before the tank was replaced, radically new tanks developed in the Soviet Union using foreign prototypes and technology were beginning to enter series production. These new tanks, produced in unprecedented numbers, would dominate Red Square parades throughout the 1930s. The T-27 tankette, based on the British Carden Loyd Mk. VI was accepted for Red Army service in February 1931, as was the T-26 light tank and soon thereafter the BT series. The line-up of Soviet tanks in the 1930s was a world away from the early attempts to copy foreign tanks which had resulted in the Russky-Reno or KS at the beginning of the previous decade.

The 1st May 1931 parade was a momentous occasion, with some 500 tanks and other armoured vehicles on display, accompanied by a flypast by the Red Army Air Force. A further demonstration, to the military hierarchy including I.V.Stalin, K.E. Voroshilov and G.K. Ordzhonikidze was held on 2nd May at the Moscow central aerodrome at Khodynka.

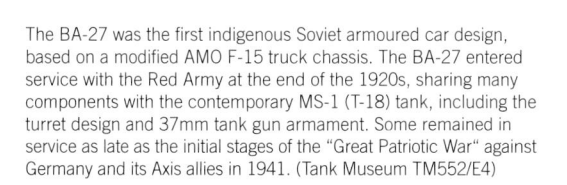

The BA-27 was the first indigenous Soviet armoured car design, based on a modified AMO F-15 truck chassis. The BA-27 entered service with the Red Army at the end of the 1920s, sharing many components with the contemporary MS-1 (T-18) tank, including the turret design and 37mm tank gun armament. Some remained in service as late as the initial stages of the "Great Patriotic War" against Germany and its Axis allies in 1941. (Tank Museum TM552/E4)

THE RED ARMY ON PARADE 1917-45

Some less commonly seen military vehicles have paraded through Red Square over the years. These YaG-5 trucks with 122mm M-1910 howitzers mounted within the cargo area rather than being towed are on parade in Red Square on 1st May 1931.

The AMO-F-15 was the Soviet Union's first series production truck. These vehicles, armed with twin 7.62mm M-1910 "Maxim" water cooled machine guns are on parade in Red Square on 1st May 1931. Early pre-series GAZ-A and GAZ-AA vehicles can be seen behind the AMO F-15s.

These AMO-F-15 based anti-aircraft searchlight vehicles were also paraded through Red Square on 1st May 1931.

Vehicles paraded in other Soviet cities over the years have often differed from those demonstated on Moscow's Red Square. These AMO-F-15 searchlight vehicles are on display on Uritsky Square, Leningrad.

In the early 1930s all eyes in Europe were on the financial and social upheavals in Germany and Italy, which would in time lead to the spectacular rise to power of Hitler and the Nazi Party in the former country and the Fascist Party under Mussolini in the latter. The Soviet Union due to its expansive geography and recent history was however also highly congniscent of ongoing activity on its eastern borders, not least that of Japan.

The situation on the Soviet Union's eastern borders deteriorated between the May and November 1931 parades, as Japanese localised aggression against China destabilised the security situation in the remote regions of eastern Siberia, raising major concerns for the Soviet Union with regard to its territory in eastern Siberia and Soviet Asia.

On 18th September 1931, the same day as the Mukden incident, Japanese troops of the maverick Kwangtung Army occupied Manchuria in northern China. Although the attack was staged against the express instructions of the Japanese high command and central government, the latter was forced to accept the fait accompli and made the reluctant decision to reinforce the Kwangtung Army as it consolidated control of its newly gained territory and established the satellite state of Manchukuo. This move raised major concerns for the Soviet Union with regard to its territory in eastern Siberia and Soviet Asia. With potential enemies on two fronts, and very recent experience of being invaded on several fronts, the Soviet Union took actions to defend itself against potential aggressors, while back in Moscow the size and duration of Red Square parades demonstrating Soviet military might increased exponentially during the early 1930s.

The Mukden incident and the subsequent establishment of the Japanese satellite state of Manchukuo in 1931 was a prelude to a series of incidents in the area during the 1930s. The military clashes in the region between Japan and the Soviet Union later in the decade were to end in specatcular defeat for the Japanese, not least as the Red Army had deployed significant quantities of tanks and armoured cars against the relatively lightly armed Japanese. These clashes, and their unfavourable result for the Japanese, would be a determining factor in Japan not pushing further militarily against the Soviet Union in the region in 1941 as war broke out between the latter and Hitler's Germany, despite massive pressures on resources at home in Japan. Japan being held in military check on the Soviet Union's eastern borders would in turn allow the Red Army to move its Siberian divisions to bolster the defence of Moscow in the late autumn and winter of 1941.

Early production MS-1 tanks moving towards Uritsky (ex Dvortsovaya) Square before the 1932 Leningrad parade.

The MS-1 (T-18) tank was paraded through Red Square at the very end of the 1920s and the very beginning of the 1930s. This photograph is interesting in that it shows the indigenous Soviet T-18 with captured British origin Mk.V tanks in the background. The respective designs were only a decade apart and yet the rapid development of Soviet tank technology in the intervening years is clearly evident.

# 7th November 1931 – 14th Anniversary of the Great October Socialist Revolution

The parade line-up for 7th 1931 November replicated the May parade, with the first generation AMO-F-15 remaining the primary transport vehicle on show, together with the recently introduced BA-27 armoured car and the MS-1 (T-18) tank. 1931 was however a year that heralded great changes in both the make-up and the scale of Red Square parades in the coming decade. The first production version of the T-26 light tank was displayed on Red Square, the twin turreted T-26 M-1931 heralding the first of a tank series based on a British design of which 11,218 would be manufactured over the next decade, in three main production variants and in 53 modifications. Six BT-2 tanks were originally planned for display on Red Square on 7th November 1931, but only three tanks were completed (without armament) at KhPZ in Kharkov in October 1931, of which two were displayed on Red Square on 7th November 1931. Series production BT-2 tanks entered service with the 1st (Kalinovsky) Mechanised Brigade (MVO) in 1932. The BT-2 was paraded in Leningrad and Kharkov in 1932.

The T-26, BT and entirely indigenous design T-28 medium and T-35 heavy tanks would become the default parade tanks of the 1930s, replacing the relatively small assortment of captured tanks and even smaller number of indigenous designs with which the Red Army had been equipped in the 1920s.

# 1st May 1932

The 1st May 1932 Red Square May Day parade began with marching columns followed by officers and other ranks of the Proletariatian Divisions, naval and marine forces, border forces, OGPU (police/secret police) forces, cavalry and horse drawn "tachanki" machine gun carts, armoured cars, motorised artillery, trucks with machine guns, searchlights and sound locators. The parade also included light GAZ-4 "pikap" vehicles and trucks with radio communications equipment. The parade was also the public debut of the T-27 tankette, in large numbers that appeared to literally swarm over Red Square.

The 1st May 1932 Red Square parade began to display the second generation of Soviet designed tanks, armoured vehicles and mechanised forces that were in some cases based on foreign technology but all developed within the Soviet Union and being manufactured in unprecedented numbers. The BA-27, at the time the still relatively new first Soviet indigenous armoured car design, made its last Red Square parade appearance before being replaced by the FA-I and BA-I armoured cars in the light and medium armoured car classes respectively. The first "series production" tank, the MS-1 was likewise nearing the end of its parade life on Red Square, the tandem file of MS-1 tanks being joined on 1st May 1932 by large numbers of T-26 M-1931 and T-26 M-1932 light tanks which were paraded in both Moscow and Leningrad. The tanks and armoured cars were followed by motorised artillery, including artillery noted at the time as mounted on gun carriages, with pneumatic rather than solid rubber tyres, GAZ-A command vehicles and GAZ-AA trucks armed with machine guns and seachlights, replacing the venerable AMO-F-15 which has served the Red Army well over the preceeding decade.

In Kharkov, the capital of Ukraine from 1919-1934, and far from the foreign observers present in Moscow, a small parade was also held on 1st May 1932 which included the Kharkov KhPZ developed T-24 tank prototype together with the Leningrad built T-26 M-1932 and the BT-2 fast tank, representing several new tank types in the light, medium infantry support and fast (cruiser) tank categories. The limited production T-24 was never displayed on Red Square in Moscow.

While life continued as normal in the Soviet capital Moscow and other large cities of the Soviet Union, the situation in some areas of the country was less optimistic. The years 1932-

The FA-I light armoured car was introduced into Red Army service from the very early 1930s. Based on the new GAZ-A chassis, the FA-I was a modern design, which replaced the heavier armed BA-27 in the reconnaissance role, while the BA-I more directly replaced the BA-27 as a medium armoured car with the capability to engage lightly armoured tanks.

The twin turreted T-26 M-1931 was developed in the Soviet Union based on technology procured from the British Vickers company. These T-26 M-1931s, named after the Polish communist and historian Julian Marchlewski and Klim Voroshilov are awaiting the Red Square parade in Moscow, 1st May 1932.

33 were stricken by failed grain harvests and a breakdown in the distribution of basic foodstuffs in the Soviet Union generally. The situation was particularly acute in Ukraine, the Soviet breadbasket, resulting in what became latterly known as the "Golodomor" - Holodomor in Ukrainian (translated as starvation rather than simply famine). The entire subject of the "Golodomor" is disputed by historians to the present day, with some politicians in modern Ukraine accusing the Soviet Union and Stalin in particular of deliberately starving the Ukraine. The situation also however affected the Caucasus republics, Kazakhstan and a large swath of the Volga region, such that the disaster was not restricted to Ukraine as sometimes alluded today, but rather to the food growing regions of the Soviet Union which were all in the southern part of the country. The more impartial viewpoint may be that the time was one of natural disaster, added to undoubtably by incompetence among party officials charged with food distribution, rather than a deliberate act to starve the population. Regardless of who was at fault, Ukraine bore the brunt of the famine as Ukraine was the default production centre where the widespread grain harvest failures occurred, and thereby suffered disproportionately as a result. Whatever the truth of the matter, while the parades were underway in Moscow and other cities of the Soviet Union, millions of citizens literally starved to death in the Soviet Union during 1932-33. Official estimates vary widely, from under 5 million souls having starved to death, to as many as 12 million. (the latter figure is double the officially documented total but the exact number may never be known). By any standards this was nevertheless a disaster in human terms, but in Soviet terms was only a foretaste of what was to come in the years ahead. To prevent a recurrence, a large scale industrial program was started, which with the exception of

T-26 M-1932 light tanks parading through Red Square, 1st May 1932. The T-26 was a Soviet development of the "Vickers 6 ton" light tank design, one of many technology transfers concluded by the Soviet Union with foreign manufacturers which exponentially increased Soviet military technology development and production in the early 1930s. The T-26, produced in massive numbers, became the default Red Army light tank of the 1930s.(TsFFKA)

a famine in 1946-47 as a result of the destruction of agricultural output caused by war, ensured that the "Golodomor" was never repeated.

As the Soviet Union dealt with failed grain harvests in agricultural regions, the Ford Motor Company was meantime completing the installation of machine tooling at the new GAZ production plant located in Nizhny Novgorod, now renamed Gorky, 400km to the east of Moscow. The new plant would initially manufacture the GAZ-A passenger vehicle and the GAZ-AA 4x2 truck in the Soviet Union based on Ford, and in the latter case Jumbo and Timken company technology, followed a few months later by the 6x4 GAZ-AAA truck. The Red Army would be a major user of all these vehicle types.

In parallel with development of its military production capacity, the Soviet Union also began to rapidly increase its mechanised forces and also their operational level armoured structures. The first mechanical brigade had been formed in 1930, and by 1932 the Red Army had two mechanised corps, the 11th Mechanised Corps in the Leningrad Military District and the 45th Mechanised Corps in the Ukrainian Military District.

T-26 M-1931 light tanks preparing for the 1st May 1932 parade on Uritsky Square, Leningrad. A single T-26 M-1932 with its 37mm armament in one turret can also be seen on the left side of the formation.

THE RED ARMY ON PARADE 1917-45

The T-27 tankette was another Vickers design which was successfully replicated under licence in the Soviet Union and modified for local requirements. These early production T-27 tankettes are in two columns only. Later parades involved massed and fast moving formations of these tankettes. The T-27 was not a particularly practical armoured vehicle, but gave Red Army tank crews significant training experience in operating tanks and in tank warfare principles. Red Square, 1st May 1932. (TsGAKFD)

The BT-2 was developed at the KhPZ plant in Kharkov based on the designs of another foreign inventor, the American Walter J. Christie. Six BT-2s were scheduled for public debut on 7th November 1931, but only three were built in time and one had an engine fire, such that two BT-2s made their public debut on Red Square in November 1931. The BT series would in time evolve into the T-34 medium tank.

Two generations of Red Army tank on parade in Leningrad. The final production model T-18 M-1930 was replaced by the T-26 light tank which during the 1930s was produced in several versions and in massive numbers.

# 7th November 1932 – 15th Anniversary of the Great October Socialist Revolution

The Soviet Union celebrated its 10th anniversary in 1932, and the 7th November parade that year was significantly larger than previous parades. The Red Square parade began by tradition with marching infantry, followed by cavalry, horse drawn "tachanki" machine gun carts and horse drawn artillery, in turn followed by a display of armoured vehicles, of which the rapidly industrialising Soviet Union had manufactured approximately 10,000 of different types, including tanks, tankettes and armoured cars in the period 1929-32.

The 7th November 1932 Red Square parade included a mass display of T-27s in columns eight vehicles wide, one of the largest displays of a single given tank type ever seen on Red Square. The T-27 was followed by early twin-turreted T-26

The 6x4 GAZ-AAA was a Soviet truck developed based on Ford Timkem technology but significantly modified for local production and service. The GAZ-AAA was used by the Red Army as a general service load carrier and weapons platform. The seating arrangement seen here was for parade purposes only. Note the sand covering the parade square surface.

M-1931 and M-1932 light tanks, the former armed with two 7.62mm DT machine guns, one in each turret, and the latter fitted with a 37mm PS-2 gun in one of the turrets and a machine gun in the other, giving the T-26 limited tank engagement capability.

The recently introduced 4x2 GAZ-AA had also been further modified within the GAZ design bureau as the 6x4 GAZ-AAA, which was duly demonstrated on Red Square during the November 1932 parade in general service configuration, with infantry riding on bench seats in the rear.

While the military parades of massed Soviet technology being displayed on Red Square impressed the crowds and the foreign defence attachés present, some of the realities of the Soviet planning system, and the incompetence and deriliction with which party appratchiks often carried through their instructions had resulted in shortages of many basic foodstuffs for the general population. As described earlier, the grain harvests failed in the Ukraine, the main agricultural production region of the Soviet Union in 1932, and would do so again in 1933, which, coupled with the disasterous mismanagement of the food distribution system led to famine. The origins of the famine, whether it was the result of deliberate policy as today claimed by Ukraine, or more likely simply mismanagement is outwith the scope of this book, but the fact remains that while the Soviet Union was strengthening and rapidly industrialising, and the military was mechanising at an unprecedented rate, the civilian population of the country was vulnerable to the consequences of a command economy system that was subject to the usual negative human factors of greed, corruption and incompetence. The Soviet Union was always a country of extremes, and the military strength on one side of the equation was matched by the brutal reality of everyday life and death for the "narod" or general population on the other. The Soviet Union would lose many more citizens to political purges in the 1930s, and another 27 million of its population to war during Stalin's tenure as "Vozhd" or leader of the Soviet Union.

This rare photograph taken in Kharkov on 1st May 1932, shows an early production BT-2, a T-26 M-1932 and the limited production and ultimately ill-fated T-24 tank. This parade through the streets of Kharkov is the only known public display of the limited production T-24.

The GAZ-AAA was used for mounting light weapons such as the 4M, consisting of four 7.62mm M-1910/30 water cooled "Maxim" machine guns mounted together on a single anti-aircraft pedestal. 7th November 1932. (O. Baronov)

The BA-27 was the first Soviet indigenous armoured car to be manufactured in significant numbers. It was introduced into Red Army service from 1927 and paraded through Red Square at the end of the 1920s and in the very early 1930s. These BA-27s are individually named "Kavkazky Komsomolets" and "Moscow Komsomolets". Red Square, 7th November 1932.

BA-27s during the same "15th Anniversary of the Great October Revolution" parade on Red Square, Moscow, 7th November 1932. The BA-27 in the background is marked "10th Anniversary of the Domestic Transport Workers Union".

THE RED ARMY ON PARADE 1917-45

T-27 tankettes pass before the newly completed and definitive version of the Lenin Mausoleum on Red Square, 7th November 1932. (O. Baronov)

Kommunar tracked artillery tractors towing 76.2mm M-1915/28 anti-aircraft guns through Red Square, 7th November 1932. The Kommunar artillery tractor was replaced by several other Soviet tractor types during the 1930s but remained in Red Army service when war broke out in June 1941. (O.Baronov)

# 1933

The year 1933 in the Soviet Union was blighted by the grain harvest failures and their consequences as described earlier. But the forces of nature were by 1933 being joined by the storm clouds of human nature in Europe as the indigenous populations in the economically hardest affected countries, namely Germany and Italy, turned to extreme views as a means of national and personal salvation.

While the Soviet Union projected its military might on Red Square, the country continued to rapidly industrialise, aided by military technology transfers from the United States, Great Britain, Germany and other countries. Events were however occuring outside the Soviet Union which would have a profound impact on the state and its citizens. On 5th March 1933, the German NSDAP - the National Socialist (Nazi) party - won 43.9% of the votes in the German Federal Elections. In direct parallel with unemployment in Germany having risen from 1.3 million in 1929 before the Wall Street Crash to 6.1 million by 1933, the previously largely irrelevant and maligned Nazi party and its leader Adolf Hitler had gone from obscurity to become by 1933 the perceived saviour of Germany. The March elections were not an outright victory for the party, but on 23rd March Hitler signed the Enabling Act, effectively installing himself as dictator, and within four months the Nazi party had consolidated its position as the de-facto Nazi government of Germany. The landscape artist who had purportedly been refused entry to the Vienna Academy of Art by a Jewish professor because he had no school leaving qualifications and not enough people in his landscape paintings had been democratically elected as Fuhrer of the Third Reich and had consolidated that position as dictator. Hitler lost no time in restoring national pride in Germany and as a powerful orator he told the German population what they wanted to hear. As Hitler consolidated his new found power, and that of Germany, he reneged on all agreements made at the Treaty of Versailles and began a major programme of re-armament, in the process terminating all military technical partnership arrangements with the Soviet Union. It was already clear in 1933 to those with direct knowledge that a clash between the highly militarised cultures of Soviet Communism and German Nazism would now be only a matter of time. The Soviet Union and Germany had both benefitted from the years of secret mutual military cooperation centred around the tank school at Kazan and the aviation school at Lipetsk deep in the Soviet Union. But for the Soviet Union the technical assistance received in the early 1930s from American companies such as Arthur McKee (steel production), Autocar, Christie, Caterpillar, Dodge, Ford, General Electric, Moreland, Wright (aircraft engines), and British companies such as Vickers was to be of far greater advantage in the years ahead than the now terminated period of cooperation with Germany. As was the more engaged relationship with those once adversarial nations, now that the emerging threat in Europe was no longer - for the moment at least - considered to be the Soviet Union and its brand of socialism.

During the two "Five Year Plans" that covered the industrialisation of the Soviet Union in the 1930s, approximately 500 new manufacturing plants were established, many with foreign assistance, with the Soviet Union paying foreign American and European companies approximately $2 billion for machine tooling and technology transfers during the 1930s, which equates to approximately $250 billion in today's monetary terms.

# 1st May 1933

As the Soviet Union observed events in central Europe from a distance, the 1st May 1933 parade was held in the early summer sunshine against a backdrop of rapidly advancing technical advancement in the military sphere, contrasting sharply with fundamental issues such as basic foodstuff supply distribution in the regions. The achievements of Soviet socialism being able to rapidly industrialise with its state driven Five Year Plans meantime contrasted sharply with the failures of the very same system, or perhaps the technically incompetent apparatchiks chosen to manage the system.

The marching parade on 1st May 1933 was the usual combination of cadets from military academies, infantry, police and border forces, with infantry of the Moscow "proletariat" conspicuously led by snipers. The parade of military equipment began with armoured cars, followed by mechanised towed field artillery, a subtlety of which was that some gun carriages were now fitted with pneumatic rather than solid tyres (allowing a higher towing speed) behind fast tractors. There were vehicles mounting air defense weapons, T-27 tankettes, high-speed BT tanks and as a parade finale the debut appearance on 1st May 1933 of both the first series production T-28 medium tank and the T-35-2 heavy tank prototype in Moscow. The parade was accompanied by a flypast of fighter and bomber aircraft.

The year 1933 might fairly be described as the year during which the Soviet military machine as portrayed on Red Square came of age, in that the sheer scale of Soviet military investment in adapting the best "pick and mix" of available foreign technology in the preceeding years of development began to be demonstrated on Red Square. The second generation of indigenously designed

Military parades involve significant planning and rehearsal. These FA-I light armoured cars are practicing parade formation in the 1930s.

tanks and armoured cars were now appearing on Red Square, together with new military transport vehicles, new ground artillery and air defence weapons and new purpose designed military tractors to tow them.

The first generation of mass production military transport vehicles also began to enter service in large numbers with the Red Army in the years 1932-33, namely the 1.5 tonne 4x2 GAZ-AA and the 2.5 tonne 4x2 ZiS-5, both of which made their public debut on Red Square during these years. Several other vehicle types, which pre-dated the better-known series production types were also produced at this time. One such was the AMO-4, developed from an original American Autocar design, which was displayed on Red Square mounting searchlights, for which the standard load carrier vehicle would later be the ZiS-12, a lengthened version of the ZiS-5 with a lowered rear cargo area.

It was however displays of tanks on Red Square that set the tone required by the Soviet leadership in the early 1930s, and from 1933 massed displays of tanks would predominate, including the introduction of what in early 1930s terms was the ultimate experssion of armoured might, the multi-turreted T-35 "land battleship". The first prototype T-35 (T-35-1) was completed at OKMO in Leningrad in August 1932. Armed with a mockup of the 76.2mm PS-3 gun in the main turret, 37mm PS-2 guns in the two subsidiary turrets and 7.62mm DT machine guns in the remaining turrets, the 50.8 tonne combat weight T-35-1 was in 1933 an impressive sight, but it was far from ready for series production. The prototype T-35-1 tank as displayed in Moscow had at the time of its debut appearance already been replaced by a second prototype, the T-35-2. The original T-35-1 had an underpowered engine and temperamental transmission together with a technically clever but complex pneumatic control system. The T-35-1 made its public debut on Red Square in Moscow on 1st May 1933, the same day the next iteration T-35-2 made its public debut on Uritsky Square in Leningrad.

The T-35-2 had a simplified hull and turret construction, a new M-17 engine, a new transmission and gearbox and a genuine 76.2mm PS-3 gun rather than a mock up in the main turret. The T-35-2 prototype was completed in April 1933 and made its parade debut in Leningrad on 1st May 1933 while the earlier T-35-1 was paraded the same day in Moscow. The T-35-1 and T-35-2 would be paraded together in Moscow on 7th November 1933 while the series production variant, the T-35A, which was developed in parallel with the T-35-2 made its parade debut in Kharkov, then the capital of Ukraine, on the same date of 7th November 1933.

The May and November Red Square parades are generally remembered for their military content, but the 1st May parades were primarily a civilian workers celebration with a military element attached. The cobbles of Red Square were often traversed by all manner of workers and sports associations, such as these columns of female gymnasts on parade in 1933. (Eh. N. Evzerikhin)

GAZ-AAAs with infantry seated on benches for parade purposes traversing Red Square in the early 1930s. The GAZ-AAA was used by the Red Army in smaller numbers than the 4x2 GAZ-AA, often in specialised support vehicle roles. (Shterenberg)

THE RED ARMY ON PARADE 1917-45

The T-26 M-1933 entered Red Army service in 1933, replacing the twin turreted T-26 M-1931 and M-1932. The new model, as seen here during parade formation practice, mounted a 45mm 20K tank gun in a turret unified with the contemporary BT-5 fast tank. (Viktor Kulikov)

The first T-35 prototype (the T-35-1) made its public debut on Red Square on 1st May 1933, while the second prototype (the T-35-2) made its public debut in Leningrad on the same day. The first prototypes were significantly different from each other and both differed from the later "series" production T-35A. (Steven J. Zaloga)

# 1st May 1933 Leningrad

The new, single turreted T-26 M-1933 with its 45mm main armament was by May 1933 paraded in massed formations through Leningrad in front of the Winter Palace, together with an equally impressive number of the earlier T-26 M-1931 model. The Dyrenkov D-13 medium armoured car and the prototype BAD-1 and BAD-2 amphibious armoured cars developed at OGPU and built at the Izhorsk plant near Leningrad were also displayed together for the first time during this 1st May parade in Leningrad. The first pre-series batch of 12 T-28 medium tanks was displayed in Leningrad and Moscow, with the majority (10 tanks) being displayed in Leningrad and two sent to the Moscow parade. The first series production T-28 tanks were subsequently sent to the 2nd Independent Tank Regiment located in the Leningrad Military Region (LVO).

The T-35-2 prototype, which was completed at OKMO in April 1933, made its 1st May public debut in Leningrad rather than Moscow.

The T-26 M-1933 entered service with the Red Army in 1933, and became the default Red Army light tank of the 1930s. These T-26 M-1933s and earlier production T-26 M-1931s are awaiting a parade on Uritsky Square, Leningrad. Note that one T-26 M-1933 has an interim turret with small turret bustle. These turrets were produced at the Mariupol plant and also used in limited numbers on the BT-5.

BT-2s during a parade on Uritsky Square, Leningrad, 1st May 1933. The tanks are without their 37mm main armament.

# 7th November 1933 - 16th Anniversary of the Great October Socialist Revolution

The 7th Nov 1933 military parade on Red Square was commanded by Mikhail N. Tukhachevsky in the capacity of deputy minister of "Narkomvoenmor", the Minsitry of Army and Navy Affairs - effectively deputy defence minister. Tukhachevsky was a rising star at the time and was at the forefront of mechanised and ground-air combined arms warfare in the 1930s. His impact on Red Army developments in mechanised combined-arms warfare was significant.

As with many of the brightest and best of the Soviet officer class he was however seen as a potential threat to the established order and to Stalin's authority as "Vozhd" or chief. Though Tukhachevsky may have been seen by Stalin as perhaps the single greatest threat to his own position, some of Tukhachevsky's futuristic and expensive technology projects were subject to a degree of financial mismanagement by those working directly under his command, and it was this that led to his sudden downfall. He was arrested as an enemy of the people, and was summarily executed in the summer of 1937, as were several of his subordinates.

The 7th November 1933 military parade on Red Square started with marching columns from the RKKA (Red Army) Academy and higher military schools, followed by infantry including engineers and chemical troops, OGPU police and secret police, Red Guards, former partisans from the Civil War and cavalry. The following mechanised part of the parade included anti-tank weapons, mortars, and perhaps most significantly various artillery types towed by tracked tractors, replacing the horse-drawn artillery still then common in most armies worldwide. Motorised infantry were paraded seated in open trucks, followed by locally designed Soviet light and medium armoured cars. A new tank prototype, the amphibious PT-1 also made a singular appearance on Red Square as doctrinal changes in the Red Army led to the development and series production of amphibious tanks.

Some particularly unusual vehicles were never displayed on Red Square. The BAD (BAD-1) and later BAD-2 amphibious armoured cars were displayed together only in Leningrad, on 7th November 1933.

The second prototype T-35 (T-35-2) and first prototype T-35 (T-35-1) were both displayed on Red Square on 7th November 1933. The second prototype had a new turret and changes in armour configuration, but retained the six road wheel running gear of the earlier prototype, which was replaced on the series production T-35A.

The first series production Soviet medium armoured car, the BAI or BA-I (BroneAvtomobil-Izhorsky) was paraded on Red Square on 7th November 1933, together with the D-8 (Dyrenkov-8) and FAI or FA-I (FordAvtomobil-Izhorskiy) light armoured cars. The early production variant of the T-37 amphibious light tank was displayed on Red Square, the parade debut of the T-37 amphibious light tank being in massed rows eight tanks wide, together with a rare parade appearance of the rival T-41, of which at least three prototypes were paraded on Red Square. On 7th November 1933, the first (T-35-1) and second (T-35-2) prototypes of the new five turreted T-35 heavy tank were paraded together on Moscow's Red Square for the first time. The first prototype had been completed at OKMO in Leningrad in August 1932, and the second prototype was built in 1933, with series production of the T-35A commencing on 1st November 1933. The SU-12 (SU-1-12) wheeled self-propelled gun was also paraded on November 1933, with the leading row based on the imported American Moreland heavy truck chassis (SU-12), and the second on the smaller and lighter GAZ-AAA chassis (SU-1-12).

Meantime, in Leningrad, the smaller 7th November parade there was attended by both the BAD (BAD-1) and BAD-2 amphibious armoured cars, both of which were developed at the Izhorsky plant near Leningrad. As with the T-35, development was now so rapid that early prototypes on parade were being replaced by improved prototypes or their production replacements almost concurrently with the parade debut of the former.

The weeks between the 7th November parade and the end of the calendar year were marked by two significant events, one of which was in the international public domain and the other somewhat more obscure. On 16th November 1933, U.S. President Roosevelt signed the official documents by which the United States formally recognized the Soviet Union as a state, the United States being the last of the international powers to do so, a full decade after Great Britain had formalised the same diplomatic recognition. Europe and the United States continued to consider the Soviet Union as an ongoing political and potential military threat, however the Soviet Union was meantime more directly concerned with pressures on its far-eastern borders.

In late December 1933, in response to mounting concerns over Japanese expansion in Asia Pacific and changing trading patterns and relations in the area along the route of the centuries old "Silk Roads", a contingent of between 2000 (and according to some sources up to 7000) Red Army troops supported by armoured cars and bombers crossed into China in an operation that remains somewhat obscure to this day. The Soviet move, today described as the Soviet invasion of Xinjiang, had the intentional or otherwise incidental effect of reducing British controlled trade between China and India to a fraction of previous levels. Although militarily a minor operation, the move for obvious reasons again raised British chronic concerns over historic Russian, and now Soviet, intent with regard to the jewel in the British political and trading empire, India.

BA-I (BroneAvtomobil - Izhorsky) medium armoured cars enter Red Square during a parade on 7th November 1933. The BA-I was the first series production medium armoured car. Several successive modifications would followed in the form of the BA-3, the BA-6 and BA-10. (Mikhail Baryatinsky)

A T-27 tankette and a T-35A heavy tank on parade in Kharkov on 1st May 1933. This T-35A is the first "series" production tank, on parade in Kharkov on the same day that the T-35-1 and T-35-2 prototypes were on display in Moscow and Leningrad respectively.

On 7th November 1933, the T-35-1 and T-35-2 prototypes were displayed together on Red Square, Moscow. Both used the same early running gear arrangement but the differences between the two prototypes are clear when viewed together. The "series" production T-35A was a further major revision of the prototype designs.

# 9th February 1934

1934 was a year of large military parades demonstrating the staggering speed of industrialisation and military mechanisation in the Soviet Union. The year started with an additional military parade by the Moscow Garrison on 9th February 1934, on the occasion of the 17th Congress of the VKP(b), yet another new date on the Soviet calendar on which a military parade was held. The parade was taken by the People's Commissar for Defence (Defence Minister) K.E. Voroshilov, with Marshals Budenny & Yegorov amongst others on the review stand. As light snow gently fell during the coldest period of the Russian winter, the parade began, reviewed by Stalin standing on the mausoleum review stand, with the foreign press and military attachés in attendance to take note and report back on a show intended to focus their attention on the Soviet Union's dramatic progress over little more than a decade since the end of the Civil War. The parade was doubtless a warning to those powers (specifically the United States, Great Britain, France and Japan that had effectively invaded the new state after the Russian Revolution and consequent decision by the new state to opt out of World War One) that any future attempt would now be even more calamitous than the previous disaster.

The out of schedule 9th February 1934 parade was to be one of the largest-ever Soviet military parades, lasting 3 hours and with the participation of 42,000 troops, of which 21,000 were infantry. The marching columns included the usual cadets of military academies, engineers, chemical troops, OGPU, border and railway security troops, machine-gunners, snipers, radio communications specialists and air force personnel, together with columns of Moscow militia. The traditional cavalry, horse drawn "tachanki" machine gun carts and horse drawn artillery followed, but it was the armoured elements of the parade, in terms of both the new types and quantities displayed that was to create the desired impression of a rapidly developing industrial economy and a rapidly mechanising Red Army.

The parade was to be a huge demonstration of virtually all the new tanks and vehicles that had recently entered series production and service with the Red Army. There were new Soviet designed and built tanks from the diminutive T-27 tankette and the larger T-26 light tank to the series production multi-turreted T-35 "land battleship", new armoured cars including the BA-I and the BA-3, indigenous military transport vehicles from GAZ and ZiS, new self-propelled artillery and an infinite variety of other Soviet weaponry.

The tank contingent of the parade began with T-27 tankettes followed by pre-series production T-37A amphibious tanks and even a few T-41 amphibious tank prototypes, followed by mass formations of twin turreted T-26 M-1931 and M-1932 and single turreted M-1933 light tanks, all paraded in columns eight tanks wide, which would have been impossible before the demolition of the Voskresensky Gate allowing access to Red Square from both sides of the Historical Museum. BT-2 fast tanks, the first series production model of the tank that would evolve in 1939 into the T-34, were displayed together with the later BT-5, the latter armed with a 45mm M-1932/34 tank gun. Multiple-turreted tanks followed, in the form of the three turreted T-28 medium, and the parade highlight, the T-35 five turreted heavy tank, which would continue to be a parade highlight until the outbreak of the Second World War.

Self-propelled artillery included the SU-12 (SU-1-12), a 76.2mm M-1927 field gun mounted on both Moreland and GAZ-AAA chassis. ZiS-5 and lighter GAZ-AA trucks were both paraded with 76.2mm field guns and with crews located in the rear cargo area for parade purposes.

Kommunar artillery tractors towed various heavy artillery through the square, including the 203mm M-1931 B-4 tracked howitzer. Another new development was the T-26T armoured artillery tractor, based on the T-26 light tank chassis, several of which towed 76.2mm regimental guns and 122mm howitzers through the square.

The 6x4 GAZ-AAA variant of the GAZ-AA was demonstrated, together with approximately 40 AMO-4 trucks with ZT-5 searchlights.

A total of 525 tanks were paraded through Red Square on 9th February, the parade demonstrating conclusively to domestic audiences and the outside world alike that the Soviet military machine had come of age; no longer reliant on civil war era or imported military technology. The first indigenously manufactured truck and armoured car, the AMO-F-15 and BA-27 respectively, had entered series production in 1927, but by 1934 the Soviet Union was mass producing GAZ passenger cars, GAZ and ZiS light and heavy trucks, light and medium armoured cars, and tanks from the T-27 tankette through to the goliath T-35. The scale and the variety of new tanks and vehicles on display was intended to create a specific impression, and that was admirably achieved.

Politically, it was the beginning of the era of Stalin's purges of the "old guard" and with that all potential domestic opposition within the Soviet Union, sometimes known as the "Great Purge", and many people on the Lenin Mausoleum review stand would fall to these purges in the following five years, including a high percentage of the Red Army senior leadership.

# 1st May 1934

Following on so closely from the massively orchestrated 9th February military parade, the military contingent of the 1st May parade was relatively benign by comparison. The parade was reviewed by Defence Minister K. E. Voroshilov, with the parade commander being the MVO commander A.I.Kork. The tanks demonstrated were the by now standard Soviet designs from the T-37A amphibious tank to the T-35 heavy tank, while the armoured cars, transport vehicles and mechanised artillery were as demonstrated in February, but in smaller quantities. The 1st May 1934 parade was accompanied per tradition by an aviation flypast.

The large scale parades undertaken on Red Square in the 1930s were as a result of considerable redesign and rebuilding at the turn of the decade. This included new cobbles laid, lamp posts removed, the Minin and Pozharsky monument moved from outside the GUM department store to near St. Basil's Cathedral and the Voskresensky Gate demolished, allowing columns of armour eight vehicles wide to traverse Red Square as seen here.

T-37A amphibious reconnaissance tanks traverse Red Square, Moscow, 1st May 1934. Due to the significant number of rivers, lakes and waterways in the Soviet Union, the Red Army was provided with several successive amphibious tank designs during the 1930s.

The definitive production version of the T-35 heavy tank appeared on Red Square from 1934. The tank, of which only 61 were built in total, was continually modified with significant changes between very small production batches. The T-35 would be a parade favourite throughout the 1930s.

# 7th November 1934 – 17th Anniversary of the Great October Socialist Revolution

The 7th November 1934 Red Square parade in celebration of the 17th anniversary of the Great October Socialist Revolution included the standard configurations of marching columns as in February and May 1934, but the armoured element of the display included new generations of armoured vehicles from both state companies and entrepeneurial designers, with the Dyrenkov designed D-8 and D-12 armoured cars being demonstrated alongside the FA-I light and heavier BA-I (BroneAvtomobil-Izhorsky) medium armoured cars. Mobile artillery was represented by the only truck mounted close-support gun deployed by the Red Army, the SU-12, again in two variants, based on imported Moreland and domestic GAZ-AAA chassis being displayed together as the SU-12 and SU-1-12 respectively. The multi-turreted T-28 medium and T-35 heavy tanks were the highlight of the 7th November 1934 parade, as they would remain for the rest of the decade, great crowd pleasers if not exactly the most remarkable of tank designs in combat. The 7th November parade was concluded per tradition with a flypast, and then Red Square was again quiet.

The political situation in the Soviet Union in 1934 was far removed from the orderly processions on Red Square, with a ramp-up in the level of intrigues and rivalry that would be inflicted on the country for several years ahead. By 1934, in order to tighten his lock on absolute authority, and fearing the unspoken opposition of more popular political characters viewed as rivals, Stalin began the background orchestration of efforts to ensure that any opposition to his supreme power would be quashed. Over time this would ultimately lead to mid decade purges that decimated any potential alternative leadership and the ranks of the Red Army's senior officer class, considered by Stalin as one and the same. The popular Leningrad Party Chief, Sergei Kirov, may also have been considered a threat though he was one of few people on good personal terms with Stalin. The reign of terror that was to sweep the Soviet political an military classes in the mid 1930s may be argued to have started with the assassination of Kirov in his offices on 1st December 1934, the motivations and "Grey Cardinal" behind which may never be known.

While the Soviet Union braced for an upcoming period of domestic terror during the years of the political purges, disconcerting events in Europe were beginning to look more international in scale. At the League of Nations Disarmament Conference in 1934, Adolf Hitler demanded that Germany be given military parity with Great Britain and France in Europe, effectively demanding the right to re-arm Germany in contravention of the Treaty of Versailles signed by Germany at the end World War One. In what became a period of appeasement, Europe, not for the first or last time, looked on helplessly as a "rogue state" with strong leadership broke free of the rules Europe had dictated to it but could not enforce when given the option of making a stand. Europe was again on the slide to total war, for the second time in the first half of the 20th Century, but there were two opposing totalitarian regimes in the mix this time, led by two equally ruthless national leaders, and which would by the time the fighting started both have amassed mechanised armies on a scale that the world had never before seen. The ultimate clash of these regimes and their respective armies would also be on a scale never before witnessed in history.

BA-I medium armoured cars parade through Red Square, 7th November 1934. Several other interesting vehicles can be seen in the background, including a D-12 (Dyrenkov-12) armoured car and SU-12 and SU-1-12 wheeled self propelled guns based on the Moreland and GAZ-AAA chassis.

THE RED ARMY ON PARADE 1917-45

D-8 (Dyrenkov-8), BA-I and other armoured cars parked on Ulitsa 25 Oktyabrya (Nikolskaya) before the 7th November 1934 military parade. Note that the armoured cars on the side columns are painted in a disruptive camouflage scheme.

A T-28 medium tank traversing Red Square, 7th November 1934. The multi-turreted T-28 medium and T-35 heavy tanks would be regular Red Square participants throughout the 1930s.

A D-12 (Dyrenkov-12) armoured car on Red Square, 7th November 1934. The D-8 and D-12 differed primarily in that the latter had a tourelle mounting on the roof for a 7.62mm PM-1910/30 water cooled machine gun for air defence.

This photograph of a BA-I traversing through Red Square on 7th November 1934 was later used in foreign recognition guides. (Tank Museum TM276/D5)

# 1st May 1935

Much had happened in Europe between the Red Square parades of November 1934 and May 1935. In Germany, Adolf Hitler had on 16th March 1935 formally renounced the Treaty of Versailles and announced his intent to re-arm Germany and to re-introduce military conscription. Re-armament had in fact been underway for some time, and before Hitler's rise to power German Wehrmacht and Luftwaffe forces had as related earlier trained with the Red Army at Kazan and the Red Army Air Force at Liptesk respectively, far from prying European eyes. The era of Soviet-German cooperation had been significant, but from a German perspective far from all encompassing. For perspective, some 220 German aircrew (120 pilots and 100 navigators) were trained at Lipetsk; by comparison 2000 pilots were trained before 1932 at the German training schools at Braunschweig and Rechlin.

There had also been significant cooperation between the Soviet Union and Germany on armaments, one such benefitting the Soviet Union being the TG series of tanks developed to various design stages (and built and tested in the case of the TG-1) under the direction of the German submarine engineer turned tank designer Edward Grote who had arrived in the Soviet Union with his design team in 1930.

The announcement that Germany was to formally re-arm was met with the expected conciliation by Europe and the League of Nations, and consternation in the Soviet Union, with which relations had effectively been frozen after Hitler came to power. To emphasize his point, Hitler held a rally including a military parade in Berlin on 20th April 1935 on the occasion of his own birthday, with the participation of armed troops of the newly formed Wehrmacht, and with new

As the Red Army rapidly mechanised and modernised in the mid 1930s, some rarely seen military equipment was paraded through Red Square in Moscow and in other Soviet cities. Here, GAZ-AAA trucks fitted with the 5AK radio station.

military vehicles and equipment on display that Germany had clearly developed in secret. Within two years the Wehrmacht had fielded 36 divisions and the arms race towards World War Two was underway.

It was within this background of events in Europe that on 1st May 1935, Stalin ordained what was in terms of overall participation the largest military parade ever held in the Soviet Union. The number of tanks was approximately 500, almost the same overall number as in 1934; however they were in May 1935 accompanied by a claimed 800 aircraft flying overhead. The Soviet 1st May parade in Moscow was clearly not a direct response to the military parade in Germany ten days prior, as there would not have been time to assemble the additional armaments and rehearse; however it was in part a direct response to events in Germany over the previous year, in addition to the Soviet requirement to effectively demonstrate its own military might. Whatever the political and military drivers, the 1st May 1935 military parade was an epically staged event.

The 1st May 1935 parade began with the usual marching units from the M.V. Frunze military academy, the Military Academy of Mechanisation and Motorisation (VAMM), the Zhukovsky aviation academy, and the V.V. Kuibyshev military engineering academy, demonstrating the exponential growth in the Soviet Union with regard to all arms of the Soviet military and their respective technological development. The academy columns were followed by Red Army infantry and naval units, the Moscow Proletarian Rifle Division and other marching troops, in turn followed by cavalry and horse drawn "tachanki" machine gun carts, a historic throwback to the era of the Russian Revolution which continues on the 7th November military prarades to the present day. Horse-drawn artillery was followed by large number of bicycle mounted troops. The mechanised section of the parade included the FA-I and BA-I

T-26 M-1933 light tanks traverse Red Square, 1st May 1935 (O. Baronov)

armoured cars, and the now common T-26 light tank, in twin turreted T-26 M-1931 and M-1932, and single turreted M-1933 variants. The massed tanks now had a greater element of the later T-26 M-1933 model with its single turret and 45mm armament, with approximately 60 T-26 tanks alone participating in the parade. Other tanks included the T-37A amphibious reconnaissance tank, the BT-5 fast tank, and the multi-turreted T-35 heavy tank. Artillery included the now standard SU-12 (SU-1-12) on imported Moreland and domestic GAZ-AAA chassis, and searchlight vehicles based on the elongated AMO-4 chassis which would in time be replaced by the ZiS-12 in the specialist anti-aircraft system role.

It was however the massed display of aircraft flying overhead that held the attention of the foreign press. Waves of TB-3 bombers and other aircraft literally filled the sky, though the overall total was achieved via a few circuits by the same aircraft. The air display of a claimed 800 aircraft began with the appearance of the Tupolev ANT-20 "Maxim Gorky", a massive passenger aircraft with six wing mounted engines and a further two engines, one "pull" and one "push" mounted in a separate module above the fuselage, accompanied by I-4 fighter aircraft, and followed by the four engined TB-3 bomber, the R-5 reconnaissance aircraft, the I-15 fighter, the prototype I-16 and the "SB" fast bomber. The "Maxim Gorky" would be involved in a fatal mid-air collision two weeks later and development of such large aircraft was temporarily discontinued. By 1935, the Red Army Air Force (VVS) possessed one of the largest military air forces in the World.

There were military contingents to the May Day parades in other cities of the Soviet Union on 1st May, including Leningrad, where BT-2 fast tanks were still being paraded on 1st May 1935, and Saratov, at which parade some unusual vehicles such as communications systems not often seen on Red Square parades were demonstrated.

While the parades were conducted in Moscow and other cities of the Soviet Union, 1935 was also the year of the first major exercises by mechanised corps near Kiev in the Ukrainian Military District (UkVO), with up to 500 T-26 and BT tanks involved in these - in German terms - "Blitzkrieg" war exercises, which also involved a new military force, the "Aviadesantnye Voiska", the air desant or airborne forces.

T-26 M-1933 light tanks parade through Red Square, 1st May 1935. The highlight of the parade was a large scale flypast, including the massive eight engined ANT-20 "Maxim Gorky" passenger aircraft. Tragically, the prototype aircraft would crash during trials two weeks later with the loss of all on board.

# 7th November 1935 – 18th Anniversary of the Great October Socialist Revolution

On 7th November 1935, Stalin stood on the Lenin Mausoleum and reviewed the latest display of military might to be put on show by the rapidly mechanising Red Army. The parade commander was the deputy to the commander of MVO district troops B.S. Gorbachev. Marching soldiers of the Moscow Proletarian Rifle Division, Red Army infantry, marines and naval units marched to the music of a large military orchestra, followed by cavalry on white horses and cavalry units including the "I.V. Stalin Independent Cavalry Division". Horse drawn "tachanki" and artillery followed per tradition, followed by massed displays of solo motorcycles armed with 7.62mm DT machine guns and motorcycle sidecar combinations. The armoured section of the parade was now of the mass proportions for which Soviet era parades would always be remembered. The FA-I light armoured car paraded across Red square in columns five vehicles wide, followed by the T-37A amphibious reconnaissance tank, the T-26 light tank in twin turreted M-1931/M-1932 and single turreted M-1933 versions as in the preceeding May, followed by BT-5 fast tanks, fitted with the same turret and 45mm M-1934 (20K) tank gun as the T-26 light tank, and providing entirely adequate armour penetration capability against concurrent potential enemy armour. T-28 medium tanks followed, with single examples racing through Red Square at high speed, followed by columns of T-28 tanks travelling at a more sedate speed, led by individually named tanks such as "Kirov", named after the recently deceased Leningrad party leader. The parade culminated in a display of highly impressive multi-turreted T-35 heavy tanks.

One of the features of the 7th November 1935 military parade was the number of different anti-aircraft systems, and the quantity thereof, on display.

T-37A amphibious light tanks pass the Lenin Mausoleum, 7th November 1935. The tank in the foreground is equipped with radio communications, with a frame antenna mounted around the hull. (O. Baronov)

Self propelled air defence systems were widely represented at this mid-decade parade, including air defense machine guns and anti-aircraft guns, searchlights and ZT sound locators mounted on AMO-4 and later ZiS-12 trucks. Artillery again included the recently accepted into service SU-12 (SU-1-12), the first Soviet wheeled artillery system, mounted both on GAZ-AAA and imported Moreland chassis. Due to poor weather, the aviation flypast was cancelled.

As the parade was progressing on the cobbles of Red Square, among the observers at the November 1935 parade, looking on impassively, were the German and Japanese foreign military delegations, who duly reported back to their respective High Command chiefs in Berlin and Tokyo as to the strength of the rapidly mechanising Red Army, as might be assumed from the displays of military might passing before them on Red Square. For the German military attaché, the Moscow parades of the late 1930s would be of great personal, and fatal, significance.

Military parades were held in other Soviet cities as usual on 7th November, including locations such as Stavropol in the south of the RSFSR and Khabarovsk in the far east of the country. The parades in these cities featured vehicles and equipment differing from that displayed on Moscow's Red Square, and sometimes included equipment which was never displayed on Red Square. Vehicles paraded in these cities included S-60 and S-65 tractors towing heavy artillery, GAZ-AA vehicles with single 7.62mm PM-1910/30 anti-aircraft machine guns and GAZ-A, GAZ-AA and ZiS-5 based radio communications vehicles.

Annual military parades were held in many Soviet cities in addition to Moscow during the 1930s. These GAZ-AA trucks, configued as anti-aircraft vehicles, are believed to be on parade in Stavropol.

The military parades held in the regions of the Soviet Union often featured different vehicles from those paraded in Moscow. These ZiS-5 trucks are being paraded in Saratov in 1935.

GAZ-A, GAZ-A 5-AK radio and GAZ-AA 5-AK radio vehicles during the same parade in Saratov in 1935.

S-60 tracked artillery tractors towing 152mm M-1909/30 howitzers during a parade in Saratov in 1935.

This rear view of the S-60 shows the distinctive horizontal fuel tank which distinguished the model from the later diesel powered S-65.

Older artillery such as the World War One era 152mm M-1909/30 howitzer was unsuited to towing behind relatively faster moving tracked artillery tractors. The gun carriages of some older artillery systems were thereby modified in the 1930s, with better suspension and the use of rubber rimmed or tyred wheels.

# 1st May 1936

In 1936, the Kazansky Cathedral at the left side entrance to Red Square that stood immediately behind the Voskresensky Gates which had been demolished in 1931 was also demolished, and officially for the same reason, to allow greater manouvering and larger scale for future Soviet military parades. This may not be entirely factual as apart from marshalling some vehicles, which during the 1930s also entered Red Square from Ulitsa 25 Oktyabrya (Nikolskaya), a small side street infront of the GUM building, the cathedral did not particularly obstruct any vehicular movement, but this is outwith the scope of this study. Buildings behind St. Basil's Cathedral on the Vasilevsky Spusk, down which gentle slope military parades egressed from Red Square towards the Moskva river were also levelled. There were plans at the time to greatly enlarge Red Square, some of which mooted the demolition of GUM, and even St. Basil's Cathedral, but even Stalin considered that a "progress" too far and the beautiful cathedral remains intact to the present day. The Minin and Pozharsky monument, originally located outside the main entrance to GUM on the side of Red Square, was moved closer to St. Basil's cathedral to give additional space for parade columns.

The 1st May parade was reviewed by the People's Commissar for Defence (NKO) Mashal K. E. Voroshilov, with the by now altogether traditional and highly impressive mass display of tanks, armoured cars, and mechanised artillery, with the massive T-35A heavy tanks concluding the parade and a flypast overhead including the I-16 fighter and the "SB" fast bomber. By 1936, only six years after the formation of the first mechanised brigade, the Red Army had exponentially developed its mechanised formations, which now included 4 mechanised corps, 6 mechanised brigades, 6 separate tank regiments and 15 mechanised brigades. The Red Army was by 1936 far closer to Germany in terms of mechanisation than some of the European nations which had been the victors in World War One, and whose military concepts had not advanced much since that time.

Columns of AM-600 solo motorcycles armed with pintle mounted 7.62mm DT machine guns traverse Red Square, 1st May 1936.

The bicycle remained a viable form of military transport worldwide in the 1930s. These sappers with accompanying dogs are wearing the new M-1936 pattern helmet.

A single column of T-35A heavy tanks passes through Red Square, 1st May 1936. The T-35 heavy tank series was the default "crowd pleaser" of the 1930s, the monumental land-battleships being particularly impressive parade participants.

The SU-12 (SU-12-1) was a wheeled self propelled gun, armed with a turntabe mounted 76.2mm M-1927 Regimental Gun. It was built in small numbers on imported Moreland (SU-12) and domestic GAZ-AAA (SU-12-1) chassis. Red Square, Moscow, 7th November 1936. (Mikhail Baryatinsky)

The T-35 was the highlight of Red Army parades on Red Square throughout the 1930s, impressive for its land-battleship appearance and sheer size if not necessarily its combat potential. The T-35A was the definitive series production T-35, but almost every tank built had specific design features. Red Square, Moscow, 7th November 1936.

THE RED ARMY ON PARADE 1917-45

In the Soviet Union's second city of Leningrad, parades were held every May and November in the convex shaped Uritsky Square (formerly Palace Square). This photograph, taken from the Hermitage on 1st May 1936 includes T-37A amphibious, T-26 M-1933 light and BT-5 fast tanks, together with wheeled vehicles and artillery. (Mikhail Baryatinsky)

THE RED ARMY ON PARADE 1917-45

May and November military parades were held in several other Soviet cities besides Moscow. These FA-I light armoured cars are parading down Kiev's main street, Kreschatic on 1st May 1936. Note the suummer parade uniforms.

Another view of FA-I armoured cars in Kiev, 1st May 1936. The FA-I was based on the GAZ-A chassis and was later modernised as the FAI-M on the GAZ-M chassis before being replaced by the BA-20.

T-37A amphibious light tanks parade along Kreschatic, Kiev in the mid 1930s, probably 1st May 1936.

These T-37A amphibious reconnaissance tanks are on parade in Minsk, Belorussia, on 1st May 1936. Though misidentified in some Soviet archive records as Khabarovsk, the distinctly modernist 1930s built government buildings and the church remain intact to the present day, positiviely identifying the location as Minsk in Belorussia.

# 7th November 1936 – 19th Anniversary of the Great October Socialist Revolution

The 7th November 1936 parade was conducted in Moscow against a backdrop of escalating conflict in Europe. Civil war had broken out in Spain in July 1936 and the Spanish Civil War with its multinational foreign volunteer brigades and bohemian adventurers including a certain American Ernest Hemingway would continue until April 1939, concluding just in time for the main event in Europe. Soviet support for the Republicans in Spain included the provision of military advisors and the supply of armoured vehicles, including 281 T-26 tanks shipped in October 1936 and a contingent of 50 BT-5 tanks, providing the Red Army with significant operational experience in armoured warfare conducted over relatively large and sparsely populated areas of terrain. Germany meantime delivered 122 Pz.Kpfw 1 light tanks. Somewhat ironically, the Soviet Union was in 1936 shipping current T-26 and BT-5 tanks to Spain, and Germany was shipping its current technology, while France delivered 64 Renault "FT-17" tanks, the very tank type on which the Soviet Union had in distant memory patterned its first indigenous tank, the KS, that had already been replaced in Soviet service by the modern T-26 and BT. It may be argued that France was sending old inventory, however considering France's current tank inventory in 1939 it was also indicative as to just how far advanced Germany and the Soviet Union were compared to the old European powers in the development of mehanised warfare. Some of the mainland European powers were clearly resting on their laurels after victory in World War One, with military leadership that still believed that the tank was no replacement for cavalry.

In Moscow, the 7th November 1936 military parade was commanded by Red Army commander 1st rank, I. P. Belov. The parade began with marching columns of the Defence Ministry and students from military academies, and the Moscow Proletarian Rifle Division, followed by cavalry including from the recently introduced "I.V. Stalin"

The "Pioner" was a relatively short-lived light artillery tractor that was demonstrated on Red Square in 1936 and 1937. The diminutive vehicle was intended for towing light artillery such as anti-tank guns, but the driver and gun crew were all exposed to the elements and shrapnel.

Pioner tractors of the Moskovskaya Proletarskaya Division parade through Red Square in 1936. The vulnerabilty of the driver and gun crew is apparent. The Pioner was replaced by the semi-armoured T-20 Komsomolets in 1937. (M. Kalashnikov)

Independent Cavalry Division. The parade even included a large display of troops on bicycles.

The 7th November 1936 parade might be considered a watershed moment, in that the balance between horse-drawn and mechanised artillery would move decidedly in favour of motorised transport from 1936 onward. The "tekhnika" part of the 1936 parade began with horse drawn "tachanki" machine gun carts, each towed by four horses, followed by 122mm M-1900/02 Howizers towed by teams of eight horses. The mechanised parade began with massed numbers of solo motorcycles armed with 7.62mm DT machine guns, followed by all manner of artillery towed by tracked tractors. The diminutive "Pioner" light tracked artillery tractor made a rare appearance in 1936 towing the updated 122mm M-1910/30 howitzer with spoked wooden rims and the 45mm M-1932 anti-tank gun. The Pioner would make an appearance again in the following year before being replaced by the armoured T-20 Komsomolets. The Komintern tracked artillery tractor featured on Red Square in 1936, towing 122mm M-1931 (A-19) wheeled and the 152mm M-1935 (Br-2) tracked howitzers and also the obsolescent 76.2mm M-1915/28 anti-aircraft gun.

The tanks and other support vehicles that crossed Red Square were from the K.B.Kalinovsky Mechanised Corps, which had been formed in 1934 in Naro-Fominsk (near Kubinka) west of Moscow, and was comprised of the 13th and 14th Mechanised Brigades and the 50th Rifle and Machine Gun Brigade. The mechanised brigades were equipped with approximately 525 tanks, including T-26, T-37A (and T-41) amphibian and BT fast tanks. BT-7 M-1935 fast tanks made individual high-speed "flypasts" across Red Square, followed by armoured columns of BT-7 M-1935 and T-28 medium tanks moving at a more sedate pace, including the still relatively new but entirely obsolescent parade centrepiece, the main series production T-35A heavy tank.

The 7th November parade was accompanied by a flypast of fighter aircraft, and the four engine TB-3 bomber.

Horse drawn "tachanki" machine gun carts were a regular Red Square parade feature since the first post-revolutionary Red Army parades. These carts usually mounted two 7.62mm PM-1910 "Maxim" water cooled machine guns. The horse drawn "tachanki" remain a parade feature of the commemorative 7th November parades to the present time.

Some very curious looking military vehicles have been paraded through Red Square. Here, ZiS-5 trucks tow trailer mounted ZT series sound locators, used to detect incoming aircraft engine noise, and in combination with searchlights and anti-aircraft batteries.

THE RED ARMY ON PARADE 1917-45

# 1st May 1937

The 1st May 1937 parade was held against a backdrop of political purges at home in the Soviet Union and ongoing Soviet involvement in supporting the Republicans in the Spanish Civil War abroad.

Stalin's purge of "old guard" detractors and enemies of the state, mixed in with those involved in pilfering state assets and funds, began in earnest in 1937, ultimately decimating the ranks of the Red Army's senior officer class that would within four years be expected to defend the country from the greatest threat it had faced since Napoleon over a century previously. With regard to the armed forces, the purges were in part an attempt to remove many of civil war era officers, many of whom were simply pensioned off rather than arrested and executed, and replace them with better educated officers more suited to the increasing technology of mechanised warfare. In this respect the purges as a modernisation of the Red Army in particular were aligned with the concepts of officers such as Tukhachevsky, however the methods and penalties were those by which Stalin earned his reputation both at home and abroad.

The 1937 May Day parade was reviewed by K.E. Voroshilov in an atmosphere of intrigue and outright terror within the country's political hierarchy and the military. The staff and students of military academies marched as usual followed by troops of the Moscow Proletarian Rifle Division, cavalry including the Independent Cavalry Regiment of the NKO, the "I.V. Stalin" Indepenent Cavalry Division and many other units.

The Red Army showed off its modern tanks, armoured cars and mechanised artillery as usual, but behind the Red Square parade showcase abject fear was the everyday scenario for the country's political and military elite, and for many others who were simply the victims of false accusations or the settling of scores.

In a nightmare scenario that only the Soviet

FA-I (Ford-Avtombil-Izhorsky) light armoured cars parade through Red Square on 1st May 1937, followed by GAZ-AA "polutorka" (1.5 tonne) trucks. (Mikhail Baryatinsky)

Union under Stalin could envisage, while the Red Army was mechanising at an astounding rate, the individual considered as the leading proponent of combined operations warfare theory in the Soviet Union, Mikhail Tukhachevsky, recently promoted to Marshal, found himself out of favour with Stalin and those who, as in the military leadership of some European countries, considered that any future war would be fought along the lines of the last one, with infantry and cavalry of the four hoofed rather than mechanised variety. The reality was that the Red Army (which included the Air Force) was the one element of the Soviet state apparatus that might oppose Stalin and prevent his absolute dictatorship. Tukhachevsky was demoted from his position as assistant to Marshal Klimenti Voroshilov and sent to the Volga Military District as Commander, where once out of the limelight he was subsequently arrested on 22nd May 1937. Tukhachevsky shared the fate of many who had travelled extensively abroad and understood the outside world order, and was thereby a potential threat to the Soviet establishment, namely Stalin himself. Marshals Semyon Budenny and Aleksandr Yegorov complied or conspired with Stalin's demands and Tukhachevsky was directly accused by Budenny the cavalry officer of leading the mechanisation of armoured units of the Red Army up a "tupik" or dead end path. Mikhail Tukhachevsky, together with seven other officers, was accused of treason. The leading inspiration behind Soviet mechanised warfare development in the 1930s was shot on 12th June 1937. The same fate almost befell Aleksandr Yegorov a few weeks later. He narrowly escaped arrest by holding off the NKVD officials who had come to arrest him at gunpoint until Stalin was called, and the unfortunate misunderstanding corrected. Many Soviet military designers and engineers were also arrested in 1937, an example being Leonid V. Kurchevsky who while senior designer at OKB-1 GAU from the beginning of the 1930s had pioneered the development recoilless weapons for the Red Army including the DRP, BPK and APK, and had mounted such weapons on T-27 tankettes and T-26 tanks. He had invented

Another view of FA-I light armoured cars during the same 1st May 1937 parade. (Mikhail Baryatinsky).

A small batch of 61 6x4 YaG-10 trucks were fitted with the 76.2mm M-1931 (29K) anti-aircraft gun, nearly all of which were paraded through Red Square in the late 1930s. (TsGAKFD)

The YaG plant in Yaroslavl produced several military vehicles used by the Red Army, such as the YaG-10 seen here. Post-war, the YaG plant would become YaAZ before production was moved to Kremenchug in Ukraine where production continued under the designation KrAZ.

many weapons, and most artillery plants had been involved in their production, but many of the projects were not suitable for mass production or unsophisticated operators. Kurchevsky was arrested in 1937 for the crime of developing "unperspective military technology". He was also shot, either in November 1937 or January 1939 according to conflated information. Similarly the engineer Pavel Grokhovsky, who had pioneered the development of desant landing equipment for airborne forces, including gliders, airborne load platforms for transporting airborne troops, vehicles and even light tanks, together with rather more futuristic projects such as armoured aerosans and hovercraft, was one of the last purge victims. He was arrested by the NKVD on 5th November 1942. He was originally recorded as having died in prison in 1946, but recently released documents show he was shot on 29th May 1943. Both these engineer-inventors had developed the very indigenous technology the Soviet Union needed, but some of their ideas were considered too impractical by a conservative leadership, and in many cases they consumed budget allocations which were not best utilised (Grokhovsky's team "wrote off" state owned cars used for airborne testing which ended up in private hands) and it was for such misdemeanours that both were arrested and subsequently shot. The Soviet Union of the late 1930s was not a time for wild spending and lack of transparency related to state property. Both military inventors were given posthumous state pardons in the post-war years.

As the May 1937 parade was being conducted in Moscow, the Spanish Civil War raged in Europe. Units from the Spanish Republican Guard marched through Red Square while the evaluation of Soviet tank performance was being closely monitored by Soviet military advisors based in Spain and fed back to Moscow.

Within a background of political repression at home and a civil war in one of the former colonial powers of mainland Europe, the May Day 1937 parade got underway. The line-up generally reflected the same vehicle types as shown the previous year, but with as usual some new additions. The marching infantry were primarily armed with the venerable Mosin-Nagant M-1891/30

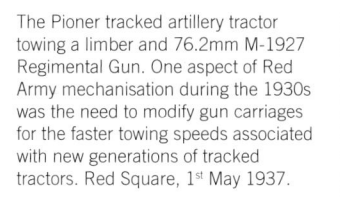

The Pioner tracked artillery tractor towing a limber and 76.2mm M-1927 Regimental Gun. One aspect of Red Army mechanisation during the 1930s was the need to modify gun carriages for the faster towing speeds associated with new generations of tracked tractors. Red Square, 1st May 1937.

bolt-action rifle, but some were equipped with new weapons such as the AVS-36 semi-automatic rifle, while the new Sh-36 (M-1936) pattern "schlem" (helmet) was now evident.

The T-38 amphibious reconnaissance tank was paraded in May 1937, almost immediately replacing the T-37A which had a relatively short production life.

The May 1937 parade clearly demonstrated the rapid replacement of cavalry and horse-drawn artillery in the Red Army with mechanised alternatives. As such the nuances were subtle but obvious to the informed. The new 76.2mm M-1936 (F-22) Divisional Gun was paraded through Red Square in a horse drawn configuration, but later in the parade there were several new types of specialised tractor developed specifically for towing artillery on the battlefield. One of the rarer examples of a specialised vehicle paraded on Red Square was the T-26T specialised gun tractor variant of the T-26 light tank, several of which paraded through the square towing the same 76.2mm F-22 divisional gun as towed through Red Square by horse teams earlier in the same parade. The small and unarmoured "Pioner" which had been seen the previous year again made an appearance on Red Square on 1st May 1937, now towing the 76.2mm M-1927 Regimental Gun. The Pioner was not considered viable due to its limited protection for the (vehicle) crew, and was thereby rapidly replaced by the T-20 Komsomolets, which was displayed during the same parade towing 45mm anti-tank guns and the 76.2mm M-1927 Regimental Gun.

Some unusual military transport vehicles were displayed in May 1935. GAZ-4 "Pikap" versions of the GAZ-A, armed with tandem 7.62mm PM-1910/30 "Maxim" machine guns were displayed together with GAZ-AAA trucks armed with the "4M" anti-aircraft machine gun system, namely four of the same 7.62mm PM-1910/30 "Maxim" machine guns mounted together on a single rotating stand within the rear cargo body. The ZiS-12 (an extended version of the ZiS-5 with a low level rear cargo body) was paraded armed with 25mm 94KM anti-aircraft guns and mounting

Another rare tracked artillery tractor displayed on Red Square in the mid to late 1930s was the armoured T-26T, based on the T-26 light tank chassis, seen here towing the 76.2mm M-1936 (F-22) Divisional Gun, Red Square, Moscow, 1st May 1937.

Z-15-4 searchlights. On an entirely larger scale, 6x4 YaG-10 trucks armed with 76.2mm M-1931 (29K) anti-aircraft guns were paraded through Red Square in columns six wide, representing almost the enire production output of this specialist anti-aircraft vehicle type (which was 61 vehicles in total).

Komintern tractors, the most powerful in Red Army service in 1937, towed 76.2mm M-1915/28 anti-aircraft guns. The first wheeled Soviet SPG , the SU-12, of which only 99 were built, on a mix of GAZ-AAA and imported Moreland chassis, was again displayed on 1st May 1937 in Leningrad, and in November in Moscow.

The highlight of the May 1937 parade was as in previous years the multi-turreted T-28 medium tanks, including the individually named tanks such as "Kirov" followed by the massive T-35A heavy tank, of which only 61 were also built. The May 1937 Red Square parade concluded with a

A rear view of the same T-26T and 76.2mm M-1936 (F-22) Divisional Gun combination on Red Square, Moscow, 1st May 1937. Although a small batch was produced and served with the Red Army, the T-26T was discontinued as an artillery tractor as it was considered an inappropriate use of a complex and expensive tank chassis.
(Mikhail Baryatinsky)

At first glance all T-35A heavy tanks parading through Red Square in the mid to late 1930s looked similar; however there were subtle modifications between the small production batches. These T-35A tanks are fitted with searchlights above the main and secondary armament for improved night fighting capability.

THE RED ARMY ON PARADE 1917-45

flypast by SB fast bombers of the LVO (Leningrad Military District) 147th Fast Aviation Brigade, together with the DB-3 long range bomber and various fighter aircraft, while small patrol boats cruised past the Kremlin walls on the river Moskva.

As was the norm in the dynamic political environment of the 1930s, much changed in the world between the May and November 1937 Moscow military parades. Fearing a future war on two fronts, Stalin in 1937 attempted to form an anti-Fascist alliance but found no interest with major European countries such as Great Britain and France. It was also clear by 1937 that despite Soviet aid, the Soviet backed Republican forces in Spain would sooner or later be defeated by General Franco. This would in turn allow Hitler to re-focus on other priorities including his decared wish for Liebenstraum (living space) for the German people, which would inevitably include the grain resources of the Soviet union, primarily located in Ukraine. Stalin, perhaps understanding the pending clash with Germany more than he is often given credit for, was in the absence of European allies forced into a pact with the very country which by 1937 was the greatest long-term threat to the Soviet Union - Germany. The Soviet-German pact which would in due course carve up Poland was from a Soviet perspective all about buying time in much in the same manner as Chamberlain acted for Great Britain. Both Stalin and Chamberlain are today often discredited as having misunderstood German intent; in reality they both understood the predicament of their respective countries perfectly, but in the Soviet Union as in

The T-37A amphibious reconnaissance tank was replaced by the T-38 from 1937. The T-38 had a lower, wider hull, providing better buoyancy and water stability, and the turret was moved to the left side of the tank. The armament remained a single 7.62mm DT machine gun.

Great Britain, decisions were made making accommodations on paper in order to allow their respective military forces and military industrial complexes to prepare for total war. To the dismay of communists and European countries alike, the Soviet Union and Germany signed a non-aggression pact in Moscow on 23rd August 1937, albeit after France, Great Britain and Poland had already done so. This allowed Hitler to prepare an invasion of Poland on 1st September 1939, with Red Army troops entering Poland on 17th September and retaking former Russian Empire territory as defined by the Curzon line after the Polish government had fled to run the following war from exile in London.

GAZ-A 5AK radio vehicles parade past the Hermitage on Uritsky Square, Leningrad, 1st May 1937. The GAZ-A was used by the Red Army in reconnaissance, transport and communications roles. (M. Albpert)

A T-28 moves past the Hermitage in Leningrad during the same 1st May 1937 parade. Although Red Square was usually the default location for parade debuts, this was not always the case, and some tanks such as the T-35 heavy tank had their public debut in Leningrad. (M. Albpert)

The original Soviet era photo caption defines this Pioner tractor as being in the Pervomaisky region of Moscow in September 1937. The specific occasion in unknown. (Fishman)

# 7th November 1937 – 20th Anniversary of the Great October Socialist Revolution

The 7th November 1937 Red Square military parade was a major event, celebrating as it did the 20th anniversary of the Great October Socialist Revolution in 1917. Whereas the 10th anniversary in 1927 had been conducted in the eye of a storm of political intrigue and infighting between political factions after the death of Lenin, and with militia cavalry holding back protests in the streets around Red Square, the 20th anniversary was held in a country very much in the firm grip of a ruthless dictator, who had emerged from the very intrigues and infighting that surounded the 10th anniversary parade.

The 7th November 1937 parade was reviewed by Defence Minister Marshal Klimenti E. Voroshilov, with the parade commander being Marshal of the Soviet Union S. M. Budenny who had been responsible for having Mikhail Tukhachevsky shot during the summer. Stalin stood on the review stand as the armed forces of the Soviet Union passed before him. The parade was attended by military attaches from various European countries including Germany, and also from distant countries such as Japan with which Soviet relations might be best described at the time as being difficult. Considering the growing political crisis in both Europe and the Far East, the parade of military equipment passing before the Lenin Mausoleum was more than a parade, it was a military statement of intent.

The parade began with the usual marching columns of students from the Red Army schools and colleges, cadets from the VTsIK academy, troops of the Moscow Proletarian Rifle Division, cavalry of the I.V.Stalin Independent Cavalry Division, NKVD secret police forces, naval forces and marines, Red Army Air Force personnel, veterans of the Civil War, and specialist forces including communications, engineering and airborne troops. There followed massed formations on bicycles and on TIZ AM-600 motorcycles.

The November 1937 parade included massed formations of BA-20 and BA-20M armoured cars, followed by huge numbers of tanks of different

By 1937, the FA-I light armoured car was being replaced in Red Army service by the BA-20, based on the modern GAZ-M1 chassis. Some vehicles were fitted with radio, for which a frame antenna was mounted around the hull. (Tank Museum: TM3202/B5)

types which filed passed the party faithful on the review stand on the Lenin Mausoleum and the assembled foreign military attaches standing nearby. Tanks displayed included T-26 light tanks, BT-5 fast tanks (which were already being superseded by the BT-7), T-28 medium and finally T-35 heavy tanks which filed onto Red Square from their traditional marshalling area on the adjacent Manezhnaya Square. In 1937 it was the turn of T-28 medium tanks to be used for single tank fast drive pasts, with named tanks such as "Kirov" impressing the crowds. Average tank production in the Soviet Union had meantime increased exponentially from an average 740 tanks annually in 1930-1931 to an average of 3139 anually in 1935-1937.

The new T-20 Komsomolets armoured light artillery tractor was displayed, replacing the recently unveiled but short-lived Pioner tractor, and towing the modified 45mm M-1937 anti-tank gun which had better armour piercing capability.

The towed artillery paraded on Red Square on 7th November 1937 now included the parade debut of the RVGK "Corps Duplex" heavy artillery, the 122mm M-1931/37 (A-19) field gun,

The YaG-10 6x4 truck and 76.2mm M-1931 (29K) anti-aircraft combination was paraded in Red Square until the end of the decade. The side boards folded down to provide a firing platform allowing 360° traverse.

The T-20 Komsomolets armoured light artillery tractor replaced the Pioner in production from 1937. It provided armoured protection for the vehicle commander and driver-mechanic, but not the gun crew, who remained seated back to back on bench seats at the rear of the vehicle. The Komsomolets was produced in three distinct production series.

modernised from the earlier M-1931 variant, and the new 152mm M-1937 (ML-20). Introduced as RVGK strategic command reserve artillery, the weapons would during the Second World War prove extremely effective tank-killers. The 152mm M-1937 (ML-20) was mounted in the wartime SU-152 and later ISU-152 self propelled guns and the 122mm M-1931/37 was mounted in the ISU-122 self propelled gun. Although labelled as SAUs or self-propelled guns, with their primary role being the destruction of field strongpoints and concrete bunkers, these vehicles performed a secondary role as highly effective tank destroyers. Wartime operators manuals nevertheless had on the introduction pages the opening statement: "SAU is not a tank!"

Air defense artillery on display ranged from new Komintern tractors towing obsolescent 76.2mm M-1915/28 anti-aircraft guns (AAGs) to YaG-10 trucks mounting 76.2mm M-1931 (29K) AAGs. The parade concluded with a flypast by 300 aircraft including the ANT-25, piloted by M.M. Gromov. In closing the 20th Anniversary of the Great October Revolution military parade, fighter aircraft "drew" "CCCP" and "20" with smoke in the sky above Red Square.

The November 1937 parade was also the last to be attended by Yakov Alksnis, who had been the Commander of the Red Army Air Force since 1931. He had also been coerced into denouncing Mikhail Tukhachevsky and was directly responsible for his execution. In the same manner as Tukhachevsky had been arrested and subsequently shot soon after the 1st May 1937 parade, Alksnis met the same fate soon after the November parade. Stalin had been advised to remove Alksnis from his post in 1935 due to the overall poor state of readiness in the Red Army Air Force; however he waited until 1938 when it was long clear that the Red Army Air Force was not ready for modern air combat, and the quantity of aircraft and aircrews which the Soviet Union had built up was not necessarily matched by quality. Alksnis was arrested on 23rd November 1937 and also subsequently shot. Stalin was at the time more concerned with his immediate surroundings than events at large in Europe, and was decimating the very officer class on which the Soviet Union would depend for its survival in the coming years. Considering the thousands of Red Army and Air Force officers who were executed on spurious charges during Stalin's purges, it says much of the Soviet military and the strength of Soviet character that the Soviet Union survived the aftermath of 22nd June 1941 when European countries such as France with no internal strife and a massive standing army would collapse within a few weeks of being attacked by the same German war machine.

The Komintern "fast" artillery tractor was introduced into service with the Red Army in 1937. Based on the chassis of the short-lived T-24 tank, the Komintern was designed to transport medium and heavy artillery while also accomodating the gun crew and a quantity of ammunition. (Kislov)

The Komintern was paraded on Red Square from 1937, towing heavy artillery such as the 122mm M-1931/37 (A-19) and 152mm M-1937 (ML-20) "Corps Duplex" heavy artillery pieces.

THE RED ARMY ON PARADE 1917-45

T-35A heavy tanks pass through Red Square, 7th November 1937. These tanks have field unit rather than parade markings.

T-26 M-1933 tanks on parade in Khabarovsk, 7th November 1937.

These rarely seen SU-5-2 self propelled howitzers, based on the T-26 tank chassis, were also paraded in Khabarovsk on 7th November 1937. (Mikhail Baryatinsky)

113

# 1938

From a foreign affairs perspective, the Soviet Union was in 1938 involved directly in the Spanish Civil War and was manoeuvering against the Japanese in the Far East in the region of Lake Khasan, which would result in direct conflict with Japan later in the year. But the Soviet Union, its military and its general population were for most of 1938 as in the previous year more concerned with the terrors of the Great Purge, actually a series of repressions and purges, first of the party and then the military, which had started in 1934 and continued into the spring of 1938. These purges which were in part related to maintaining Stalin's personal position and ensuring there was no competition for his position as "Vozhd" or leader, and in part bringing order where there were elements of chaos, cost the lives of an unrecorded number of Soviet citizens. The death toll is believed to be around 600,000, including a very large proportion of the senior officer class of the Red Army and the Red Army Air Force, including pragmatic and forward thinking senior officers such as Mikhail Tukhachevsky and Yakov Alksnis.

While the state apparatchiks of the Soviet Union were in 1938 more inwardly concerned with late night knocks at the door than international events, Germany's rise to political power in Europe now began to unfold militarily, such that within a period of months Stalin would in order to save the country be forced to make amends such as were possible with the very officer class he had recently permanently purged of some of its best talent along with the less capable. As rehearsals for the 21st anniversary of the Great October Revolution military parade were underway in Moscow, Germany on 1st October 1938 annexed areas of Czechoslovakia referred to as the Sudetenland, and as Germany consolidated both land and additional military manufacturing capability, the slide towards war in Europe began to gather pace.

Meanwhile in the Far East, the chronic build up of tensions which had started with the Japanese invasion of Manchuria in 1931 resulted in July 1938 in a direct clash between Soviet and somewhat maverick Japanese Kwangtung Army forces in what was known as the Battle of Lake Khasan, which took place between 29th July and 11th August 1938. The Red Army contingent included 354 tanks, of which the overwhelming majority were T-26 light tanks (including 10 KhT-26 flamethrowers), a significant number of BT-5 fast tanks and a few BT-7 fast tanks; and even fewer SU-5-2 self-propelled guns based on the T-26 light tank. The Japanese were decisively defeated, for the loss of 9 tanks destroyed and a further 76 damaged in combat. The clash was in the scale of things to come perhaps insignificant, but was proof if needed that the Red Army was by the second half of the 1930s both highly mechanised and well versed in combined arms operations. The incident was a minor battle, but the decisive defeat was for Japan all encompassing, and had a direct bearing on events to come in World War Two. As the Soviet Union was having to deal with the German invasion in the summer of 1941, Japan had its chance to conquer long coveted territories in mainland Asia Pacific and even to strike for eastern Siberia within the territory of the Soviet Union. But it did not, in large part due to the disastrous outcome of the engagements with the Red Army at Lake Khasan in 1938 and the Khalkin Gol in 1939. The lack of action on the part of the Japanese allowed Stalin to release the Red Army Siberian divisions to reinforce the defence of Moscow and other Russian cities in the European part of the Soviet Union, which had a decisive effect in halting the German onslaught. Meantime, the resource starved Japanese, struggling with among other things an oil embargo imposed by the United States, struck at the resource-rich Asia Pacific colonies then belonging to Great Britain, Holland and the United States. In order that the move in Asia Pacific be successfully consolidated, the Japanese attacked the major United States naval base on the main island of Hawaii which provided naval protection in the region - Pearl Harbour.

# 1st May 1938

The 1st May parade was nearly identical to that of November 1937; however it was held against a backdrop of the latter stages of Stalin's ongoing political repression in the Soviet Union, which included the oppressors turning on their own. Genrich Yagoda, who had been replaced as People's Commissar for Internal Affairs (the NKVD) by Nikolai Yezhov in the role in September 1936 was among those arrested in the "Great Purge". He was executed on 15th March 1938.

The YaG-10 is again seen on parade in Red Square in an anti-aircraft vehicle configuration, mounting the 76.2mm M-1931 (29K) anti-aircraft gun. Relatively small numbers of YaG-10 trucks were used by the Red Army, primarily in technical support vehicle roles.

The T-35A was by 1938 an anachronism, but remained a crowd pleaser on Red Square right up until the last pre-war parade in May 1941. Meanwhile, design work on next generation heavy tanks such as the SMK, T-100 and the KV (later KV-1) was by 1938 underway at the LKZ plant in Leningrad.

T-26 M-1933 light tanks parade through Uritsky Square, Leningrad, on 1st May 1938. The lead vehicles are command tanks fitted with radio and a frame antenna round the turret, followed by standard line tanks.

# 7th November 1938 – 21st Anniversary of the Great October Socialist Revolution

On 7th November 1938, Moscow celebrated the 21st anniversary of the Great October Socialist Revolution within a backround of increasing tensions in Europe and the Far East. Japanese aggression in Manchuria which had been ongoing since 1931 had by 1938 begun to encroach on Soviet territory, with the Battle of Lake Khasan at the beginning of August having been critical in that although not a major battle it definitively arrested Japanese aggression in the region. Meantime in Europe, fearing war and determined to avoid such a war at all costs, the heads of State of Germany, Great Britain, France and Italy had on 29th September 1938 signed the Munich Agreement, with Neville Chamberlain signing on behalf of Great Britain. The agreement effectively sealed the fate of Czechoslovakia, which was incorporated into the German sphere of influence, including its much valued military manufacturing capacity. The 7th November parade in 1938 was set against a background whereby the focus of the Soviet Union was returning to international politics rather than the internal political terrors that had gripped the nation in recent years.

The November 1938 parade had as with all parades some specific features, with a large number of military academies being represented among the marching infantry columns during this parade. The many and varied academies present included the RKKA (Red Army) military academy in the name of M.V. Frunze, the N.E. Zhuvovsky aviation academy, the RKKA Academy of Motorisation and Mechanisation, the V.V. Kuibyshev military engineering academy, the Military Academy of Chemical Defence in the name of K.E. Voroshilov, the military veterinarian academy, and the military-legal academy amongst others. The parade for the first time included participants from the artillery academy named after F.E. Dzerzhinsky, the Military-Political Institute in the name of V.I. Lenin, the 1st Moscow Artillery School, the Military-Railroad School, border guards, NKVD

The Red Army employed a significant number of motorcycles, such as these AM-600s parading through Red Square on 7th November 1938. AM-600s, which were built at Taganrog Instrument Plant, were sometimes designated in full TIZ-AM-600. Note the pintle mounted 7.62mm DT tank machine gun.

THE RED ARMY ON PARADE 1917-45

and not least the Military Musical School. Soon after the parade, on 25th November 1938, a new People's Commissar for Internal Affairs took control of the NKVD, an individual by the name of Lavrenty Beria.

The mechanised part of the parade began with a massed display of TIZ AM-600 motorcycles, produced in Taganrog. BT-7 M-1937 fast tanks performed single tank high speed drive pasts across Red Square ahead of the main armoured columns. The single turreted T-26 M-1933 was displayed as the main tank type, as it was in Leningrad in May and November of 1938. Tracked tractors towed artillery across the square, the armoured T-20 Komsomolets towing the 76.2mm M-1927 Regimental Gun and the larger Komintern towing the always impressive 203mm B-4 tracked howitzers. Various wheeled military transport included the ZiS-5, GAZ-AA and GAZ-AAA, while air defence vehicles included the GAZ-AAA fitted with the 4M anti-aircraft machine gun (AAMG) system in the cargo body and the ZiS-12 armed with the 25mm 94KM AAG.

The BA-20 was modified as the BA-20M, with mechanical and layout changes, the most obvious of which was a new conical turret providing better internal working space. Early radio-equipped BA-20Ms retained the hull frame antenna, but this was later replaced by a dashpot mounted whip antenna.

The GAZ-AA (GAZ-MM) was the standard 1.5 tonne general service truck used by the Red Army in the 1930s. The bench seating was for parade purposes only.

The ZiS-12 was a lengthened version of the ZiS-5 4x2 truck, used to mount specialised equipment, including the 25mm M-1940 anti-aircraft gun and de-mountable searchlights, as seen here on Red Square on 7th November 1938. Stalin and his predecessor both look down on the proceedings from their posters on the GUM department store wall.

The GAZ-AAA was a 6x4 version of the GAZ-AA used by the Red Army primarily for specialised technical support and weapon mounting roles. These GAZ-AAAs are fitted with the 4M anti-aircraft system, which consisted of four 7.62mm PM-1910/30 "Maxim" water cooled machine guns mounted on a single pedestal within the cargo body.

THE RED ARMY ON PARADE 1917-45

The 6x4 ZiS-6 performed a similar role to the lighter capacity GAZ-AAA. These ZiS-6 vehicles on display during a November parade in the late 1930s mount the strange looking ZT-5 sound locator system, which was more usually mounted on a trailer.

ZiS-6 searchlight vehicles parade through Red Square, 7 November 1938. The ZiS-6 was produced until the autumn of 1941 when the ZiS plant was evacuated from Moscow to several cities including Miass in the Urals.

The Komintern was purpose designed "fast" tracked artillery tractor which entered service with the Red Army in the late 1930s. These Komintern tractors, on parade on 7th November 1938, are towing 122mm M-1931 (A-19) guns with their barrels locked in the transport position. The 122mm M-1931 was updated in 1937 as the 122mm M-1931/37, with the carriage and wheels modified for higher towing speeds.

Komintern medium artillery tractors towing 203mm M-1931 (B-4) tracked howitzers through Red Square on 7th November 1938. The Komintern would soon be joined by the more powerful Voroshilovets heavy artillery tractor which was more suited to towing heavy tracked artillery such as the 203mm B-4 and 152mm Br-2.

THE RED ARMY ON PARADE 1917-45

The 203mm M-1931 (B-4) was an obsolescent looking but highly effective artillery piece, normally assigned to the RVGK (the strategic command reserve). It was mounted on a tracked chassis to provide a stable, but all-terrain capable firing platform, which required a powerful tracked tractor to tow it. It was used for the demolition of hardened defences and for destroying buildings at short range such as in the streets of Berlin in April and May 1945. Post-war it was remounted on a wheeled chassis as the B-4M.

The T-26 M-1933 was the default Red Army light tank during the second half of the 1930s. Note that the tank in the centre column is fitted with searchlights above the main armament, providing an element of night fighting capability.

The T-26 M-1933 was the definitive Red Army light tank of the 1930s, built in large numbers and innumerable specialised versions. Although sometimes maligned due to the numbers destroyed in the early stages of "Operation Barbarossa", the tank was armed with a relatively powerful 45mm M-1932/34 (20K) tank gun and was comparable to or better armed than the majority of light tanks employed by contemporary armies.

The T-26 was the Soviet Union's first truly mass production light tank, representing the backbone of Red Army tank forces in the late 1930s. Its planned replacement, the heavier and far more complex T-50, was due to enter service as war broke out, due to which its production was curtailed as it was too complicated for wartime manufacture. These are T-26 M-1933 line tanks, some fitted with searchlights for the turret armament.

THE RED ARMY ON PARADE 1917-45

The T-28 was by 1938 also something of an anachronism, as although impressive on Red Square the tank was at the time still armed with relatively low velocity 76.2mm KT-28 tank gun. It also presented a very large target with considerable vertical armour. Red Square, Moscow, 7th November 1938.

The T-28 would enter combat in Finland the year after this photograph was taken, and would suffer badly at the hands of Finnish anti-tank gunners. Final production model T-28 tanks would be armed with the improved 76.2mm L-10 tank gun and feature additional armour. Red Square, 7th November 1938. (RGAKFD)

BT-7 M-1937 fast tanks parade through Minsk, Belorussia in 1937. The BT-7 was the Soviet development of the original "cruiser tank" concept suggested by Walter J. Christie, which was turned down by the United States Army but adopted by other countries including Great Britain, and not least the Soviet Union. Within two years of this parade, the BT-7 would have morphed via the A-20 and A-32 into the T-34 mdium tank.

# 1939

The year 1939 is etched into history as the year in which Germany invaded Poland and World War Two began. Having acquired the Sudetenland in October 1938, Germany acquired the balance of Czechoslovakia in March 1939. On 1st September Germany invaded Poland and Europe was at war. In the early months of 1939, the Soviet Union remained however as much preoccupied with events in the Far East as it was with events in Europe, while the Unites States would not become embroiled in the war until after the Japanese attack on the American naval base at Pearl Harbour, an event then still two years in the future. While European history concentrates on the German onslaught in Europe in 1939, with Soviet participation in the division of Poland, the collective Soviet memory for 1939 is more vivid as regards the disasterous Russo-Finnish "Winter War" of 1939-40 than events in old Europe. Having in the late 1930s refused Stalin's attempts at a military alliance to contain the German threat, the very countries that had declined that alliance found themselves in 1939 fighting the German threat alone, while the Soviet Union was for expediency purposes temporarily allied to the very country that was the source of the threat. 1939 would herald the beginning of World War Two in Europe, but for the Soviet Union in 1939 a war on home territory which was the reality for much of Europe in 1939 was still two years distant. And as Germany put its "Blitzkrieg" tactics into practice in the lowland countries of western Europe, it was, for the moment, the Finns and the Japanese that were the primary concern for the Soviet leadership in the Kremlin.

# 1st May 1939

For the May Day Parade in 1939, the "GUM" department store building was decorated with slogans in German, somewhat ironically with hindsight, but in the fluid politics of pre-war Europe allies were allies and the old saying of keeping one's friends close and enemies closer held true for the Soviet Union as much as any other country. The 1st May 1939 parade included marching columns representing the NKO (Defence Ministry), the higher and middle RKKA schools, infantry, air force and naval personnel, civilian aircrew, artillery, border troops, cavalry, horse drawn "tachanki" machine gun carts, motorised infantry, trucks with 7.62mm 4M anti-aircraft machine guns and larger calibre anti-aircraft weapons, artillery towed by tracked tractors and tanks and armoured cars. The parade concluded with a flypast.

In the 1930s it had been not uncommon to put the prototypes of future tank designs on display on Red Square before they were officially accepted for service. The T-28 medium and T-35 heavy tank prototypes were for-instance displayed in public as design work on the series production variants was being completed, while various prototypes which were not ultimately accepted for service had also made cameo appearances on Red Square. The 1939 parades were from this perspective an anomaly, as were those of 1940 and May 1941, in that the Soviet Union deliberatley chose not to display the latest tank technology in

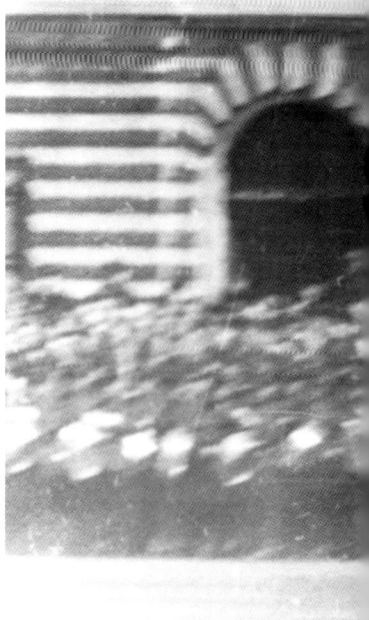

A BT-7 M-1937 fast tank parading through Red Square, Moscow, 1st May 1939. The tank is undergoing a dramatic high speed run through the square, with its red flag billowing above the turret.

public. The May Day parade in 1939 included the BT-7 M-1937 fast tank, which was also one of the main tank types paraded in Kiev the same day in a city where older generation tanks were the norm during such displays. The May 1939 parade had all the usual secondary armoured vehicles, truck mounted air defence sytems and towed artillery coupled to modern tracked artillery tractors. The parade highlight was as usual the multi-turreted T-35 heavy tank, with the standard "M-1933" (T-35A) production model now joined by the final production variant with sloped conical turrets. But the parades had changed significantly in scope just as geopolitics in Europe had shifted, and with the benefit of hindsight are more interesting from the perspective as to what was not demonstrated rather than for what was on display. The world was changing in 1939, and the Red Square parades in Moscow were defaulting back to the Soviet art of "maskirovka" or military deception.

At the beginning of May 1939 Soviet tanks paraded on Moscow's Red Square in accordance with standard peacetime traditions. At the end of the same month, Soviet tanks were in combat against the Japanese Army on the Soviet Union's far eastern borders. A series of clashes between combined Soviet and Mongolian forces and the Japanese Army in late May resulted in a military defeat for Japan on 28th May. The clashes nevertheless escalated in June, with Japanese forces crossing the river Khalkin Gol in July, resulting in larger scale set battles with Red Army forces commanded by Zhukov. The tanks and armoured cars then being displayed on Red Square were the same types being actively used in combat against the Japanese, with BA-3, BA-6 and BA-10 armoured cars and T-26, BT-5 and BT-7 tanks being the main Red Army armour used during these battles. A Soviet counter-attack in August involved 3 rifle divisions, 2 tank divisions and 2 tank brigades, with some 498 BT-5 & BT-7 tanks in action - no longer minor clashes. A major offensive by 50,000 Mongolian and Soviet troops begun on 20th August resulted in the Japanese being defeated in combat by 31st August. Total Soviet losses in these ongoing clashes were approximately 9703 killed, with 253 tanks destroyed, of which up to 80% were destroyed by anti-tank gun fire, with 133 armoured cars also destroyed in combat. These clashes were as stated more of a preoccupation for the Soviet high command in 1939 than events in Europe, though the stalling of Japanese

The same tank from the rear. The final production BT-7 tanks, sometimes designated BT-7M were fitted with the same V-2 diesel engine design as later mounted in the T-34 medium tank. Red Square, 1st May 1939.

advances in the far east in 1939 and Japanese reticence to restart hostilities thereafter would have a direct influence on the Red Army defence of Moscow in the autumn of 1941. The Japanese military remaining dormant on the Soviet union's eastern orders allowed the battle hardened Soviet Siberian divisions to move west to bolster Red Army defences on the Soviet "Western" front in Europe.

Meantime in Europe, having failed to secure treaties with other European nations to form a defensive pact against Germany, the Soviet Union signed the Mototov-Ribbentrop Non-Aggression Pact with Germany on 23rd August 1939. The Pact theoretically gave Hitler access to the resources of the Soviet Union, particularly the agricultural production of Ukraine, a political means of obtaining basic food resources which were the bedrock of German stability. Germany was ready to sell modern equipment and technology in return for food exports from the Soviet Union; while the other European countries and the United States had demanded hard currency or gold in payment.

From a Soviet perspective, the pact gave Stalin and the Soviet Union time to prepare militarily for the inevitable onslaught with Germany, and to recover from the self-inflicted decimation of the Red Army's officer cadre.

At 04:44 on 1st September 1939, Germany invaded Poland from the west. Great Britain presented an ultimatum to Germany related to its own defensive pact with Poland, which was ignored, and by 3rd September Europe was at war. With Europe at war with Germany for having invaded Poland from the west, the Soviet Union on 17th Septem-

The T-35A heavy tank received a major and final update at the end of the 1930s. The final "M-1938" production model was provided with conical main and subsidiary turrets and many other detail changes, such as foreshortened suspension side shields to prevent the build up of mud around the drive sprockets. This final production T-35 tank is following a "standard" production T-35A across Red Square, 1st May 1939.

ber invaded from the east. The next Red Army "military parade" was thereby held on 22nd September 1939, in the town of Białystok (Belastok) in north-eastern Poland. The Białystok parade included BA-20M light and BA-10A and BA-10M medium armoured cars, BT-5 fast tanks, S-65 tractors and other military vehicles actively employed in Poland in the previous days, displayed together with Wehrmacht armoured vehicles, a brief interlude of cooperation between the fascist and communist superpowers. The occasion was a meeting of German and Soviet forces in the city in order that Wehrmacht forces that had occupied the city handed the region over to the Red Army before returning to their own pre-agreed demarcation lines. Red Army and Air Force losses had been minimal, under 1500* killed during the short campaign. The occasion was a unique meeting of two then aligned armies, with officers and men smoking cigarettes together and inspecting each other's military vehicles. Behind the apparent co-operation between Germany and the Soviet Union there was pragmatism on the part of the Soviet leadership. Besides the stated Soviet reconquest of former Russian territory to the Curzon line, the former border with Poland was only 30-40km from Minsk, the capital of the Belorussian Soviet Republic. In the event of a Blitzkrieg war, Minsk could be taken within 48 hours of an invasion, and the border being pushed westward would buy the Red Army additional time. As would the concrete gun emplacements of the "Stalin Line" of defensive bunkers which would soon thereafter be built to the immediate west of the city. Two years later, these same forces would be engaged in arguably the most bitter conflict in world history.

Several subsequent parades were held in eastern Poland, which remained under Soviet military control from 1939 to 1941. There was also a joint Wehrmacht/Red Army military parade on the same date in Brest, today in modern Belarus, with a single column drive-past of T-26 M-1933 and later production model T-26 M-1939 tanks.

The tanks and armoured vehicles paraded in cities other than Moscow were often very different to those displayed on Red Square. These OT-130 flamethrower tanks are parading through Kalinin (today Tver) north of Moscow, 1st May 1939. (Photographer: Shamov)

* Russian MoD official statistics, 1993

# 7th November 1939 – 22nd Anniversary of the Great October Socialist Revolution

The 7th November 1939 Red Square parade featured some incremental improvements of existing tank and armoured vehicle designs, but as in May there was none of the new military technology which would earlier in the 1930s have been showcased for domestic and foreign press consumption.

The late production model T-26 M-1938 was displayed on 7th November 1939, now with sloped turret armour and searchlights mounted above the gun barrel providing an element of night fighting capability. Late production model T-35A heavy tanks, also fitted with armament searchlights, were paraded alongside standard T-35A tanks and the final T-35 production model with its new conical turrets. The usual artillery towed by Komsomolets and Komintern artillery tractors was on display, together with the new Voroshilovets heavy artillery tractor, but there were no new tank prototypes in sight, no prototype SMK or T-100 heavy tank or any other revelations. The SMK and T-100 prototypes would soon be tested in combat but would never appear on Red Square. The T-34 and the KV would meantime both enter combat long before their first (and only) public appearance at the same venue.

The 7th November 1939 military parade was held at a moment in time when war had been declared in Europe but for Great Britain the period was known as the "Phoney War", in that Hitler's Germany was still gathering its military and industrial strength (in which the subjegated Czech manufacturing plants would play a major role), the low countries of western Europe had yet to be invaded and the island fortress of Great Britain made

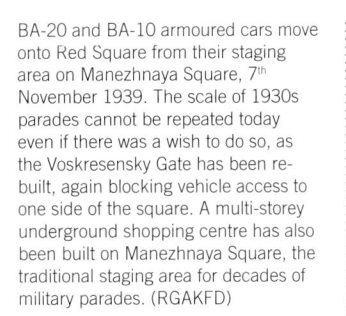

BA-20 and BA-10 armoured cars move onto Red Square from their staging area on Manezhnaya Square, 7th November 1939. The scale of 1930s parades cannot be repeated today even if there was a wish to do so, as the Voskresensky Gate has been rebuilt, again blocking vehicle access to one side of the square. A multi-storey underground shopping centre has also been built on Manezhnaya Square, the traditional staging area for decades of military parades. (RGAKFD)

THE RED ARMY ON PARADE 1917-45

The T-26 light tank underwent further modernizations in the late 1930s. These T-26 M-1938 tanks have a new welded turret with sloped armour, which was followed by the M-1939 with additional hull armour shielding. These tanks also have searchlights mounted above the main armament. Moscow, 7th November 1939.

BT-7 M-1937 fast tanks begin to move from their marshalling area on Gorky Street (today Tverskaya) across Manezhnaya Square and on to Red Square, 7th November 1939. The buildings to the right and the Central Telegraph building in the background look almost the same today.

preparations for a potential invasion by sea which would never come. The Soviet Union meantime, having held the Japanese in check on its eastern borders, was about to enter a short but brutal war on its western borders in northern Europe.

By the end of November 1939, the Red Army was engaged in the bitter Russo-Finnish war, which began on 30th November 1939. Compared to the lightning invasion of Poland, the war in Finland, fought against the Finns on their home territory, and in the depths of winter, was a blow to the morale of the Red Army. Notwithstanding that the Red Army had in recent years lost many of its senior officer class, and was perhaps not as well led as it might have been in the Finnish campaign, the Finns fought ferociously on their own territory and Red Army losses of men and equipment were atrocious. The war continued until the early spring, with a peace agreement being signed on 13th March 1940. As the Soviet Union prepared for the 1st May 1940 May Day parade, the country had behind it the bitter experience of a war lasting less than four months in which the Soviet Union had taken and retained 10% of Finnish ter-

T-28 tanks marshalled on Manezhnaya Square before the 7th November 1939 Red Square parade. Note the large red star with border on the side of the lead tank. The National Hotel in the background remains the same hotel today. (TsGAKFF)

ritory at a cost of over 25,000 Finnish lives, but had itself lost almost 127,000* killed in action and nearly 265,000* wounded, together with massive amounts of military equipment, including some of the Red Army's newest designs. The military leadership of countries such as France might in 1939 have been accused of living on past glories and in consequence being somewhat asleep to the reality of the threat of new armoured "Blitzkrieg" war that was moving inexorably in their direction. After the Finnish campaign, the leadership of the Red Army was fully awake, and the combat experiences in Finland had a direct bearing on the Soviet tank development, some of which would be seen on Red Square during the very next parade.

After the United States recognized the Soviet Union in 1933, American diplomats and military attaches for many years had offices in the building adjoining the National Hotel on Mokhovaya Street. The building looked directly out onto Manezhnaya Square, which was particularly useful for intelligence gathering purposes as tanks were being marshalled for military parades, as this interesting overhead view of a T-28 shows. (Steven. J. Zaloga)

T-28 tanks assembled on Manezhnaya Square awaiting the 7th November 1939 Red Square parade.

The final production model T-35 was as magnificent for parade purposes as its predecessors. The new conical turrets, curtailed suspension side skirts and new track guards are all apparent in this view.

* Russian MoD official statistics, 1993

THE RED ARMY ON PARADE 1917-45

BA-10A armoured cars on parade in Leningrad in 1939. The Soviet banner is flanked by banners of Marx and Engels and Lenin and Stalin, all hanging from the walls of the Hermitage Palace, home to the last Russian Tsar Nicholas II and his family until the Russian Revolution of 1917.

T-20 Komsomolets armoured artillery tractors towing 45mm M-1937 anti-tank guns and their limbers parade through Minsk, Belorussia, probably in November 1939. Compare the machine gun sponson with the Komsomolets tractors paraded in Moscow

T-35A and final production model T-35s staged for the 7th November 1940 Red Square parade. Note the minor construction differences between the two nearest T-35A tanks. Note also the American flag flying from the U.S. Embassy offices next to the National Hotel. (TsGAFF)

# Soviet Military Parades in the Pre-War 1940s

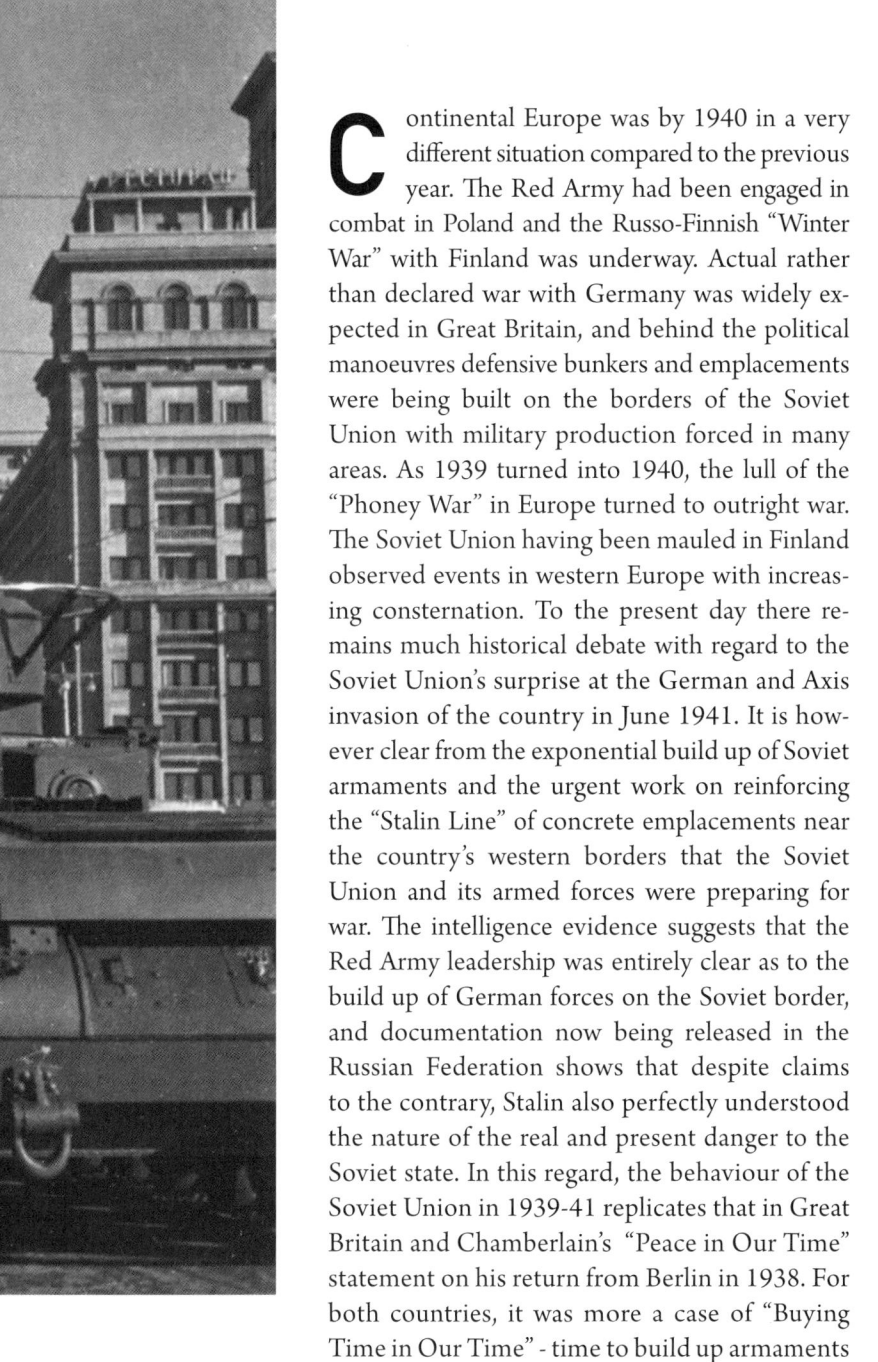

Continental Europe was by 1940 in a very different situation compared to the previous year. The Red Army had been engaged in combat in Poland and the Russo-Finnish "Winter War" with Finland was underway. Actual rather than declared war with Germany was widely expected in Great Britain, and behind the political manoeuvres defensive bunkers and emplacements were being built on the borders of the Soviet Union with military production forced in many areas. As 1939 turned into 1940, the lull of the "Phoney War" in Europe turned to outright war. The Soviet Union having been mauled in Finland observed events in western Europe with increasing consternation. To the present day there remains much historical debate with regard to the Soviet Union's surprise at the German and Axis invasion of the country in June 1941. It is however clear from the exponential build up of Soviet armaments and the urgent work on reinforcing the "Stalin Line" of concrete emplacements near the country's western borders that the Soviet Union and its armed forces were preparing for war. The intelligence evidence suggests that the Red Army leadership was entirely clear as to the build up of German forces on the Soviet border, and documentation now being released in the Russian Federation shows that despite claims to the contrary, Stalin also perfectly understood the nature of the real and present danger to the Soviet state. In this regard, the behaviour of the Soviet Union in 1939-41 replicates that in Great Britain and Chamberlain's "Peace in Our Time" statement on his return from Berlin in 1938. For both countries, it was more a case of "Buying Time in Our Time" - time to build up armaments and military preparedness for the inevitable outcome of events.

In the last two years before war broke out between the Soviet Union and Germany on 22nd June 1941, the Red Square parades were significant as much for what was not on display as opposed to what was. By contrast with the 1930s, the Red Square Parades of 1939, 1940 and even May 1941 it was the lack of new technology being displayed on Red Square that was notable. Though the T-34 medium and KV heavy tanks were in series production by 1940 and could have been paraded in Red Square as early as 1940 or certainly by May 1941, they were not. While the archaic T-28 and T-35 continued to trundle through Red Square, the T-34 and KV remained hidden from public gaze as an unpleasant surprise for the approaching German Army in the summer of 1941. Much is made today by some historians of Stalin and the Red Army's unpreparedness for "Operation Barbarossa", but as with the background to Chamberlain's famous announcement in Great Britain, much of the politics of "bonhomie" was conducted out of a pragmatic need to buy time to build up military capability. The debate on the Red Army preparedness for war in June 1941 is outwith the scope of this book; however the build-up of Soviet armaments in the years 1939-41 was by any standards immense; the country was preparing for war.

The parades of 1939, 1940 and May 1941 did not feature any of the new tank types which were at prototype stage, and in cases such as the T-34 and KV were already in series production. Whereas the Red Square parades of the 1930s had often included prototypes or limited production vehicles, in the two years before war tanks such as the T-100 and SMK, and even the prototypes for the KV heavy tank which together with the A-34 prototype had been tested in Finland would have been reeled out for the cameras for effect. These tanks were not demonstrated; but neither were the T-34 medium and KV heavy tanks already in series production by 1940 and which would have in other times undoubtably been paraded in Red Square in 1940 or May 1941. They were not, and the parades were significant in that the Soviet Union was now holding back on what it wanted the world - in particular Germany - to see.

# 1st May 1940

The May Day 1940 parade was reviewed by Marshal K. E. Voroshilov, with the parade commander being Marshal Semyon Mikhailovich Budenny. The parade was relatively low key, begun with the brass band of the Moscow Military Music School. Marching columns were formed from the NKO central command, a battalion of VMF (Naval) forces, students and cadets from the M.V. Frunze Military Academy named after V.I. Lenin, Military-Political Academy, and columns of RKKA infantry. The infantry were followed by the mechanised procession, with massed columns of BA-20 armoured cars, a mix of hybrid BA-20s with frame ariel around the hull, and later BA-20Ms with a whip antenna followed by BA-10A and BA-10M medium armoured cars. Tanks were represented by the BT-7 M-1937, the V-2 diesel engined BT-7 M-1939 (BT-7M), T-28 medium tanks (now fitted with additional "ekrany" armour around the turrets as a result of combat experince in the 1939-40 Russo-Finnish "Winter War") and the venerable T-35A land battleship heavy tanks including the final production variant with sloped turrets. The artillery and related tracked tractor vehicles were all very much current, including the STZ-5 towing 76.2mm M-1939 (USV) and 122mm M-1910/30 field guns, together with larger Komintern and Voroshilovets tractors towing larger

This overhead view of the final production model T-35 was taken by American Embassy staff based at the U.S. Embassy offices, which were in the 1930s conveniently located next to the National Hotel, outside which the Red Army staged much of its hardware before Red Square military parades. (Steven J. Zaloga)

This late production T-35A moving towards Red Square has several modifications, the most obvious of which is the shortening of the armoured side skirts protecting the complex suspension, so that mud does not build up on the drive sprocket.

BT-7 M-1937s traverse Red Square at speed, 1st May 1940. Despite the T-34 medium tank and KV heavy tanks being in series production, the BT-7 was even the following May still the most modern tank on display.

calibre long-range 122mm, 152mm and 203mm artillery pieces. The parade was overflown by 634 fighter, bomber and reconnaissance aircraft, including the TB-7 bomber. The latest generations of Soviet tanks remained however conspicuous by their absence during the May Day parade. Meantime on 1st May 1940, military parades were held in other cities of the Soviet Union with older vehicles still on display, with the FA-I armoured car for-instance still being paraded in Kiev.

As the Red Square military parade was being reviewed in the still peactime Soviet Union, the "Phoney War' in Europe was over and combat hostilities had begun in earnest. War now raged in Europe and for the future Allies of the Soviet Union the war was not going at all well. Germany had invaded Denmark and Norway on 9th April, and on 10th May, Germany invaded France and Belgium in a lightning Blitzkrieg war that would result in the French Army and the British Expeditionary Force fighting a rearguard action in France which would later that month result in the infamous evacuation from Dunkirk, followed on 14th June 1940 by the capture of Paris, and three days later by the capitulation of France. The mighty French Army, victorious in World War One, had been defeated in just over one month of combat. Holland had surrendered on 15th May, and Great Britain stood alone awaiting its fate, protected from immediate invasion by the English Channel. Fully aware that events unfolding in Europe would soon be replicated in the east, the Soviet People's Defence Committee (NKO) in early 1940 demanded the creation of 9 new mechanised corps by 6th July 1940, and in February-March 1941 the NKO demanded another 20 be created. Despite the historical received wisdom that the Soviet Union was taken by surprise in June 1941, all defence deci-

THE RED ARMY ON PARADE 1917-45

BA-10M medium armoured cars move from Manezhnaya Square on to Red Square, 1st May 1940. The BA-10M featured additional fuel tanks on the rear wheel mudguards and other detail construction changes. (Mikhail Baryatinsky).

BA-10A (left) and BA-10M (right) medium armoured cars preparing to move on to Red Square (located to the right of the photograph) from Manezhnaya Square, 1st May 1940. The removable "overall" tracks were moved to the hull rear on the BA-10M. (Tank Museum TM276/C2)

sions suggest that the country and its leadership were fully aware that war was approaching, and were taking the appropriate actions to build up defensive capability while the leadership prepared for war. The main difference between the United Kingdom and the Soviet Union was that the party leadership of the latter had dismissed, and in some cases arrested and executed a large proportion of the Red Army's senior command structure, which was not as easy to replace and build up again as armaments. The Soviet Union had in turn also executed many of those who had been the formal executioners. Nikolai Yezhov, who had replaced Genrikh Yagoda as People's Commissar for Internal Affairs in September 1936 and had served in that position until 1938 followed his predecessor's fate. Replaced by Lavrentiy Beria in the head of the NKVD in that year, Yezhov was himself later arrested as an enemy of the people, and executed in February 1940.

The ZiS-12 was an extended chassis version of the ZiS-5 with a low profile rear cargo area used primarily for transporting demountable searchlights such as the Z-15-4 and the 25mm M-1940 (94-KM) anti-aircraft gun systems.

THE RED ARMY ON PARADE 1917-45

STZ-5 tracked artillery tractors tow 152mm M-1938 (M-10) howitzers through Red Square, 1st May 1940.

STZ-5 tracked artillery tractors towing 76.2mm M-1939 (USV) Divisional Guns with their ammunition limbers through Red Square, 1st May 1940.

STZ-5 tracked artillery tractors towing 122mm M-1938 (M-30) howitzers through Red Square. The STZ-5 was a purpose designed tracked artillery tractor that could accommodate the gun crew and a quantity of ammunition in addition to being the gun prime mover.

Massed formations of AM-600 (TIZ-AM-600) motorcycle combinations pass through Red Square, 1st May 1940.

THE RED ARMY ON PARADE 1917-45

The final production model of the T-28, with its distinctive conical turret, was displayed both in Leningrad and Moscow in November 1940, but in Moscow the tank had only a cameo appearance at the end of a parade of earlier production T-28 tanks. Leningrad, 7th November 1940.

Komintern "fast" tracked artillery tractors parade through Red Square, 7th November 1940. The Komintern, which was based on the chassis of the aborted T-24 medium tank, was intended for towing medium and heavy artillery while also accommodating the gun crew and a quantity of ammunition.

# 7th November 1940 - 23rd Anniversary of the Great October Socialist Revolution

In November 1940, with France and the lowland countries defeated and Great Britain being bombarded by the Luftwaffe during the months of the Blitz, which had at the time been seen as a prelude to a land invasion, the Soviet Union celebrated the 23rd anniversary of the Great October Revolution with its traditional military parade on Red Square. Lenin and Stalin were both featured on the posters on the walls of the GUM department store. The Lenin Mausoleum had now been modified with an additional level added thereby increasing the number of people that could be accommodated for parade review purposes. The foreign military attaches of several countries including Germany, the United States, Great Britain and Japan were in attendance at the 7th November parade, at which the mood was significantly more sombre than in previous years.

The 7th November 1940 Red Square parade started as usual with marching infantry, marines and cadets from military academies, infantry including troops of the 1st Moskovskaya Motor-Rifle Division, armed with the new 7.62mm PPD sub-machine gun, the precursor to the famous wartime PPSh. The usual elements of naval forces, marines, NKVD border troops and the Red Army Air Force were followed by cavalry of the NKO Independent Cavalry Brigade.

The armoured component of the parade consisted as in the previous May of massed late pro-

THE RED ARMY ON PARADE 1917-45

The T-28 fared badly during the 1939-40 Russo-Finnish "Winter War", as a result of which it was up-armed and up-armoured. These T-28 tanks seen on parade in 1940 have the new 76.2mm L-10 tank gun but have not been up-armoured.

As a direct consequence of the Red Army experiences in Finland, the T-28 was up-armed with the 76.2mm L-10 tank gun and provided with additional armour, particularly on the turrets as seen here on these T-28Э (Eh) tanks parading on Red Square on 7th November 1940.

The same tank viewed from the rear. The additional armour on the main and subsidiary turrets is evident when compared with the standard T-28 tank below.

The final production model T-35 featured sloped armour on the main and subsidiary turrets and other detail changes such as extended track guards. The T-35 had been replaced by the new LKZ produced KV by 1940, but for parade purposes the T-35 remained the most modern heavy tank the Red Army chose to demonstrate.

As with the T-35 heavy tank, the T-28 remained the latest medium tank that the Red Army chose to demonstrate in 1940, despite the T-34 having entered series production. These T-28s on parade on 7th November 1940 are individually named "Kirov" (after the former Leningrad party leader) and "Andrey Zhdanov" (after the then current one).

This T-28 tank awaiting the 7th November 1940 parade is fitted with the more powerful 76.2mm L-10 tank gun as main armament.

duction model BA-20 and BA-20M armoured cars displayed together, including the interim model with the conical turret but a frame antenna from the earlier BA-20. Theses were followed by BA-10M medium armoured cars, the final production variant of the BA-10 series. Tanks included both the petrol engined BT-7 M-1937 and the V-2 diesel engined BT-7 M-1939 (BT-7M), some of which were individually driven through Red Square at full speed for effect. The main medium tank on display remained the venerable T-28, albeit the M-1940 T-28Э (Eh)production variant with additional armour on the turret and armed with the more powerful 76.2mm L-10 tank gun. The T-28 had been up-armoured as a direct result of recent combat experience in Finland where the Red Army had lost significant numbers of tanks to Finnish anti-tank gun fire. The T-35 heavy tank was as late as 1941 the only heavy tank on display despite its KV-1 replacement being in series production at LKZ in Leningrad. The T-35A tanks displayed included the final production model with sloped turret armour as before. Military transport included the usual GAZ-AA, GAZ-AAA and ZiS-5 trucks. Komintern tracked artillery tractors towed 122mm M-1937 (ML-20) howitzers, while air defence weapons as in previous years included the YaG-10 truck armed with with 76.2mm M-1931 (29K) AAG, but the new generations of tanks entering series production were nowhere to be seen.

THE RED ARMY ON PARADE 1917-45

BA-20M armoured cars staged on Manezhnaya Square awaiting the 7th November 1940 Red Square parade. The later BA-20M featured a conical turret. Some early production radio equipped BA-20M vehicles still featured the earlier frame antenna rather than the dashpot mounted whip type that became a later standard feature.

The YaG-10 mounting the 76.2mm M-1931 anti-aircraft gun was again on parade on 7th November 1940.

BA-10 medium armoured cars staged on Ulitsa 25 Oktyabrya (Nikolskaya), adjacent to Red Square. The large number of armoured vehicles paraded in the late 1930s required them to be staged on Manezhnaya Square, Gorky Street and other side streets around Red Square.

BT-7 M-1935 and BT-7 M-1937 fast tanks at the 7th November 1940 military parade in Riga, Latvia. (Mikhail Baryatinsky)

BT-7 M-1937 fast tanks move through Red Square at speed, 1st May 1941. The BT-7 was the most modern tank paraded on Red Square as war approached. The May 1941 Red Square parade was as significant for what was omitted from display as for what was shown to the crowds including the German and Japanese foreign missions present. (O. Baronov)

# 1st May 1941

On 1st May 1941, the Soviet Union celebrated the traditional May Day workers holiday under the gentle sun of early summer. Dark clouds were forming on the country's western borders however, and the 1st May 1941 was to be the last peacetime parade held on Red Square before the outbreak of World War Two on the Eastern Front. As the Red Army paraded on Red Square, German forces were assembling near the borders of the Soviet republics of Belorussia and Ukraine. Within weeks of the parade, the Soviet Union would be at war with Germany.

In order to demonstrate the might of the Red Army and the potential consequences of attacking it, the 1941 May Day parade was particularly large in scale, though the parade still did not feature the latest armaments available to the Red Army, an again entirely deliberate omission. The usual Soviet hierarchy was standing on the Lenin Mausoleum review stand, including I.V. Stalin, M.I. Kalinin and K.E. Voroshoilov. The parade was reviewed by Marshal of the Soviet Union Semeon. K. Timoshenko, initially from on horseback, with the parade commander being Red Army General I. V. Tulenev. Timoshenko gave the parade speech from the Lenin Mausoleum podium, with Stalin, Molotov, Beria and others other looking on. Marshal Timoshenko made a point of personally greeting the invited military attachés and guests from foreign embassies, including the military attachés and foreign press who were expected to carry the news of the parade back to their respective countries as a warning as to the scale of Soviet military might.

With high stakes and war foreseen as inevitable, the May Day 1941 parade was one of the largest of all parades and a particularly large show of Red Army strength. Foreign embassy military attachés were in attendance together with the world's press for the last peacetime Soviet military parade.

The foreign delegations present under the

clear skies and warm sun of this particular May Day parade included the German military delegation. As Ernst Köestring and Colonel Hans Krebs stood under the Mausoleum looking across at giant posters of both Stalin and Lenin on the wall of the GUM department store building on the opposite side of the square, war was raging in Europe. On Red Square meantime a military parade of what was within weeks to be the Wehrmacht's newest - and as events transpired, its fiercest - combat adversary, the Red Army, was about to commence. For Colonel Krebs, the parade would be a defining moment in both his life and his ultimate death.

The parade started later than usual, at 12.00. The marching element included students of the M.V. Frunze Military Academy, the Military Academy of Motorisation and Mechanisation (VAMM), the V.I. Lenin Military-Political Academy, the F.E. Dzerzhinsky Artillery Academy and the V.V. Kuibyshev Engineering Academy, the S.K. Timoshenko Chemical Defence Academy, the Military Veterinarian and Military Judicial Academies, the N.E. Zhukovsky Aviation Engineering Academy and the Military Aviation (VVS) Academy. There were parade participants from the 1st Moscow Artillery School and students of the military faculty of the State Institute for Physical Culture. There were marching battalions of VMF

T-35A heavy tanks parade through Red Square on the eve of war, 1st May 1941. After this parade, Hans Krebs, the German military attaché present, reported to Hitler that the Red Army was 20 years behind the Wehrmacht in terms of technology and training. Meanwhile, the T-34 and KV were both in series production but nowhere to be seen on Red Square, a quite deliberate omission at Stalin's behest. (O. Baronov)

(naval forces), the M.F. Frunze Higher Military Naval Academy, engineering troops and internal security NKVD and NKVD border guards. Some infantry units were armed with PPD sub-machine guns and SVT automatic rifles in addition to the venerable Mosin-Nagant bolt-action rifle, which had served the Red Army throughout its entire existence. Cavalry units followed, including the horse drawn "tachanki", the horse drawn carriages with their 7.62mm PM-1910/30 "Maxim" machine guns. Massed bicycle formations were followed by solo and tandem motorcycles, armed with 7.62mm DT and 7.62mm DP machine guns. Massed columns of BA-20 and BA-20M light and smaller numbers of BA-10A and BA-10M medium armoured cars were paraded, followed by mechanised infantry seated in GAZ-AA and ZiS-5 trucks. The immensely powerful "Voroshilovets" tracked artillery tractor towed the 203mm M-1931 B-4 tracked howitzer assigned to the RVGK reserve through the square.

Tanks displayed on Red Square infront of the Soviet hierarchy and foreign military attaches included the BT-7 M-1937 and BT-7 M-1939 (BT-7M) fast tanks traversing the square in columns four abreast, some 40 BT-7 tanks in all, followed by late model T-28 M-1940 T-28Э(Eh) tanks armed with the 76.2mm L-10 tank gun traversing the square in columns two wide. Two columns of T-35 heavy tanks taking up their traditional place in the pre-war parade line-up, being a mix of T-35A and the final production model with sloped turret armour. The up-armoured T-28Э (Eh) tanks had as stated previously been modifed as a result of the short but brutal Russo-Finnish "Winter War" where the Red Army had lost a significant quantity of armour to Finnish anti-tank gunners.

Some Soviet era publications indicated that the T-34 and KV were paraded through Red Square on 1st May 1940; however this is inaccurate. The tank parade was nevertheless highly impressive, not least the aviation element which included the newly introduced to service Petlyakov Pe-2, Mikoyan MiG-3 and other new combat aircraft designed by Gurevich, Gorbunov and Gudkov flying over Red Square. But although prototype and early production versions of both the T-34 medium and KV heavy tanks had seen combat during the 1939-40 "Winter War" in Finland, and both had been in series production for some time, there were still no T-34s and no KVs in sight on 1st May 1941. Both the T-34 medium and the KV heavy tank had originally been scheduled to attend the May Day parade in 1940, but two weeks before the parade an official directive was issued forbidding their participation. The non-appearance of the T-34 and KV was yet again a deliberate decision; and the tanks designated for appearance during the May 1940 parade were reassigned to "frontal" areas.

Towed artillery on display included Komintern tractors towing the 152mm Br-2, and Voroshilovets tractors towing the 203mm M-1931 B-4 tracked howitzers, and separate gun barrels. These tracked heavy artillery pieces dating from the early and mid 1930s looked archaic even in 1940, but they were highly effective and stable firing platforms, and would exactly four years later be photographed on the streets of Berlin. Anti-aircraft sytems included YaG-10 trucks mounting the 76.2mm M-1931 (29K) anti-aircraft gun and ZiS-12 trucks with Z-15-4 searchlights.

The military parade was accompanied by a huge flypast which was made a powerful impression on the crowds below, foreign dignitaries included. Aircraft on display over Red Square included LaGG-3, MiG-3 and Yak-1 fighters, and Petlyakov Pe-2 dive bombers which were just then entering service with the VVS, the Red Army Air Force.

One individual who was not impressed by the 1st May 1941 parade, as least in formal written reports, was Colonel Krebs, the military attaché at the German embassy in Moscow. He reported back to Berlin that from his observations the Red Army officer class would take twenty years to reach Wehrmacht levels of professionalism. Despite the precision of the military parade he had observed, it is entirely possible that his report also took into consideration his personal (but undefined in writing) understanding of the purges and

Before World War Two the Red Army used a variety of motorcycles in both solo and sidecar combination configurations. The M-72 motorcycle would during the war become the default Red Army military motorcycle, replacing the earlier Soviet AM-600 and A-750 designs. The Red Army would also make use of Lend-Lease motorcycles from foreign manufacturers such as Harley Davidson.

their overall effect on the Red Army, the recent Red Army debacle in Finland the previous winter, and his own personal observations of the Red Army since being posted to the German embassy in Moscow in 1936. In the circumstances of his position and the time concerned, it is also highly likely that Krebs simply reported back to Berlin exactly what he expected Hitler wanted to hear. Only days after the parade, Krebs would be appointed as General-Lieutenant of the Wehrmacht and would go on to a career on the German General Staff. Perhaps more than any foreign parade attendee that has observed the military parades on Red Square, Krebs would come to understand the reality of the Soviet ability to absorb and then deal out immense destruction, the unequivocal hidden weapon behind the military hardware on display, or indeed the equipment that in May 1941 was deliberately not on display. Exactly four years later, Krebs was on 1st April 1945 promoted from Deputy Commander to Commander of the Oberkommando der Wehrmacht (OKW) - the German Supreme High Command during the final days of the crumbling defence of Berlin. The technically backward Soviet war machine and its unprepared officer class he had reported on after his last Red Square parade attendance in Moscow in May 1941 was after four years of brutal war now within sight of the Reichstag in his own capital city. It was Krebs that would visit General Colonel V.I. Chuikov at the staff headquarters of the 8th Guards Tank Army in Berlin to advise the Red Army commander in fluent Russian of Hitler's suicide four hours earlier, and to present the German surrender to Chuikov for consideration by Stalin as he attended the 1st May 1945 Red Square parade in Moscow. His four years spent in Moscow as military attaché and his report to Hitler after the May 1941 parade were doubtless not lost on him as he offered the surrender papers to Chuikov.

A Soviet era artwork depicting the historic 7th November 1941 parade, with the first snows of winter arriving in Moscow.

T-60 small and BT-7 fast tanks parked on Gorky Street before the historic 7th November 1941 parade. The tanks arrived at 06:00 from staging areas at Khoroshevskoe Shosse (near modern-day Begovaya Metro station) and Serebryanny Bor (between modern day Sokol and Oktyabrskoe Pole Metro stations).

# 7th November 1941 – 24th Anniversary of the Great October Socialist Revolution

The six months between the May and November 1941 Red Square military parades can only be described as tragic for the Soviet Union. On 22nd June 1941, Wehrmacht forces including 17 Panzer Divisions crossed the Soviet border fulfilling the carefully laid plans for "Operation Barbarossa". Initial Soviet losses in terms of both manpower and equipment were staggering, with Red Army losses of armoured vehicles in the first weeks of the conflict equating to the rest of the world's combined tank park being eliminated. Huge swathes of territory had been lost and those manufacturing centres not over-run were in the autumn of 1941 evacuated to newly established centres behind the Ural Mountains in Siberia. The Soviet government had made arrangements to re-establish in Kuibyshev (today Samara) on the river Volga should Moscow fall. By November, Axis forces were within 70km of the Kremlin, advanced units even closer, and the enemy was literally at the gates.

In the circumstances, holding a ceremonial parade in Moscow to celebrate the 24th anniversary of the Great October Socialist Revolution would perhaps not have been seen as a major priority, but Stalin insisted that a parade would nevertheless be held. By November 1941 the Battle for Moscow was well underway, and though Axis forces were close to Moscow and Leningrad, German losses of troops and equipment had escalated in the previous weeks as the Red Army recovered from its initial losses, and having given up huge swathes of territory had formed new defence lines that were

# The Wartime 7th November Military Parades

Stalin made the decision to hold a parade on 7th November 1941 despite Moscow's precarious situation from his temporary underground offices on the central platform of the Mayakovskaya Metro Station. The underground station is unchanged today.

beginning to hold. Broadcasting a parade from Moscow would provide a massive boost to Soviet morale just when the war might conceivably be at a turning point. Stalin decreed that the Soviet Union would on 7th November hold its traditional military parade in commemoration of the Great October Socialist Revolution.

The German Army had orders from Hitler to take Moscow by 16th October, and although some post-war legends indicate that Hitler had his own plans for a German military parade on Red Square, the actual instructions to the Wehrmacht were to encircle Moscow and Leningrad and destroy both cities by artillery fire. Three weeks after the German deadline to take Moscow, the traditional 7th November parade was held on Red Square, with the Red Army participating as usual.

With enemy forces almost within artillery range of central Moscow, and Luftwaffe sorties already finding targets in the city, the 7th November 1941 parade was conducted on the direct orders of Stalin in defiance of Moscow's precarious situation. Holding a parade on Red Square in November 1941 was nevertheless a risky undertaking and if the weather was good the parade would be vulnerable to attack from the Luftwaffe. For perspective, on 6th November, the very day before the parade, with many of the tanks and other vehicles scheduled for the parade assembled at their staging areas at Khoroshevskoye Shosse and Serebryanny Bor, several waves of Luftwaffe bombers, taking advantage of clear skies, had bombed strategic targets in central Moscow.

As Luftwaffe bombers sortied over Moscow, Stalin personally conducted the final review of plans for the 24th Anniversary of the Great Octo-

THE RED ARMY ON PARADE 1917-45

# Official Map of the 7th November 1941 "Military Operation" on Red Square

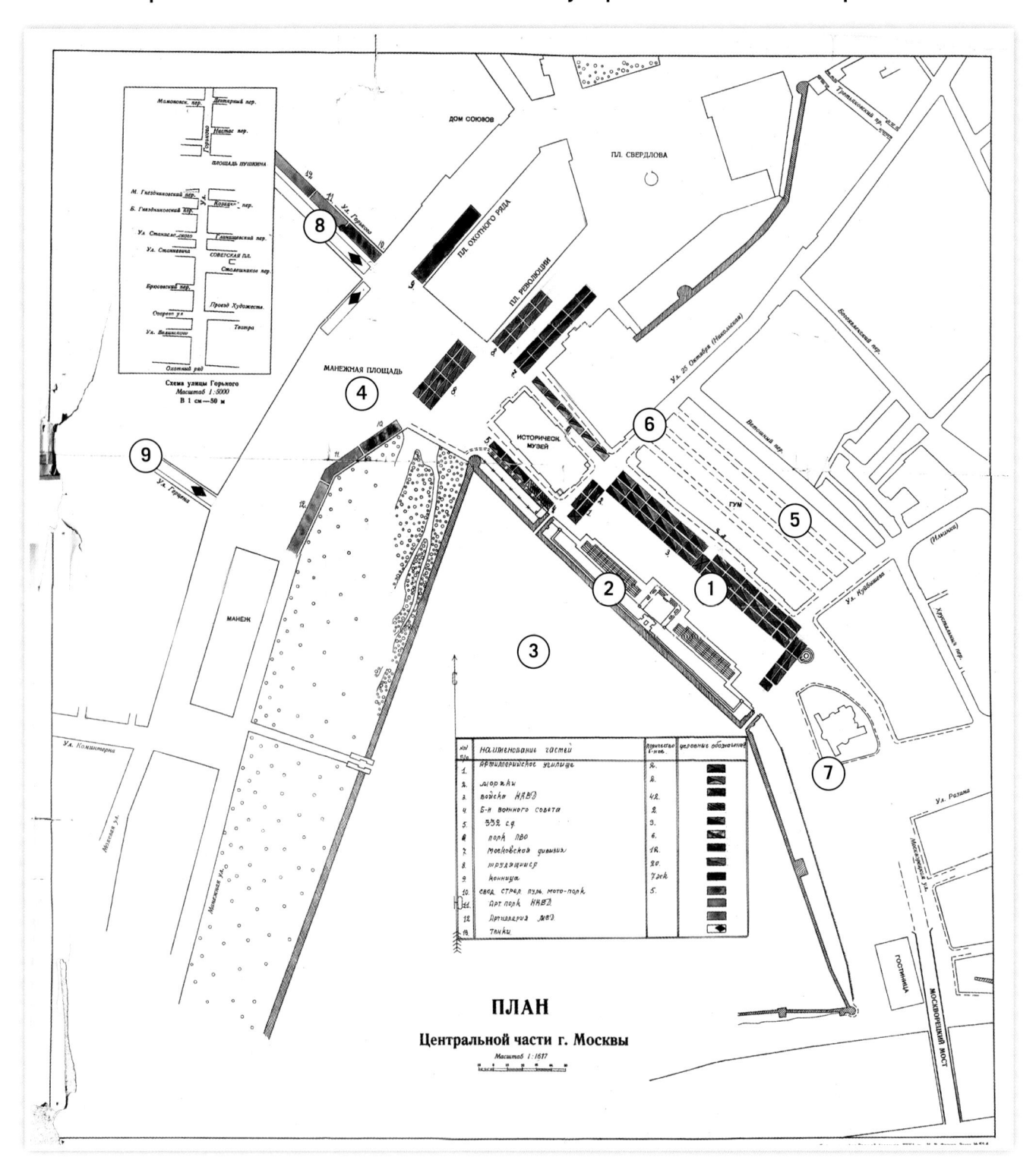

This is the original plan of the 7th November 1941 parade layout. The parade was largely made up of NKVD troops with units from the Moscow garrison and armoured units as described.

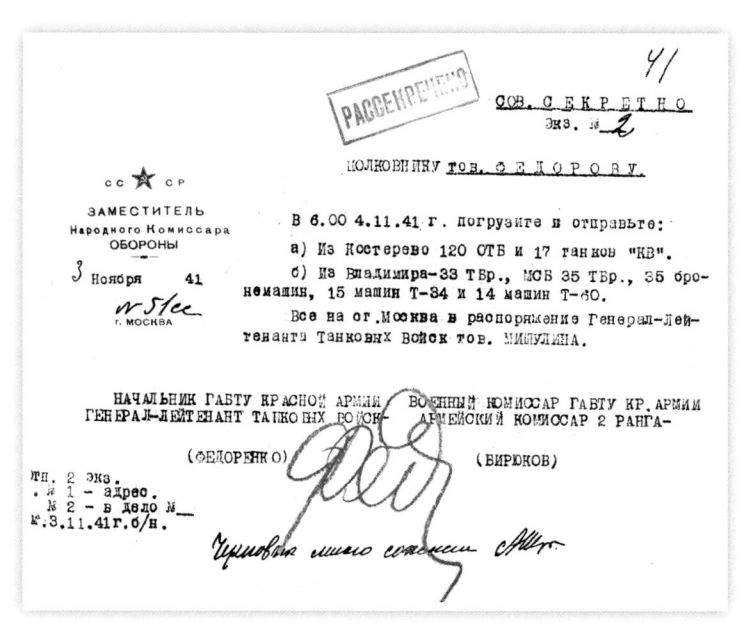

The NKO order dated 3rd November 1941, instructing Colonel Fedorov to arrange loading and dispatch of tanks to Moscow by rail on the following day, 4th November, at 06:00. 17 KV tanks from the 120th Separate Tank Brigade were to be loaded and dispatched from Kosterevo, and 35 armoured vehicles, 15 T-34s and 14 T-60s of the 33rd and 35th Tank Brigades were simultaneously to be dispatched from Vladimir. The order is co-signed by the Chief of GABTU, Federenko and the Military Commissar of GABTU Biryukov. This movement began precisely three days before the parade, leaving no time for final rehearsals on Red Square.

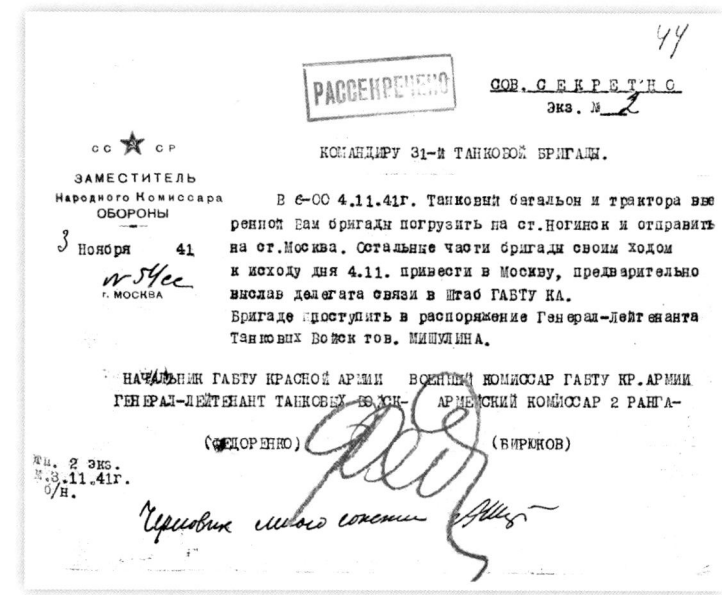

A corresponding order also dated 3rd November 1941, ordering the commander of the 31st Tank Brigade to load and dispatch tanks and tractors at Noginsk railway station destination Moscow on the same day and hour as the 33rd and 35th Tank Brigade had been instructed.

**Map Reference, opposite**

1. Red Square
2. Lenin Mausoleum
3. Kremlin
4. Manezhnaya Square
5. GUM department store
6. Ulitsa 25 Oktyabrya (Nikolskaya) Street
7. St. Basil's Catherdral
8. Gorky Street
9. Gertsen Street

**Original Map Index**

1. Artillery College (2 battalions)
2. Naval troops (2 battalions)
3. NKVD troops (42 battalions)
4. Battalion of the Military Council
5. 332nd Rifle Division
6. Regiment of Air Defence troops (6 battalions)
7. Moscow (Rife) Division (12 battalions)
8. Workers (20 battalions)
9. Cavalry (7 Squadrons)
10. Combined rifle/machine gun motor-cycle regiment
11. Artillery Regiment NKVD
12. Artillery of the Moscow (Rifle) Division
13. Tanks

ber Revolution parade from the relative safety of the central underground platform of the Mayakovskaya Metro Station, during which he formally announced that the traditional 7th November military parade would go ahead as usual. This was clearly known to the Red Army in advance, as the units required for the parade had already been assembled in Moscow and parade precision is not an overnight practice. Although the 7th November 1941 military parade on Moscow's Red Square has gone down in Soviet history as the ultimate act of defiance under wartime adversity, large scale military parades were actually held in three cities on 7th November 1941, namely Moscow, the "reserve" capital of Kuibyshev and Voronezh.

The decision to hold the Moscow parade was fraught with risk, as at the time Axis forces were within 70-100km of Moscow on different sectors of the front line, and the parade was as noted highly vulnerable to air attack. Stalin had nevertheless authorized the parade from his temporary location on the central platform of Mayakovskaya Metro Station where high level government meetings were conducted. The traditional timing was however changed at the last minute to 08:00 rather than the traditional 10:00 to allow tanks to be assembled during the winter pre-dawn darkness. Large numbers of Soviet fighter aircraft patrolled above central Moscow to ensure no German bombers could penetrate the city defences during the parade. In the event, the weather that morning was overcast, with heavy cloud cover and light snow which prevented any precision bombing of targets by the Luftwaffe. Soviet fighters nevertheless patrolled overhead as weather conditions allowed.

The November 1941 parade as recorded for posterity requires some interpretation. The parade was prepared in great secrecy, and was described in official documents as an "operation" rather than a parade. The parade as noted began at 08:00 rather than the usual 10:00 start time, dawn in the Russian winter, which was done in order to protect the parade from potential Luftwaffe air attack, for which emergency instructions were issued to all parade participants.

The parade was taken by the Deputy Defence

T-60 tanks enter Red Square for the dawn parade on Red Square, 7th November 1941. The 1941 parade was the public debut and only parade appearance of the T-60.

Minister of the Soviet Union, Marshal of the Soviet Union Budenny, who took the parade on a black horse. The parade commander was General Lieutenant Pavel Artemiev, commander of the MVO, the Moscow Garrison, also mounted on a black horse.

Stalin had taken on the role of Defence Minister personally a month after the 1st May parade, and with Axis forces within a few kilometres of the Kremlin, he as "Vozhd" or leader of the nation personally made the speech from the Lenin Mausoleum podium, the only time he directly addressed the nation from the Lenin Mausoleum in all the parades he had observed as leader. The parade speech being made personally by the Soviet premier was repeated only once in history, in 1990 when Mikhail Gorbachov made the last speech delivered from the Lenin Mausoleum as the Soviet Union slipped into history.

With the future of the Soviet State in the balance but the German Axis advance facing strengthening resistance as it reached the suburbs of Moscow, Stalin told the assembled troops, and the nation at large, that Germany would be defeated. The archive footage of the speech was filmed later however, on a reconstructed background, as at the time he actually made the speech it was still almost dark. There are also conflicts in the archive footage, the majority of photographs showing light snow cover but the official "cine" version of the parade shows the parade passing over dry cobblestones. The "cine" version also shows BT-7 fast tanks parked in a line directly in front of the Historical Museum, which was never a practice during actual parades as they would obstruct vehicles moving onto Red Square through the relatively narrow cobbled entrance ramps. The 7th November 1941 parade was in fact run twice, the main parade conducted in the dawn of the early Russian winter being re-staged later

T-60 tanks pass the Lenin Mausoleum, 7th November 1941. The T-60 had been intended for production at Plant №37 in Moscow, but by the time of the parade the plant had been evacuated from the city.

T-60 tanks parade through Red Square, 7th November 1941. These tanks represented the first T-60 production output from the GAZ vehicle plant in Gorky. Some of the tanks had the conical turret from the T-30 rather than the octagonal welded turret designed specifically for the T-60.

BT-7 M-1937 fast tanks moving towards Red Square, 7th November 1941. The snowfalls and rapidly lowering tempeartures which were in evidence on the day would be a major asset for the Red Army in the weeks ahead. (Mikhail Baryatinsky)

BT-7 M-1937 fast tanks pass the Lenin Mausoleum and assembled Soviet hierarchy during the 24th Anniversary parade of the Great October Revolution, 7th November 1941. (O.Baronov)

The Red Square debut of the T-34 was on 7th November 1941, the only appearance of the original 76.2mm armed T-34 on Red Square during the war. These early M-1941 tanks, with welded turrets, have the early pattern reserve fuel tanks, including non-standard additional tanks and in contrast with other parades are in full combat order. Due to a shortage of V-2 diesel engines at the assembly plant, these tanks were fitted with M-17T petrol engines. (O. Baronov)

in the day with synchronised film and sound for the benefit of the press and the cameras when the light was better for propaganda purposes. It is this second, staged parade that is today documented in most film and photograph archives.

The Archives of the MO (Defence Ministry) of the USSR list all the tanks and vehicles that participated in the historic 7th November 1941 parade. The parade started with a march by 69 infantry battalions, totalling 19,044 personnel, followed by 160 tanks and 140 artillery pieces. The official parade plan confirms that the "cine" version of the parade often cited as the actual parade was a later re-run, not least as several battalions of infantry were staged from a position directly in-front of the Historical Museum, where the BT-7s are conveniently parked on the official wartime "cine" version of the parade. That the parade was restaged for the purposes of what would today be called marketing distribution is entirely understandable, and indeed the tanks were presented on the day infront of the Soviet political and military leadership, but were re-filmed (and photographed) later for expediency purposes. The actual reason for the later filming of the parade re-run was according to some anecdotal evidence also a case of human error. Although the low light levels would have made early dawn "cine" filming difficult, the film crews were not actually present to start filming as the parade got underway at 08:00, apparently as the crews were not informed of the belated change in start time, so the re-staging may also have been a technical necessity. Nevertheless, filming the parade was critical in that the film was distributed throughout the Soviet Union to assure the Soviet people that Moscow was still in Soviet hands and that victory was ultimately assured.

The 7th November 1941 parade was the traditional mix of marching infantry, cavalry, tanks, motorized infantry, artillery and anti-aircraft weapons. Marching columns included regiments from the 2nd Moskovskaya Rifle Division, the 332nd "Frunze" Division, and cavalry of the

The same T-34 M-1941 tanks parade past posters of Lenin and Stalin hanging from the State Universal Store (GUM) which forms the eastern side of Red Square.

"Dzerzhinsky"division. It is significant that of the 69 infantry battalions that marched through Red Square on 7th November 1941, 42 battalions were NKVD, there being an understandable shortage of front line Red Army infantry battalions available for the parade as they were at the time actively involved in the defence of Moscow. The parade began with cadets of the artillery schools with the music provided by the orchestra of the MVO General Staff, led by Vasily Agapkin. The marching parades were followed by cavalry, horse drawn artillery and "tachanki" machine gun carts, each towed by four white horses, followed by the armoured section of the parade.

The November 1941 parade was in part made up of available combat vehicles located in the immediate Moscow region, consisting of T-60s, BT-7s and T-34s from 2nd Tank Brigade and the 2nd Independent Tank Battalion. The BT-7 M-1937 fast tanks were standard fare at the parade, but were joined by three new and particularly influential tank types on 7th November 1941.

The T-60 small, T-34 medium and KV heavy tanks all made their public debuts during the 7th November parade. The T-34 and KV-1 were in service in considerable numbers before the events of June 1941, however the November parade was their first public outing together with the T-60 tank which had entered series production only in September. The 48 T-60 tanks of the 33rd Tank Brigade paraded through Red Square in November 1941, the only appearance of the T-60 on Red Square, were a mix of early production types with the conical turret built at Plant №37 for the T-40/T-30 and assembled at GAZ using these turrets evacuated from Moscow and standard production models with the octagonal turret used on later production models.

The T-34 also made its public debut on Red Square during the 7th November 1941 parade, with several T-34 M-1941 production models parading through the square, the only time the original 76.2mm armed T-34 would appear on the square. The tanks had begun their move to Moscow on the night of 4th November 1941 and after an 04:00 wake-up reveille had at 06:00 on the morning of 7th November begun moving down Gorky street onto Red Square.

The KV heavy tank also made its public debut at the same parade, with a handful of these tank types rolling through Red Square. The KV tanks displayed on Red Square were Chelyabinsk

THE RED ARMY ON PARADE 1917-45

Tanks from the Military Academy of Mechanisation and Motorisation of the RKKA (VAMM) at the time of the November 1941 parade. This mixed column of training tanks on the streets of Moscow is led by a T-35A heavy tank, by November perhaps the last surviving example.

(ChKZ) production tanks, assembled in Siberia from October 1941, armed with the 76.2mm ZiS-5 tank gun and fitted with additional cylindrical fuel tanks on the track guards.

The T-60 small, T-34 medium and KV heavy tanks all made their only parade appearance on Red Square during the 7th November 1941 parade, during which, in contrast to all peacetime parades, all tanks carried a full ammunition complement, some tanks moving directly back to the front lines after the parade. Noticeably, the tanks entered and traversed Red Square in rough and at times almost random formations, in sharp contrast to the pre-war and immediate post-war parades. The reason was simply that the crews were conscripted combat crews who had no time to prepare for the parade as their tanks were in transit until literally the day before the parade, in contrast with the usual weeks of meticulous preparation as was the norm in peacetime.

One of the tank commanders participating in the parade was Commander of the 31st Tank Brigade, Andrey Kravchenko. During subsequent fighting later in November, the brigade lost every last one of its tanks in combat. Kravchenko himself survived the war and, doubtless a very changed individual, would participate in the Soviet Victory Parade held on Red Square on 24th June 1945.

The motorized forces paraded in November 1941 consisted of a mix of vehicles and weapons. GAZ-AAs passed the Lenin Mausoleum with infantry, tandem 7.62mm PM-1910 "Maxim" anti-aircraft machine gun mounting and 14.5mm PTRD anti-tank rifles. GAZ-AAAs transported 76.2mm M-1927 Regimental Guns and towed 76.2mm M-1939 (USV) Divisional Guns through

KV-1 heavy tanks pass the Lenin Mausoleum and assembled Soviet hierarchy, Red Square, 7th November 1941 parade. As with the original T-34, the 1941 was the first and last parade appearance of the tank type on Red Square. Note the disruptive camouflage paint on the Kremlin building walls.

A KV-1 passes the Pushkin monument on Pushkinskaya Ploshad (Pushkin Square) moving towards Red Square, 7th November 1941. These Chelyabinsk (ChKZ) built KV-1s were shipped to Moscow specifically for the parade.

KV-1 tanks move through Red Square past the GUM department store. The banner for the 24th anniversary of the Russian Revolution proclaims the destruction of the power of imperialism; and somewhat ironically in the circumstances also proclaims peace between the peoples of the world.

KV-1 tanks pass the Lenin Mausoleum during the same parade. The first snows of winter did not melt in 1941, and the temperature continued to drop as the enemy stalled at the gates of Moscow.

the square, while GAZ-AA and ZiS-5 trucks towed World War One era 76.2mm M-1900/02 and "Lender" howitzers, and Soviet M-1915 (ZU-25) and M-1915/28 anti-aircraft guns, both obsolescent weapon types being covered in tarpaulins. ZiS-5 trucks towed French built Polish 75mm field guns captured in 1939, perhaps a subtle reference for the foreign military attaches present at the parade or simply a refection that most modern Red Army artillery was in service at the front.

The November 1941 parade was the most poignant of all Soviet military parades to held on Red Square. Defended by Soviet fighter aircraft, which some Russian sources claim downed 34 enemy aircraft in the vicinity of Moscow on the day, many of the parade participants were dispatched directly from the parade to the front to defend the city, many if not most never to return. The parades in other cities were equally impressive but far from the public gaze. The Kuibyshev parade was as significant in scale as the Moscow parade, complemented by a 600 aircraft fly-past, but it was the Red Square parade in Moscow that held the attention of the nation, and indeed the world.

On 7th November 2011, on the 70th Anniversary of the original November 1941 parade, wartime tanks and transport vehicles were displayed as a historical re-enactment in commemoration of the original parade. As with the return of the May Victory Parades in 2008, the historical 7th November Red Square emembrance parades have now become an annual event.

# The 7th November 1941 parade from recently declassified Russian sources*

Although the 7th November 1941 parade was described accurately in the following morning's edition of "Pravda" as the 24th Anniversary of the "Great October Socialist Revolution", recently uncovered documents indicate that in the circumstances of a country at war it was actually defined as a military operation by the Red Army. The actual make-up of the parade was also obscured until long after the event itself, despite the primary propaganda intent of the parade. The 8th November edition of "Pravda" described the passage of 200 undefined tanks through Red Square, starting with "tankettes" that kicked up clouds of snow, followed by light, medium and heavy tanks. For years the composition of the parade remained officially secret despite the newsreel and photographic evidence. It was only at the end of the first decade of the 21st Century that declassified documents were released, describing the parade as an "operation" rather than a "parade". These documents also give a fascinating insight into the complex and severely time-limited organisation behind the wartime, parade, and the fate of the Red Army units which participated in that historical parade.

The head of GABTU KA, General-Lieutenant Tank Forces Ya. N. Federenko, who clearly had many things on his mind at the time, was advised by Stalin only on 31st October 1941 that the annual 7th November parade would be held as usual in Moscow in 1941, enemy at the gates or not. Federenko immediately issued Directive № 44ss, instructing the commanders of the 31st, 33rd, 35th, 143rd, 145th and 146th Tank Brigades to prepare tanks, vehicles and crews for the parade, with all equipment to be ready in situ, serviced and inspected by 5th November.

Infantry were to parade in winter uniform, and in columns 12 wide and 8 deep. Wheeled vehicles were to parade in 3 columns, light tanks in 5 columns, medium and heavy tanks in 3 columns. Directive № 48ss was sent to Stalin, informing him that the parade "operation" would be conducted by the 31st Tank Brigade (located at Noginsk), the 33rd Tank Brigade (located at Vladimir), the 120th Independent Tank Battalion (located near Kosterevo) and the 128th Tank battalion (located in the Sormovo region). Within these units there were 68 tanks, namely 36 T-60 small, 15 T-34 medium and 17 KV heavy tanks.

The 31st Tank Brigade located at Noginsk had 4 KV-1, 13 BT-7 and 14 T-26 tanks.

The 33rd Tank Brigade located in the Vladimir region had 7 KV-1, and 24 T-60 tanks.

The 120th Independent Tank Battalion located in the region of Kosterevo had 7 KV-1 and 24 T-60 tanks.

The 128th Independent Tank Brigade located in the region of Sormovo had 2 KV-1, 16 BT-7 and 13 T-34 tanks.

The T-34s within the 128th Independent Tank Brigade were early production tanks assembled at Plant №112, the "Krasnoe Sormovo" plant in Gorky. Due to a defecit of V-2 diesel engine at the time of initial production at the plant, all these tanks were fitted with the M-17T petrol engine as decreed by GKO Resolution №1 dated 1st June 1941.

Stalin agreed to Federenko's proposals, incorporating the above units within the Strategic High Command Reserve (RVGK) for the duration of the parade. Federenko the same day instructed the head of the Moscow ABTU training school, Colonel Fedorov, and the commander of the 31st Tank Brigade, Colonel Kravchenko, to arrange transit of the 120th Tank Brigade and 17 "KV" tanks from

---

* From material originally published in the article "Neozhidanniy Parad" by Colonel (Retired) Igor Zheltov, Rolling Wheels N° 1 2012. With thanks to Igor Zheltov for permission to use his original research.

Red Square in November 1941, almost deserted as the Russian winter approached, as it did in 1941 with a vengeance, to the great advantage of the Red Army defending Moscow.*

GAZ-AA "polutorka" (1.5 tonne) trucks parade through Red Square, 7th November 1941.

GAZ-AAA trucks with 76.2mm M-1927 Regimental Guns located within the load areas for parade purposes traverse Red square during the historic November 1941 parade.

GAZ-AAA trucks towing 76.2mm M-1939 (USV) field guns across Red Square. The temperature on Red Square was a few degrees below zero on the day, but considerably lower in the regions.

Kosterevo, and the 33rd Tank Brigade and the Motor-Rifle Battalion of 35th Tank Brigade, with a total of 35 tanks, including 14 T-60 small tanks and 15 T-34 medium tanks. Transport to Moscow was to be by rail for the more distant units, with units closer to the city moving under their own power on 4th November.

Specific instructions related to rail and armoured column shipments, including new tanks to be delivered directly from the assembly plants were detailed in Letter № 56ss issued by the Deputy Commander of GABTU, General-Major Lebedev. In typical Soviet manner, the instructions were precise and detailed:

1. 31st Tank Brigade, Load at Noginsk Station, destination Moscow. Columns -1, 60 tonne railcars - 10, load time 07:00 04.11.41. Echelon № 41171.

2. 120th Independent Tank Brigade, Load Kosterevo Station, destination Moscow. Columns - 2, 60 tonne railcars - 27, load time 07:00 04.11.41. Echelon № 41172-73.

3. 33rd Tank Brigade, Load Vladimir Station, destination Moscow. Columns - 4, 60 tonne railcars -10, load time 07:00 04.11.41. Echelon № 41174-77.

4. 35th Tank Brigade, Load Vladimir Station, destination Moscow. Columns - 2, 60 tonne railcars - 10, load time 07:00 04.11.41. Echelon № 41178-79.

5. 128th Independent Tank Brigade, Load

---

* Typical mean November early winter temperatures in 1930s Moscow were +1°C to -3°C. In the winter of 1941-42, as the Wehrmacht stalled near Moscow, Field Marshal von Bock, Commander of Army Group Centre recorded in his field diary on 5th November a temperature of -29°C, which continued through December. The Soviet Union's harsh climate, in the form of "General Winter" was a major factor in the Battle for Moscow, as the Red Army had everything it required (from winter clothing to specialised winter engine lubricants, and even propeller driven "aerosani" snow vehicles) to operate in conditions the Wehrmacht had simply not expected or planned for in what was expected to be a short summer and autumn campaign.

THE RED ARMY ON PARADE 1917-45

The 7th November parade was by necessity a combination of available equipment not deployed at the front line. The tanks were specially shipped to Moscow; but the parade featured several curious combinations, such as these new Voroshilovets heavy artillery tractors towing obsolescent 76.2mm M-1915/28 anti-aircraft guns.

Horse-drawn tandem 76.2mm M-1927 gun limber combinations, minus the guns which were transported in the rear of GAZ-AAA trucks during the same parade.

Sormovo Station, destination Moscow. Columns - 1, 60 tonne railcars - 10, load time 07:00 04.11.41. Ecehelon № 41180.

In addition, the following rail consignments were instructed:

1. № 22923 from Chelyabinsk Station, addressed to Kosterevo, to be re-addressed to Moscow, Serebranny Bor Station on the Moscow Circular Rail Line (8 KV tanks)

2. № 22924 from Chelyabinsk Station, addressed to Kosterevo, to be re-addressed to Moscow, Serebranny Bor Station on the Moscow Circular Rail Line (8 KV tanks)

3. № 22926 from Stalingrad Station, addressed to Kosterevo, to be re-addressed to Moscow, Serebranny Bor Station on the Moscow Circular Rail Line (22 T-34 tanks)

4. № 22927 from Stalingrad Station, addressed to Kosterevo, to be re-addressed to Moscow, Serebranny Bor Station on the Moscow Circular Rail Line (15 T-34 tanks)

5. № 22999 from Gorky Station, addressed to Kosterevo, to be re-addressed to Moscow, Serebranny Bor Station on the Moscow Circular Rail Line (20 T-60 tanks)

The tanks duly arrived in Moscow after their relatively short (by Soviet geographical standards) journeys and were assembled in Moscow on 5th for inspection by Federenko personally.

At 06:00 on the morning of 7th November, two hours before the 08:00 parade start, which was two hours earlier than usual for reasons already described, the tanks moved down Leningradsky Prospekt and Gorky Street (today Tverskaya) in columns. The first column consisted of 49 T-60s in columns of 3, which were assembled on Manezhnaya Square. 70 BT-7 tanks followed, also assembled in columns of 3. The third column consisted of 41 T-34 medium tanks, which were parked on Ulitsa Gertsena. Four KV heavy tanks were also parked on Manezhnaya Square awaiting the parade start.

The parade started on schedule at 08:00 with Stalin's speech being followed by a procession of infantry, cavalry and other non-mechanised components as per normal parade protocol. The tanks began to move onto Red Square at 09:00, moving at a convoy speed of 20km/h as light snow billowed around them, the tanks returning to their marshalling point as usual via Vasilevsky Spusk, along the embankment beneath the Kremlin, along the Sadovoe Koltso (the "Garden Ring") back to Mayakovskaya Square, where they moved onto Leningradsky Prospekt and Khoroshovskoye Shosse back to their original assembly points, without breakdown or incident. For the next two days the tank brigades and independent battalion were held near Khodynka, where the very first post-revolutionary Red Army parade had been held, as "Stavka" high command reserve.

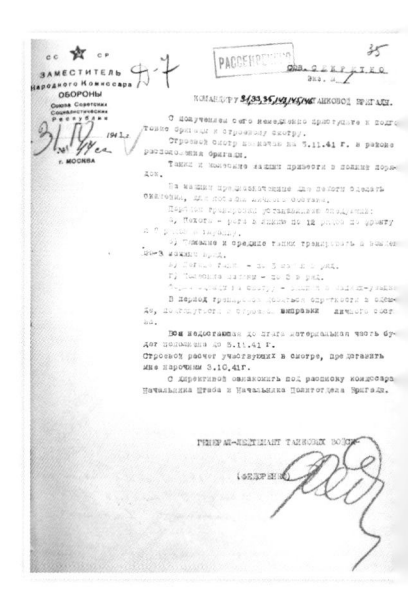

The original order from General Lieutenant of Tank Forces Federenko dated 31st October 1941 instructing the 31st, 33rd, 35th, 143rd, 145th and 146th Tank Brigades to immediately prepare for an inspection parade in the locality on 5th November. The parade formation was to be in columns of 3 for medium and heavy tanks and wheeled vehicles, and in columns of 5 for light tanks, with all personnel to be in winter uniform. All preparations were to be finalised by 3rd November, which, unstated, was the night before the tanks were to be loaded pre-dawn onto trains destined for Moscow

*There were occasional ad-hoc displays of equipment by the Red Army in Moscow during the war years, such as this World War One vintage 122mm howitzer located on Mayakovskaya Square in the winter of 1941.*

*A column of newly ChKZ built KV-1 tanks used in the Red Square parade in November 1941, moving along Leningradskoe Shosse.*

The letter dated 13th November from General Lieutenant Tank Forces Federenko and Military Commissar GABTU Biryukov to Defence Minister Comrade Stalin regarding the dispatch of tanks after the Red Square parade in compliance with his direct order. The letter advises that the following tanks and other vehicles were despatched from Moscow at 14:00 on 13th November 1941 and were now under the command of the Western Front:

31st Tank Brigade – KV (21), T-34 (24), T-60 (21), BT (11), T-26 (14), T-37 (5) and associated motor-rifle battalion, air defence and other components of the brigade.

145th Tank Battalion – KV (20), T-34 (24), T-60 (48) and ten "English transporters" together with an incomplete strength motor rifle battalion.

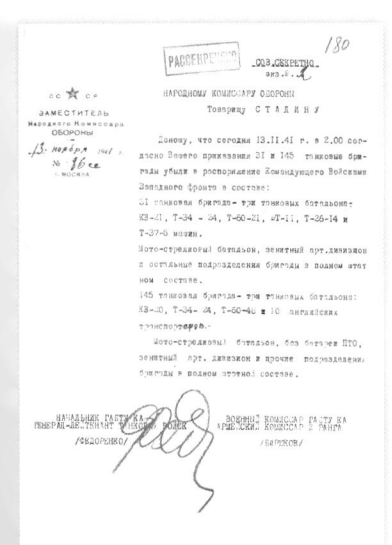

There has always been much speculation as to the fate of the military units, tanks and equipment which participated in the 7th November 1941 parade. It was always understood that with the front lines nearby, the units would be deployed to the front line or perhaps held in reserve, but the recent release of previously classified documents now confirms their fate. Two months after the 7th November parade, Federenko on behalf of GABTU KA advised Stalin on 9th January 1942 that in compliance with his instruction, the 33rd Tank Brigade, with 16 T-60s, 11 T-34s and 4 KVs had after the parade moved west to the region of Golitsino and joined the forces of the Western Front under the command of General Zhukov. The 120th Independent Tank Battalion, with 20 T-60s, 4 T-34s and 6 KVs had been loaded onto rail cars at Krasnaya Presnya rail station at 14:40 on 9th November 1941, and the 128th Independent Tank Battalion with 16 BT-7s, 9 T-34s and 6 KVs had been loaded onto rail cars at Boinya station at 19:00 on the same day, both routed to the 4th Army of the Leningrad Front under the command of Meretskov. The 31st Tank Brigade, was meantime increased from two tank battalions to three, and at 02:00 on 13th November departed Moscow under its own power heading due west. The brigade had a total of 5 T-37 amphibious tanks, 14 T-26 light tanks, 11 BT-7 fast tanks, 24 T-34 medium tanks and 21 KV heavy tanks. After a 152km road march, tanks of the 31st Tank Brigade entered combat near the town of Serpukhov approximately 100km due south of Moscow. By 15th November it had lost a T-26, two T-34s and a KV tank in combat.

In the first days of December 1941, T-34 crews of the 31st Tank Brigade committed to combat in the region of Lugovaya and Sukharevo north east of Moscow, where today stands the "History of the T-34 Tank" Memorial Museum. The 31st Tank Brigade official accounts, dated January 1943, confirm that the 31st Tank Brigade received new tanks on 30th October 1941, with the 31st Tank Brigade placed in the reserve of the RVGK. Being within the RVGK reserve, the tanks of the 31st Tank Brigade received their orders directly from the Red Army High Command until assigned to Corps or Army level command.

Exactly one month after the 7th November Red Square Parade, on the other side of the world, another event took place which would ultimately help secure the survival of the Soviet Union, strengthen its armed forces during the war and ultimately bring Allied victory in World War Two. The event was the aforementioned Japanese bombing of Pearl Harbour which brought the reluctant United States of America into the war against both Japan and its Axis allies in Europe.

THE RED ARMY ON PARADE 1917-45

T-20 Komsomolets light artillery tractors towing 45mm anti tank guns at the military parade in Kuibyshev, 7th November 1941. (RGAKFD)

# 7th November 1941 - Military Parade in Kuibyshev

The famous military parade on Red Square on 7th November 1941 was one of three major parades held that day, the others being held in Kuibyshev (today Samara) and Voronezh. By November 1941, the majority of the Soviet government, its military command and their families had been evacuated to Kuibyshev where the city had been prepared to be the Soviet Union's wartime capital in the event Moscow fell to the advancing Axis forces. A specialised bunker system had even been constructed deep under the city by the builders of the Moscow Metro ready to act as Stalin's wartime command centre. In the event the bunker would never be required to perform operationally.

The 7th November 1941 military parade on Kuibyshev's main square was taken by Marshal of the Soviet Union Klimenti Voroshilov, with the parade commanded by General-Lieutenant Maxim Purkaev. The parade in Kuibyshev was attended by foreign delegations and military attaches, including from the United States and Japan, and was as much a display for foreign consumption as was the more famous parade on Red Square. The large scale parade in Kuibyshev lasted 1.5 hours, and consisted of infantry and marines, followed by tanks in columns three wide followed by secondary vehicles most of which were in colums four wide, with the parade being accompanied by a large scale flypast involving a claimed 600 aircraft.

The tanks and other military vehicles displayed in Kuibyshev were entirely different to those displayed in Moscow. T-38 amphibious light tanks were paraded alongside three generations of T-26, the mainstay T-26 M-1933 and final production model T-26 M-1938 with its conical turret, and even a few early twin turreted T-26 M-1931 tanks. T-20 Komsomolets light armoured artillery tractors towing 45mm M-1937 anti-tank guns were followed by SKhTZ (KhTZ-3) "agricultural" tracked tractors towing 122mm M-1910/30 howitzers in columns four wide. Anti-aircraft systems included GAZ-AAA trucks armed with the 4M quad 7.62mm M-1910/30 "Maxim" anti-aircraft gun system and ZiS-12 trucks with Z-15-4 searchlights.

T-38 amphibious reconnaissance tanks on parade in Kuibyshev, 7th November 1941.

ZiS-12 searchlight vehicles parade through the main square in Kuibyshev, 7th November 1941.

T-26 tanks on parade in Kuibyshev, 7th November 1941. The lead T-26 M-1938 tanks are fitted with radio and night fighting searchlights, followed by T-26 M-1933 line tanks.

# 7th November 1941 – Military Parade in Voronezh

The third city in which a major military parade was held on 7th November 1941 was the industrial city of Voronezh. At the time of the parade, the city was the Red Army South West Front "shtab" or general headquarters. In the preceeding weeks the city had evacuated 117 manufacturing plants and as the morning dawned in Voronezh on 7th November for what would be a misty morning, Axis forces were less than 120km to the west of the city.

The parade, held on "20 Years of October" square in Voronezh was taken by Marshal of the Soviet Union S. K. Timoshenko and General Lieutenant I.Kh.Bagramyan, with the parade commander being General Lieutenant F. Ya. Kostenko. In attendance on the review stand was the 1st Secretary of the Central Committee of the Communist Party (TsK KPSS), a certain Nikita S. Khrushchev who would later become one of the more colourful Soviet premiers.

The Voronezh parade is the least documented of all the 7th November military parades, but the parade began with marching infantry of the 327th Rifle Division, followed by columns of motorcycle combinations, T-28 medium tanks and tracked artillery tractors towing 76.2mm M-1939 (USV) divisional guns.

# 1942-1944

In the winter of 1941-42, invading Axis forces were stalled across all fronts, and from 1942 the tide began to turn against the invading Axis forces. Having on 7th November 1941 decisively demonstrated that Moscow had held back the enemy at the gates, Soviet military parades were for obvious reasons shelved for the next four years as the war gradually turned in the Soviet Union's favour. The next military parade held on Red Square would be on 1st May 1945, with the war all but over in Europe, and the Soviet war against Japan just about to begin. There were however ceremonies for the delivery of tanks to newly formed units, for 1st May celebrations and for combat victories. On 16th July 1944 a Victory Parade was held by partisans in Minsk, Belorussia celebrating the successful outcome of "Operation Bagration". The parade involved 30,000 Soviet partisans and an eclectic mix of horse-drawn artillery and solid fuel powered vehicles, led somewhat curiously by a goat adorned with collected German Iron Crosses.

There were no parades or formal military ceremonies on Red Square during the mid war years of 1942-1944, but there were ceremonies for the delivery of tanks to newly formed tank units in the field, often based on subscriptions from plant workers, towns, Soviet republics and even the Russian Orthodox Church.

THE RED ARMY ON PARADE 1917-45

A column of BA-20M light and BA-10M medium armoured cars during a field parade celebrating the May 1942 workers holiday. Russian Western Front, 1st May 1942. (Mikhail Baryatinsky)

A BT-7 M-1937 fast tank during a presentation and parade in Mongolia, 1943.

A ZiS-21 4x2 truck during the Minsk Victory Parade. The ZiS-21 was a ZiS-5 variant powered by burning solid fuel (i.e. wood) - known as "gas generator" vehicles in the Soviet Union - which allowed independent operation where fuel was scarce.

# 1st May 1945

The second and last Soviet wartime parade on Red Square was held on 1st May 1945. With the Red Army fighting in the streets of Berlin, and the war effectively over, Moscow could again afford to have the luxury of a military parade. In contrast with the previous wartime parade on 7th November 1941, and now with no threat of interruption, the parade reverted to its pre-war departure time of 10:00, and Stalin reviewed the parade under bright skies and gentle sunshine without himself feeling the need to make a speech to the nation. General Antonov as Head of the General Staff took the parade on a black horse before making the parade speech, praising the wartime leadership and Stalin who stood in silence beside him. The parade featured new elements including a new Soviet nation anthem, while it was announced that henceforth the Red Army would be known as the Soviet Army, with the formal change of designation taking effect on 25th February 1946.

The 1945 May Day parade started with infantry of the Moscow garrison followed by a large-scale mechanized parade that now featured a significant number of Lend-Lease vehicles. As might be expected, the composition of tanks, military vehicles and artillery on parade was significantly different than in November 1941, reflecting the technological advances in arma-

Ya-12 artillery tractors towing 122mm M-1931 (A-19) guns through Red Square, 1st May 1945. Hans Krebs, who as German military attaché had attended the last pre-war 1st May 1941 Red Square parade, had offered Germany's initial surrender terms to the Red Army in Berlin as the 1945 May Day parade was being held in Moscow. (Shirokov)

GAZ-AA 1.5 tonne trucks towing 45mm anti-tank guns and their limbers through Red Square, 1st May 1945. These are pre-war production trucks rather than the simplified wartime model.

UralZiS-5V trucks with airborne forces markings and "desant" paratroopers on parade, an early indication of what would become a major development in the post-war Soviet Army - the Soviet airborne (VDV) forces.

In May 1945, the IS-2 heavy tank was on parade in Red Square, Moscow, and also to be found on the streets of Berlin. The new IS-3 heavy tank was entering production, and would have its public debut at the Allied Victory Parade in Berlin rather than on Moscow's Red Square.

ments brought about by four years of total war. Two GAZ-67 vehicles led the mechanised parade, followed by GAZ-AAs with infantry in the rear cargo areas. A large number of Studebaker US6 trucks followed, with some towing Soviet 100mm 100mm M-1944 (BS-3) dual purpose guns and 85mm M-1939 anti-aircraft guns. ZiS-5 anti-aircraft vehicles paraded through Red Square, mounting twin 12.7mm DShK machine guns in the rear cargo body and towing 37mm M-1939 anti-aircraft guns. Perhaps the most iconic Soviet artillery systems of World War Two followed, in the form of the 132mm BM-13N, 82mm BM-8-36 and 300mm BM-31-12 "Katyusha" multiple rocket launchers, all mounted on Lend-Lease Studebaker US6 truck chassis, followed by more Studebaker US6 trucks with infantry. After what was significant display of Lend-Lease vehicles, the parade reverted to Soviet built types, with Ya-12 tracked artillery tractors towing 152mm M-1937 (ML-20) and 122mm M-1931/37 (A-19) "Corps Duplex" towed artillery pieces which had that month performed stellar service levelling the centre of Berlin. Voroshilovets tracked tractors

THE RED ARMY ON PARADE 1917-45

Though designated as a self propelled gun, the ISU-122 was a close support weapon and often used as a powerful long range tank-killer.

towed 152mm Br-2 tracked howitzers through the square, while Lend-Lease Allis-Chalmers tracked tractors towed 305mm Br-18 heavy howitzers of the RVGK, the Red Army Strategic Command Reserve, split into gun cradle and barrel loads.

The tanks and other armoured vehicles followed, SU-76Ms in columns five vehicles wide, T-34-85s, some bearing scars and armour patches, and finally SU-100s, ISU 122s and ISU-152s. The late war SU-100 and ISU-122 had proven potent heavy tank killers, while the 152mm ML-20S howitzer mounted in the ISU-152 had performed an excellent job of destroying tanks, and whole apartment buildings when required, as when snipers had proven troublesome during street fighting. The KV (KV-1) heavy tanks of November 1941 were now replaced with the Iosif Stalin 2 (IS-2) heavy tank, named after the Soviet leader who now impassively watched on from the mausoleum podium as they rolled past infront of him on Red Square. Softskin vehicles included GAZ-MM trucks towing older 45mm M-1937 anti-tank guns and Ya-12 tracked tractors towing 152mm M-1937 (ML-20) howitzers. The ground parade was accompanied by a massive aircraft fly-past.

As the 1st May Red Square parade was being held in Moscow, events in Berlin were coming to their inevitable conclusion. The city had since

ISU-152 self propelled howitzers moving down Gorky Street towards Red Square, 1st May 1945. The building in the background is today the Moscow Mayor's office.

16th April been under assault from the combined forces of three Soviet fronts, with according to Russian primary sources a combined force of over 2.5 million men (including nearly 79,000 Polish troops) some 6250 tanks, 7500 aircraft, 3255 "Katyusha" rocket launchers and 41,600 artillery pieces, supported by some 95,000 military transport vehicles. By 20th April the city centre was being shelled by Soviet artillery and Red Army tanks and troops were moving towards the centre from the suburbs, while the more pragmatic and consciencious German commanders moved their units and men strategically westward in order to surrender to Allied forces approaching from the west in order to spare their lives in what was clearly now seen by most Wehrmacht officers as a lost cause. As the 1st May celebrations and military parade were underway in peaceful and sunny Moscow, T-34-85 medium and IS-2 heavy tanks named after Stalin were parked up beneath the ruined walls of the German Reichstag building.

The German surrender had been formally offered, and after four years of war during which the Soviet Union had lost an estimated 27 million people, peace was returning to Europe. The Red Army armoured "steamroller" had crossed Europe and was in control of Berlin, having initially bypassed the city and then returned from the west for reasons that had more to do with the post-war order in Europe and the development of rocket technology than the immediate war with Germany and the capture of its nominative capital city.

Hans Krebs, now Commander of Oberkommando der Wehrmacht (OKW) - the German Supreme High Command of the German Land Forces defending the city, may have reflected on his days as German military attaché to Moscow in the late 1930s, and specifically on the Red Square parade he had attended as military attaché to the German Embassy in Moscow on 1st May 1941, exactly four years earlier to the day. After attending that last pre-war Red Square parade Krebs had, as noted earlier, advised Hitler that in his professional military opinion the Red Army that he had observed at that Moscow parade was far behind the Wehrmacht in technical capability and military preparedness. That same army had in recent days fought its way street by street through the remnants of Berlin and Hitler's dreams of a "1000 Year Reich". Hitler committed suicide on 30th April 1945, and Krebs as OKW Commander, to which position he had been promoted only on 1st April 1945, found himself in the unenviable position on 1st May of being responsible for offering Germany's surrender terms, as dictated by Goebbels, to Chuikov at his 8th Guards Tank Army headquarters located at Karlshorst in Berlin. As the first Red Square military parade since 7th November 1941 was underway in Moscow, and the Soviet Union celebrated 1st May in the spring sunshine, Krebs waited in the smoking ruins of Berlin for a response from the Kremlin.

As the May Day parade passed before him, the first since the fateful parade of November 1941 when the enemy was literally at the gates, Stalin considered the surrender terms offered by Krebs relayed to him via Chuikov's headquarters in Berlin. Stalin's response after the parade was that the Soviet Union would accept nothing less than total surrender. This was duly relayed back to Krebs, who dutifully submitted Stalin's response to Goebbels - who was now Reich Chancellor after Hitler's suicide. Stalin's demands were rejected outright, and Krebs ordered to advise Stalin of this decision, as before via Chuikov's Berlin headquarters. As he left the

An elderly and wounded German Volkssturm soldier observes as an IS-2 heavy tank leads a column of T-34-85s through the streets of Berlin.

The IS-2 heavy tank together with the T-34 symbolised the Soviet "armoured steamroller" which spearheaded the Red Army's drive into Axis territory in the last two years of the war. (Viktor Kulikov)

OKW headquarters within Hitler's Bunker, Krebs may well have again reflected on his own personal attendance at his last pre-war Soviet military parade, witnessed as the German defence attaché in Moscow in May 1941. The Red Army that he had told Hitler only four years before was far behind Germany in terms of military capability, was now annihilating the last remaining old men and boys of the "Volkssturm" defending what was left of Berlin. What thoughts he had that day will never be known, as his memoirs were never published. Rather than presenting the unrealistic official German OKW response to Chuikov's headquarters, and perfectly understanding the situation, the intelligent, cultured and fluent Russian speaking Krebs, who was one of the few German officers to have witnessed the Red Army on its home territory before the outbreak of war, on the morning of 2nd May shot himself dead. The same day, the German, and now unconditional, surrender was presented to Chuikov by General Helmuth Weidling, the Berlin garrison commander. The war in Europe was over.

Meanwhile, as events were unfolding in Berlin, other foreign military attaches were doubtless under no illusion as to what was on the horizon for them. Among the invited guests at the 1st May 1945 parade in Moscow stood the Army and Naval military attachés of the Japanese Embassy in Moscow. They observed a very different parade to that of May 1941, the result of four years of unrelenting military conflict and the rapid development of military technology that was an inevitable result of a war for survival. Stalin had recently re-iterated the Soviet promise to the Allies that three months after the end of war in Europe, the Soviet Union would declare war on Japan and enter the war in south east Asia. Precisely three months later, with the war in Europe over, and three days after the American B-29 "Superfortress" long-range bomber "Enola Gay" returned to base from dropping the first atomic bomb on Hiroshima on 6th August, the Red Army launched land attacks on Japan, with armoured spearheads driving into inner Mongolia, Manchuria and on Sakhalin Island (the south of which was until 1945 the northernmost island of Japan), obliterating the Japanese Kwantung Army in a decisive three week campaign.

T-34 tanks await the 1st May 1945 parade on Dvortsovaya Ploschad (Palace Square) in Leningrad*. These tanks have all been damaged in combat, repaired and rebuilt. One of the tanks has an early T-34 M-1940 hull with a later T-34 M-1942 turret. The Hermitage is to the distant right of the photograph. Wartime photographer: Fedoseev (TsGAKFFD)

---

* Dvortsovaya Ploschad (Palace Square) was renamed Ploschad Uritskogo (Uritsky Square) in 1918 after Moisei Uritsky the assassinated Petrograd People's Commissar of Internal Affairs. The square reverted to its original name in January 1944.

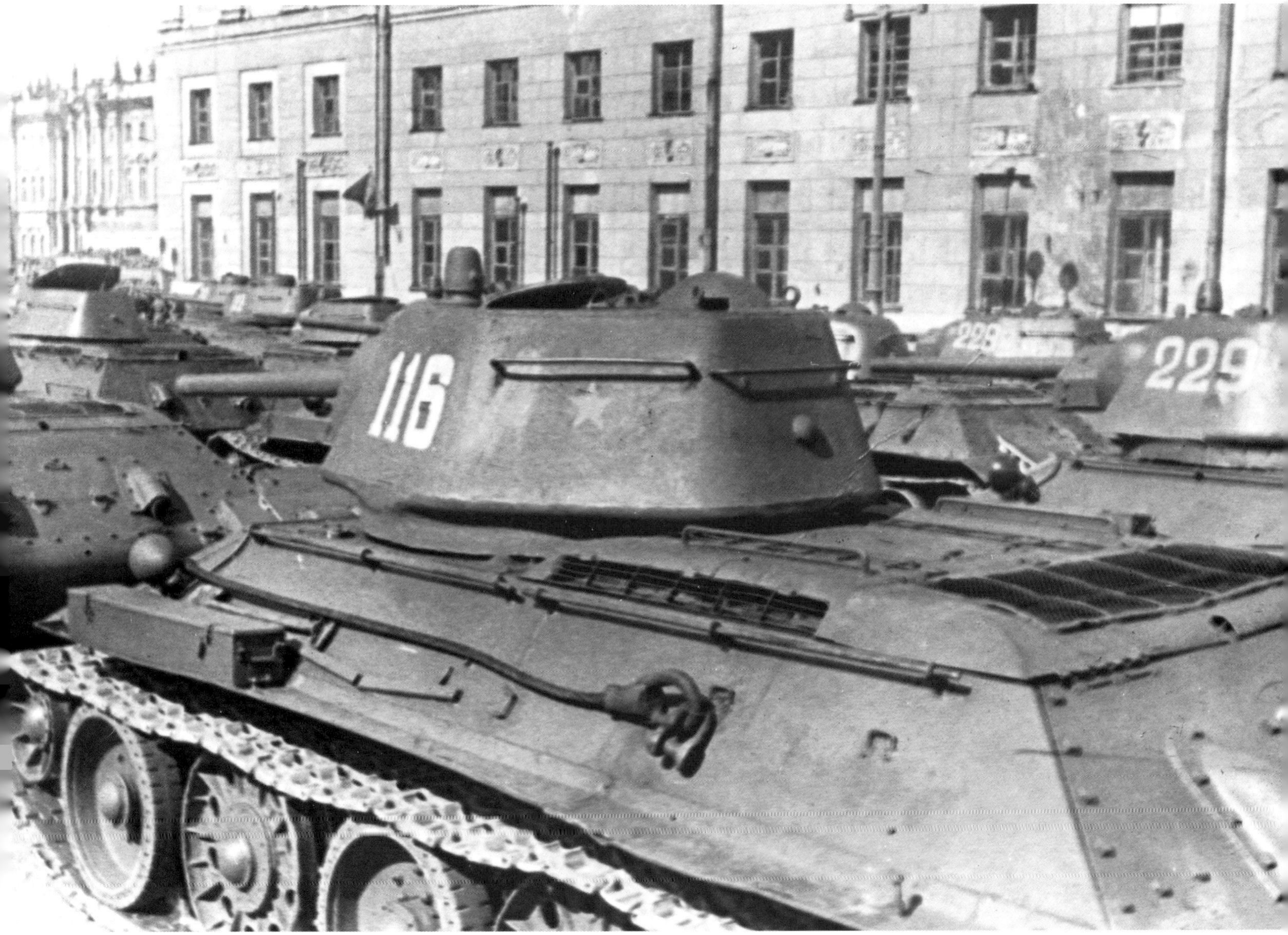
116
229

Red Army T-34-85 tank crews and infantry are entertained by a song and dance troupe, as the war comes to an end in Europe.

# Soviet Victory Parades in 1945

## 9th May 1945 – Victory in Europe

On 8th May 1945 war was declared officially over in Europe. The time of the signing was such that it was already the following day in Moscow, hence the Soviet Union celebrated (and the Russian Federation to this day continues to celebrate) Victory in Europe (VE) Day on 9th May rather than on the 8th as in western Europe.

As the population of the Soviet Union celebrated on Red Square, the streets of Moscow and in every town and village throughout the country on that day in 1945, the decision was taken to hold a formal Soviet Victory Parade, to be organized as quickly as possible. Two weeks later, General Antonov received an order to gather a Regiment of veterans from each Soviet Front to participate in the victory parade, and have them assemble in Moscow for parade rehearsals by 10th June. On 19th June, all captured German standards including the Soviet flag raised over the Reichstag were flown in a Lend-Lease C-47 "Dakota" aircraft from Berlin to Moscow for display at the parade.

Compared with the pre-war parades, the parade training was far from straightforward in the June of 1945, in that neither infantry nor tank crews had any experience of ceremonial formations. They were battle-hardened combat veterans that had known only combat in the field and had never had the time nor the need to learn ceremonial duties such as driving in formation.

By the winter of 1941, Hitler had expected German tanks to be on Moscow's Red Square. After four years of bitter conflict, Red Army tanks were by the spring of 1945 parked outside the Reichstag building in Berlin, with the Soviet flag flying from the roof.

A battle hardened IS-2 tank crew pose with other Red Army officers and soldiers at the 18th Century Brandenburg Gate in the centre of Berlin.

THE RED ARMY ON PARADE 1917-45

Decorated Red Army tank officers pose by their IS-2 heavy tank after Victory in Europe in 1945. The battle-hardened tank crews are clearly not interested in smile for the camera "propaganda" photographs and are to a man lost in their own thoughts, perhaps for their fellow crewmen who died in combat during the war.

SU-76M self-propelled guns parked on Manezhnaya Square awaiting the Victory Parade on 24th June 1945.

# 24th June 1945
# - The VE Day Victory Parade

The Soviet Union celebrated its first Victory in Europe parade on 24th June 1945 after which there would be a hiaitus of 20 years until the next VE Day celebration on 9th May 1965. There would be a 20 year haitus until it was celebrated again on 9th May 1985, during which time the country reverted to its conventional 7th November parades to demonstrate its latest military technology, with military elements to the 1st May parades also continuing until 1968. The 24th June Victory Parade thereby holds a particularly prominent position in Soviet and Russian military history, commemorating rather than celebrating the end of a war in which combined Soviet military and civilian losses were almost 50% of the total human losses of all the other combattant powers involved in the war combined. Germany had lost an estimated 6.9-7.4 million souls, Great Britain including the Commonwealth countries had lost approximately 451,000, the United States 420,000, and the Japanese, for whom the war was not yet over, would lose an estimated 2.5-3.1 million souls. The actual Soviet numbers will never be known, but are today accurately estimated at 27 million. The pre-war alliances, wartime and post-war politics of the Soviet Union and its leader Stalin can be debated ad-infinitum, but it is clear even to the mathematically minded with no knowledge of history that had Germany not invaded the Soviet Union in June 1941, and had the Soviet Union not pre-occupied

THE RED ARMY ON PARADE 1917-45

For the large scale 24th June 1945 Victory Parade, tanks and other vehicles were marshalled on Manezhnaya Square, Gorky Street (today Tverskaya) and in several other streets in the immediate vicinity of Red Square.

OT-34-85 flamethrower tanks pass through Manezhnaya Square towards Red Square for the 24th June Victory Parade.

IS-2 heavy tanks moving towards Red Square during the 24th June Victory Parade, past what is today the State Duma (parliament) building.

There were no early wartime tanks paraded on Red Square during the Victory Parade. This single T-34 M-1941 was paraded on 7th November after a wartime journey that started in Voronezh and ended in Prague.

and absorbed the majority of the German war machine on the Eastern Front until the opening of the "Second Front" in 1944, then mainland Europe would simply not exist in the form it does today, and perhaps Hitler's "1000 Year Reich" would already be into its 8th decade in Europe.

On 24th June 1945, the Soviet Union celebrated victory over Germany with victory parades held across the country. The Soviet Victory Parade on Moscow's Red Square was naturally the one which was most documented, attended as it was by the foreign diplomatic corps and press, and it has gone down in history as the most iconic military parade in history. Preparation for the parade was complicated as in November 1941 by the combat veterans not being versed in ceremonial duties; and repeated practice runs were held at the Central Aerodrome located on the former Khodynka field, with the equipment gathered being for the most part newly manufactured rather than returned from combat units.

The Soviet Victory Parade celebrating Victory in Europe over Germany and its Axis allies began at 10:00 on 24th June 1945. The weather was not ideal, with heavy rain during most of the parade. In attendance there were 24 Marshals of the Soviet Union, 249 generals, 2536 officers and 31,116 other ranks, 77 Heroes of the Soviet Union and an unprecedented 1850 items of military "tekhnika" – tanks, armoured vehicles and other military equipment.

For the 24th June 1945 Victory Parade, tanks were stacked the length of Gorky Street as a typical Russian summer shower rained down.

THE RED ARMY ON PARADE 1917-45

THE RED ARMY ON PARADE 1917-45

Tank columns marshalled on Gorky Street awaiting the Victory Parade. The scale of the parade is evident. The street view, with the Central Post Office on the right and the right entrance ramp to Red Square in the distance is readily familiar today.

The parade was reviewed by Marshal of the Soviet Union, Georgy K. Zhukov, mounted on a white horse. The story of the search for two white horses for the Victory Parade after a war when most horses had been killed and the surviving horses were emaciated is in of itself an interesting account, but beyond the scope of this study. The parade commander was Marshal of the Soviet Union Kontantin K. Rokossovsky, mounted on a black horse. The parade procession was under the direct supervision of the MVO (Moscow Garrison) commander, General-Colonel Artemiev.

Stalin stood silent on the review stand atop the Lenin Mausoleum. There was from him no speech, no minute of silence for the dead, and no single word of thanks to those who had made the ultimate sacrifice for the nation*. Among the Soviet political and military hierarchy present was a young Major-General Leonid Brezhnev, Chief of the Political Command of the 4th Ukrainian Front, who marched during the parade together with General Yeremenko, the Commander of the 4th Ukrainian Front. Twenty years later, as the Soviet Union celebrated the 20th Anniversary of the 9th May 1945 Victory Day in Europe, Leonid Brezhnev would stand on the Lenin Mausoleum review stand as the leader of the Soviet Union. In his time as Soviet premier, Brezhnev would later attend Red Square military parades in 18 consecutive years.

The cine filming of the parade was done separately in black and white and colour, using cameras located in the same positions. The Victory Parade was filmed in colour using Agfa film repatriated from Germany. The film coverage from the cameras is different, but both types record the actual parade rather than a reconstruction as had occurred in November 1941.

The infantry parade consisted of marching units including combat veterans from the 10 Soviet fronts which were active in the final days of World War Two. The banners of all ten

---

* Stalin made a speech during celebrations within the Kremlin after the parade, thanking the Russian (rather than Soviet) people for their sacrifices during the war.

THE RED ARMY ON PARADE 1917-45

OT-34-85 flamethrower tanks, SU-100 self propelled guns and M-72 motor-cycle combinations stacked on Gorky Street awaiting the Victory Parade. The morning had started dry, with a brief rain shower falling as the armour began to move, almost as if tears for the dead from mother nature. The first snowfalls of winter also often coincided with the post-war 7th November parades.

OT-34-85 flamethrower tanks stacked on Gorky Street awaiting the Victory Parade. These factory fresh tanks were used due to a shortage of T-34-85 gun tanks, at the time still mainly located in Germany and other countries in Europe.

fronts were represented, namely the Karelsky, Leningradsky, 1st Pribaltisky, 1st, 2nd and 3rd Belorussky, and the 1st, 2nd, 3rd and 4th Ukrainsky fronts, together with what is now understood to be a copy of the original Soviet banner raised above the Reichstag in Berlin by the Red Army soldiers Egorov, Kantaria and Berest. (see p.195)

The culmination of the infantry parade, which consisted of Red Army, Red Army Air Force and VMF (naval) units, with the majority of infantry being from the Moscow garrison and training schools, was the ceremonial throwing of captured German standards onto the ground below the Lenin Mausoleum.

After the infantry and cavalry, the parade included horse drawn "tachanki" maching gun carts, a throwback to the days of the Russian Revolution.

The meticulously marshalled mechanised part of the parade followed, with wheeled vehicles staged on Manezhaya Square and surrounding streets moving onto Red square followed by the balance of the parade including more vehicle columns, tanks and self propelled guns which were stacked up on Gorky Street beyond Pushkinskaya Square.

The mechanised part of the parade began with ZiS-5 trucks with troops in the rear cargo bodies and also early wartime production original ZiS-5 vehicles towing 37mm M-1939 anti-aircraft guns, ZiS-12 trucks with 25mm M-1940 (94KM) anti-aircraft guns in the rear cargo area and Z-15-4 searchlights, eight ZiS-6 trucks with ZT-4 sound locators. GAZ-67Bs were used as lead vehicles before each contingent of vehicles on parade.

Massed columns of Lend-Lease Studebaker

THE RED ARMY ON PARADE 1917-45

ISU-152 heavy self-propelled guns move towards Red Square for the 1945 Victory Parade. The ISU-152, armed with the 152mm ML-20S howitzer, was used for providing heavy close support fire. (Viktor Kulikov)

ISU-152 heavy self-propelled guns crossing Red Square during the Soviet Victory Parade held on 24th June 1945. (Photographer I. Shagin) RGAKFD

ISU-122 heavy self-propelled guns parked on Gorky Street awaiting the Victory Parade. The ISU-122 was armed with the 122mm A-19S, based on the towed 122mm M-1931/37 (A-19) gun, and was a potent tank killer, destroying tanks by sheer projectile weight. (RGAKFD)

US6 trucks followed, firstly with seated infantry, followed by Studebaker US6 mounted BM-8-48 and BM-13N "Katyusha" multiple rocket launchers, the latter having been standardised as the main chassis for BM-13 installation after a variety of other Soviet and Lend-Lease chassis had been used previously. The 72 round BM-8-72 was developed at the very end of the war and also mounted on the Studebaker US6 chassis.

ZiS-5 trucks towing 160mm M-1943 mortars were followed by Dodge WC51/WC52 ¾ tonne trucks towing 57mm M-1943 (ZiS-2) anti-tank guns, GAZ-AAA trucks towing the highly effective 76.2mm ZiS-3 dual purpose gun, followed by more Studebakers towing 100mm M-1944 (BS-3) dual purpose guns and ZiS-5 trucks towing 122mm M-1938 (M-30) howitzers. Lend-Lease Jeeps acted as parade column lead vehicles. Heavy artillery was represented by 152mm Br-2 and 203mm B-4 tracked howitzers towed by Lend-Lease supplied Allis-Chalmers HD-10W tracked tractors and the carriages and barrels from 305mm M-1939 (Br-18) howitzers towed by Soviet built Voroshilovets tracked artillery tractors. The 122mm M-1931 (A-19) and 152mm M-1937 (ML-20) "Corps Duplex" heavy artillery pieces were both towed by Ya-12 tracked tractors, the former being both the original M-1931 model with spoked road wheels and the modernised M-1931/37 then in front line service in western Europe. Red Army airborne forces were represented, seated in ZiS-5 trucks. There were vast formations of motorcycle combinations in columns six motorcycles wide, followed by at least 70

These ISU-122 self-propelled guns assembled on Gorky Street before the June Victory Parade include an ISU-122S in the second column, armed with the 122mm D-25S gun, with a modified breech and new gun mantlet. (RGAKFD)

IS-2 heavy tanks parked on Gorky Street awaiting the 1945 Victory Parade.

SU-100s stacked on Gorky Street awaiting the 24th June 1945 Victory Parade. The 100mm D-10S gun mounted in the SU-100 would (as the D-10T) become the standard armament on the post war T-54 and T-55 main battle tanks.

BA-64B armoured cars, the wartime designed and produced BA-64 making its public debut (as the BA-64B) on Red Square in columns five vehicles wide. Self propelled artillery was represented by the SU-76M, with over 40 vehicles paraded in columns five wide, and by the SU-100, ISU-122 and ISU-152 self propelled artillery units in columns four wide. The tanks paraded at the end of the parade were T-34-85s (actually newly manufactured OT-34-85 flamethrower tanks rather than standard T-34-85s) and the IS-2 heavy tank, both paraded in columns of four. The T-34-85 and IS-2 represented the epitome of Red Army armoured might, having been used in large numbers in the final drive through Germany to Berlin.

Being on such an unprecedented scale, the 24th June 1945 Victory Parade parade took considerable marshalling. Tanks and other vehicles were as related earlier stacked the length of Gorky Street, the GAZ, Studebaker and ZiS trucks were parked up on Manezhnaya Square adjacent to the entrance to Red Square, and tanks and vehicles were also located in the smaller streets near the entrances to Red Square and Manezhnaya Square, with the columns which took up all of Manezhnaya Square, and including the majority of transport vehicles and wheeled anti-aircraft systems moving onto Red Square before the motorcycles which led the armoured element of the display onto Red Square for the parade finale.

The 1945 Soviet Victory parade lasted an impressive 2 hours and 9 minutes, one of the longest-ever Soviet military parades. The next commemorative Soviet Victory Parade, now held on the original "VE" day date of 9th May, would not be until 1965, with the next parade being on 9th May 1985. After the demise of the Soviet Union and the 7th November parades celebrating the Great October Revolution of 1917, military parades were re-introduced onto Red Square in 2008, since when the 9th May commemorative parade has become an annual event.

THE RED ARMY ON PARADE 1917-45

SU-100s move down Gorky Street towards Red Square on the morning of 24th June 1945. (Photographer: Yakov Khalip)

Marshals of the Soviet Union Semeon Budenny (left), Iosif Stalin (centre) and Georgy Zhukov (right) watch the 1945 Red Square Victory Parade from the Lenin Mausoleum.

BM-13N "Katyusha" multiple rocket launchers traverse Red Square. The "Katyusha" was mounted on a variety of chassis at the beginning of the war, including the ZiS-6 and STZ-5 tracked artillery tractor, but was later in the war standardised on the Lend-Lease Studebaker US6.

The generic term "Katyusha" was used for several calibres of weapon, 82mm, 132mm and 300mm. All were latterly standardised on the on the Lend-Lease Studebaker US6 as seen here during the 1945 Victory Parade.

ZiS-5V trucks with tandem 12.7mm DShK anti-aircraft guns and Lend-Lease American "Jeep" lead vehicles parked on Manezhnaya Square before the Victory Parade.

THE RED ARMY ON PARADE 1917-45

BA-64B armoured cars parading through Red Square. The diminutive BA-64 armoured car was produced at GAZ, which began assembly of the GAZ-AA and GAZ-AAA trucks in the early 1930s and assembled the T-60 and T-70 tanks and the SU-76 self-propelled gun during the war.

The original flag raised over the Reichstag in Berlin was flown to the Moscow Central Aerodrome at Khodynka on 20th June 1945 for the Victory Parade. At the head of the ceremonial column is Captain Valentin I. Varennikov.

Marshal of the Soviet Union Georgy Zhukov crosses Red Square on a white stallion at the beginning of the Victory Parade.

Red Army sappers with mine-detecting equipment and search dogs participated in the Victory Parade.

These "tachanki" machine gun carts date from before the Russian Revolution, but continue to be used in ceremonial parades to the present day. Considerable effort was expended in finding healthy horses, particularly white ones, for the 1945 Victory Parade after four years of war.

The Victory banner as hoisted above the Reichstag, with those involved in the historic event (from left to right) Captain K.Ya. Samsonov, Junior Sergeant M.V. Kantariya, Sergeant M.A. Egorov, Senior Sergeant M. Ya. Sonyanov and Captain S.A. Neustroev.

195

THE RED ARMY ON PARADE 1917-45

Ya-12 tracked tractors towing 122mm M-1931/37 (A-19) howitzers across Red Square. These tractors were displayed in 1945-1947 before being replaced by the post-war M2.

S-65 tracked artillery tractors towing 152mm M-1935 (Br-2) tracked heavy guns across Red Square during the 24th June Victory Parade. The 152mm Br-2 tracked gun and 203mm B-4 tracked howitzer were used during street fighting to destroy entire buildings where snipers were located or hardened resistance encountered.

The 24th June 1945 Victory Parade included the casting of German banners onto the ground in front of the Lenin Mausoleum, ceremonially concluding the war in Europe and consigning Hitler's "1000 Year Reich" to history.

As the war turned in the Soviet Union's favour from late 1942, the Red Army began to accumulate war trophies, some of which were put on public display at Gorky Park in Moscow, with a formal public exhibition being organized from 22nd June 1943, exactly two years after the beginning of the war.

Captured Axis artillery on the river embankment at Gorky Park. The Krymsky Bridge over the River Moskva is in the background, and remains in place today.

# Military Exhibition, Gorky Park, 1945

In 1945, a temporary open-air exhibition of tanks, aircraft, artillery and other equipment captured from German Axis (and later also Japanese) forces was set up on the embankment of the Moscow river in Gorky Park. The exhibition was a vast display entitled the "Vistavka Obraztsov Trofeinogo Vooruzheniya Zakhvatchennogo U Nemtsev 1941-45" (exhibition of samples of armaments captured from the Germans 1941-45). The exhibition remained in place as an almost permanent structure for a long period after the war before eventually being dismantled in October 1948. Some of the tanks were shipped back to the Kubinka tank proving grounds (via which many had arrived after being evaluated there), but the majority of the extensive collection of German artillery and aircraft was scrapped.

# 12th August 1945 - Parade of Physical Culture

On 12th August, Moscow staged a Parade of Physical Culture on Red Square. It was a purely civilian parade in nature, with massed displays by Soviet sportsmen and women, particularly gymnasts. Such parades had been held on Red Square since the 1930s, but the 12th August 1945 parade was impressive in terms of its sheer scale, with 23,000 participants, not dissimilar to the number of troops that participated in a typical Red Square militray parade. The parade was attended by foreign dignitaries including Dwight Eisenhower, then Supreme Commander Allied Forces in Europe. Six years later Eisenhower would become the first Supreme Commander of NATO, and two years later the President of the United States. His attendance in Moscow had current military significance, in that the previous week the United States had dropped atomic bombs on Hiroshima and Nagasaki, while on 9th August the Red Army had as promised by Stalin attacked Japan in Manchukuo, Mengjiang (Inner Mongolia), Sakhalin Island and Korea. As Eisenhower attended the physical culture parade in Moscow, the Soviet Union and the United States were allies in the final defeat of Japan, and the machinations of post-war Europe were yet to unravel.

THE RED ARMY ON PARADE 1917-45

The Red Army participated in the Allied Victory Parade in Berlin held on 7th September 1945. IS-3 heavy tanks of the 71st Guards Tank Regiment parade along Charlottenstrasse in Berlin.

# 7th September 1945
# - The Allied Victory Parade - Berlin

The Allied Victory Parade in Berlin was staged along Charlottenstrasse by the Brandenburger Gate, and was attended by troops from France, Great Britain, the Soviet Union and the United States. The Soviet head of delegation was Georgy Zhukov, and his American counterpart General George Patton.

The parade was a mix of infantry and armour; however the parade was dominated by a display of 52 IS-3 heavy tanks of the 71st Guards Tank Regiment of the 2nd Guards Tank Army, the latest of the Red Army's heavy tank series bearing the name of the Soviet leader. The shock appearance of these tanks was palpable. While the armoured might of the Red Army was visible in the ruins of Berlin for all to see, the appearance of such a sleek and heavily armoured tank design, with its heavily sloped armour, "inverted frying pan" low profile turret and "schuka" (pike) nose was viewed as an advance that even seasoned foreign commanders had not expected to see from a country weakened by four years of war for survival. The intelligence shock generated by the appearance of the IS-3

The IS-3 heavy tank was a shock to the Allied forces assembled for the Berlin Allied Victory Parade, as the war weary Soviet Union had not been expected by Allied commanders to field a "next-generation" tank with such obvious advanced armour configuration.

cannot be underestimated. Just as in 1941, when the T-34 and the KV-1 had been a shock to advancing Wehrmacht forces, the appearance of the IS-3 was a similar surprise for the Soviet Union's wartime allies now in the process of re-aligning their post-war allegiances. The numerous design and construction faults of the IS-3 heavy tank would become known later, but the appearance of the IS-3 heavy tank within the already massively powerful Red Army tank forces resulted in emergency heavy tank design programs being launched in the United States, the United Kingdom and France, with the American M-103 and British "Conqueror" heavy tanks being developed in direct response to the perceived threat generated directly by the shock appearance of the 52 IS-3 tanks that rumbled down Charlottenstrasse in Berlin during the Allied Victory Parade of 7th September 1945.

The public debut of the IS-3 at the Allied Victory Parade in Berlin was not incidental. The first production IS-3s had been shipped to Berlin as a demonstration to the Allies that the Red Army, though exhausted by four years of war, was capable as always of delivering unexpected surprises.

THE RED ARMY ON PARADE 1917-45

The IS-3 heavy tank was without doubt the unexpected highlight (or from an Allied perspective perhaps lowlight) of the Allied Victory Parade in Berlin. The tank mounted the same 122mm D-25T tank gun as the fabled IS-2 tank that had spearheaded the Red Army assault on Berlin, but had a radically improved armour layout.

The IS-3 tanks paraded in Berlin were from the first production batch, assembled too late for the IS-3 to see active service in World War Two, but by September 1945 they were the highlight of the Allied Victory Parade.

THE RED ARMY ON PARADE 1917-45

The initial production IS-3 as paraded in Berlin had design features such as the mounting of the turret radio antenna and the design of the front track guards which were distinct to those tanks built before September 1945, and paraded in Berlin.

IS-3 tanks of the 71st Guard Tank Regiment parade along Charlottenstrasse in Berlin. This single appearance led to urgent heavy tank development programmes in France, Great Britain and the United States.

THE RED ARMY ON PARADE 1917-45

Field Marshal Bernard Montgomery presenting Marshal Georgy Zhukov with an award at the first Allied Victory Parade held in Berlin on 21st July 1945. Montgomery would in the post-war years become Officer Commanding the British Army on the Rhine and the Deputy Supreme Commander of NATO. (Vladimir Nikitin)

Marshal Georgy Zhukov and Major-General Lewis Lynne (Commander 7th Armoured Division and Allied Forces Berlin) at the first Allied Victory Parade Berlin, 21st July 1945 (Vladimir Nikitin)

Field Marshal Montgomery, Marshal of the Soviet Union Zhukov, Major-General Lewis Lynne and a British military interpreter at the Allied Victory Parade Berlin, 21st July 1945. (Vladimir Nikitin)

Field Marshal Montgomery with Marshal Zhukov at the Allied Victory Parade Berlin on 21st July 1945. (Vladimir Nikitin)

Marshals Montgomery and Zhukov share the stand at the Allied Victory parade on 21st July 1945. The July Victory Parade was primarily a British event with invited Allied guests. Zhukov attended both the July and September Allied Victory parades, with the British being represented at the latter by General Brian Robertson. (Vladimir Nikitin)

Red Army IS-2, ISU-152 and ISU-122 tank crews receiving instruction at the Military Academy of Armoured and Mechanised Troops of the Red Army, 9th August 1945. The Soviet Union declared war on Japan just after midnight that day, exactly three months after the war in Europe was declared officially over, as promised by Stalin to the Allies at the Yalta Conference.

# 16th and 24th September 1945 – Victory Over Japan (VJ Day) Parades in Harbin & Voroshilov

The Soviet war against Japan is not as documented, nor as well understood as the war against Germany in Europe, but was nevertheless a significant contributor to the overall Allied war effort. The short war against Japan in the early autumn of 1945 would culminate in a Red Army victory parade in the former Manchurian city of Harbin, today located in north east China, on 16th September 1945, celebrating Victory over Japan (VJ Day).

The Soviet Victory Parade in Harbin was the culmination of a series of skirmishes and then major clashes which had begun in the late 1930s, long before World War Two broke out in Europe. In late 1931, the maverick Japanese Kwangtung Army invaded Manchuria and captured several major cities including Harbin, with control of the region being established under the auspices of the Manchukuo regime, directly controlled by the

THE RED ARMY ON PARADE 1917-45

Victory over Japan (VJ Day) parades were held in several cities in the Far East after the short but decisive Soviet-Japanese war. These Lend-Lease Harley Davidson WLA-42 motorcycle combinations participating in a Victory Parade in Mongolia in September 1945 are armed with 82mm mortars.

The Red Army VJ Day parades included equipment that was very different from the Moscow Red Square parades, all drawn directly from front line units, including these Lend-Lease Harley-Davidson WLA-42 motorcycle combinations with 14.5mm PTRD anti-tank rifles. Mongolia, September 1945.

A BT-7 M-1937 fast tank passes the temporary review stand during the Victory over Japan parade at Voroshilov, 24th September 1945*. Many tank types that had been destroyed early in the war in Europe survived in the Far East until 1945 and beyond. (Mikhail Baryatinsky)

Japanese. During Japanese occupation, the population of Harbin, at the time 70% ethnic Chinese and 30% ethnic Russian, was subjected to medical experiments carried out by Unit 731 of the Japanese Kwangtung Army. As with all statistics related to war the truth is the first casualty, but it is estimated that from three and up to twelve thousand local men, women and children died as a result of these biological experiments.

The Soviet declaration of war on Japan on 8th August 1945 was the result of Allied agreements made at the Tehran conference in November 1943, where Stalin had committed that once Germany was defeated in Europe, the Soviet Union would join the Allies in the fight against Japan. As the war in Europe was drawing to a close this commitment had been reiterated at the Yalta conference in February, with Stalin declaring that the Soviet Union would invade Japan precisely three months after the official concluson of the war in Europe. On 8th August 1945, exactly three months to the day after Victory in Europe (VE Day) was declared in Europe, Molotov on behalf of the Soviet Union declared war on Japan. By the evening of the following day Red Army tank forces were deep inside Japanese controlled Manchukuo. The combined Soviet and Mongolian operations against the Japanese Kwangtung Army spread through Mengjiang (Inner Mongolia) and into northern Korea. The Harbin-Kirin, Khingan-Mukden and Sungari offensives were undertaken from 9th August to 2nd September 1945, under the command of Marshal Aleksandr Vasilevsky, and spread through Manchuria and the surrounding regions, a not insignificant geographical area. Units of the Red Army belonging to the 1st Far East Front under the command of Marshal K.A. Meretskov took Kirin and Harbin on 20th August 1945, following which a victory parade was organised as the more remote regions were also being quickly captured.

On 10th August, Soviet forces landed on the Kuril Islands, and the following day advanced on Sakhalin Island, with the latter offensive completed on 25th August and the former, in the remote Kuril Islands, completed by 1st September.

The Soviet Victory over Japan (VJ Day) pa-

---

* Soviet archives are conflated with regard to the parades at Harbin on 16th September and Voroshilov on 24th September. Most indicate that the background with the single poster of Stalin is Voroshilov, but other archives indicate the same parade as Harbin. Both parades are nevertheless Victory over Japan parades held in September 1945, with most photographs being from the Voroshilov parade.

THE RED ARMY ON PARADE 1917-45

S-65 tractors towing 122mm M-1931 guns at a Victory over Japan Parade. The photograph is labelled Harbin 16th September 1945 in Soviet archives but is the same background as more often quoted as the parade in Voroshilov on 24th September 1945.

The largest parade was held the former Manchurian city of Harbin, today located in northern China, held on 16th September 1945. Red Army soldiers stand above a municipal building on the day of the parade.

SU-76M self-propelled guns on parade in Harbin. As is obvious, these vehicles are parading in the opposite direction to the other parades cited as being Harbin, with dual posters of both Lenin and Stalin in the background.

rade was held by the Red Army in Harbin on 16th September 1945 as planned. The parade was taken by General A. Beloborodov, with the parade commander being General K. Kazakov. This parade was significantly different from the Moscow Red Square parades, in that the tanks, armoured vehicles and artillery displayed were all taken directly from combat operations completed only days before, many of the tanks on parade having evident battle damage.

The Victory in Japan (VJ) parade held in Harbin consisted of mixed columns of tanks and military vehicles taken directly from front line combat only days before, and ranging from T-34 and T-34-85 tanks in single file to columns three abreast depending on the vehicle type. There were a significant number of Lend-Lease vehicles on parade, from Harley Davidson motorcycles mounting anti-tank rifles and mortars to Allis-Chalmers tracked tractors, together with BT-7 M-1937 and early 76.2mm armed T-34 tanks, few of which had survived on the Soviet "Western" Front, complemented by newly delivered 1945 production model T-34-85s. The venerable S-65 tracked artillery tractor towed 122mm A-19 field guns infront of the temporary review podium. The parade was in scope and content very much a soldier's parade, a display of military might celebrating a quick victory in what could have been a brutal drawn out conflict, and concluding Soviet participation in the Second World War.

A victory parade was also held on 24th September 1945 in the town of Voroshilov on the Ussuri river in the Soviet far east. The city was known as Nikolsk Ussuriysky until 1935 when it was renamed Voroshilov after Marshal Klimenti Voroshilov. The town was subsequently renamed again, now to Ussuriysky, in 1957, hence the victory parade is sometimes designated Voroshilov-Ussuriysky in Russian sources.

SU-76M self-propelled guns on parade at Voroshilov on 24th September 1945.

Three T-34 tanks at a Victory over Japan parade, also cited as Harbin. The 1942 production model T-34 "M-1941", which has evident repaired combat damage, is flanked by two mid-war production T-34 M-1943 tanks.

A T-34 M-1941 model produced at Plant № 112 in 1942 passes the review stand at the Victory Over Japan parade, Voroshilov, 24th September 1945. The tank is marked "Za Stalina" (for Stalin).

This T-34 M-1942 believed to be at the same Voroshilov Victory Parade as the SU-76M self propelled guns shown overleaf, has evident service and combat damage. Note the lost and damaged track guards and the frontal glacis armour patched after shell damage.

THE RED ARMY ON PARADE 1917-45

Two T-34 M-1943 tanks followed by a T-34-85, Voroshilov, 24th September 1945. The lead tank is painted with the slogan "Privyet ot Tankistov" ("hello from tankers"), the second is marked "Za Rodinu" ("for the motherland").

T-34-85s at the same parade, cited as Harbin but evidently the same parade as elsewhere cited as Voroshilov. The lead tank is marked "Slava Krasnoi Armii" (Glory to the Red Army). Note these tanks have come directly from combat and have evident service damage rather than having been tidied up for parade purposes.

209

THE RED ARMY ON PARADE 1917-45

A T-34-85 passes the review tribunal at speed during the same Victory over Japan parade at Voroshilov. The turret is marked "Pobeda" (Victory). The parade is also cited as Harbin, 16th September but the conflation as noted in the footnote applies to all these photographs.

Another T-34-85 passes the review tribunal at the same Victory over Japan parade at Voroshilov. Note the two Russian Orthodox Church priests to the left of the review stand.

IS-3 heavy tanks during parade formation training. The public debut of the IS-3 at the Allied Victory Parade in Berlin consisted of virtually the entire production output at that time. The IS-3 would appear on Red Square only the year following the end of the war in Europe and the Far East.

# 7th November 1945 - 28th Anniversary of the Great October Socialist Revolution - The First Post-War November Parade

In November 1945, with the war in Europe having now been over for six months, and the short war in Japan also now consigned to history, the Soviet Union returned to its pre-war tradition of annual 7th November military parades being held on Red Square.

The 7th November 1945 parade was not dissimilar in terms of tanks and vehicles present to the 24th June Victory in Europe (VE Day) parade. The parade did however feature a tank with a definitive link to the recently won war. The mechanised part of the parade began with the demonstration of T-34 №0460 which was paraded through Red Square on 7th November 1945 having returned from an epic journey to the heart of Europe. The 76.2mm armed T-34 "M-1941"* production tank was built in September 1942 and delivered to the 4th Guards Tank Corps. The tank had been engaged in combat near Stalingrad and thereafter travelled steadily west to finish the war intact after a wartime journey of over 10,000km.

The single wartime and combat experienced T-34 was followed onto Red Square by massed columns of T-34-85 tanks belonging to the Kantemirovskaya Tank Division, these being of post-war "Krasnoye Sormovo" plant production, with split turret ventilators, replacing the OT-34-85 flamethrower tanks which had been displayed at the victory parade held in June that year. Ya-12 tracked artillery tractors towed heavy artillery through Red Square as in the June parade. There was one subtle change, the introduction of an element of mechanised VDV (airborne) forces in the form of immediately post-war ZiS-5V trucks in VDV markings with desant paratroopers sitting in bench seats in the rear cargo area. The VDV air-

---

* The T-34 M-1941 production model as described was designed in 1941, but production continued until 1942.

Early production IS-3s practice driving in parade formation. The Victory Parades in 1945 were more difficult than most in that the time available for rehearsals for the combat hardened crews was limited.

Maintaining precise distance and alignment between columns of tanks with limited visibility at best is not an art mastered in a few minutes. These early production IS-3s have non-standard single reserve fuel tanks fitted on each side during practice.

ISU-152s marshalled on Gorky Street awaiting the 7th November Military Parade. The view in the background from the theatre to the Central Telegraph building is unchanged today. (Viktor Kulikov)

borne element of post-war Soviet parades would grow at a rapid pace as the Soviet Union took a lead in the development of mecahnised airborne forces in the post-war era.

As the last vehicles departed Red Square at the end of the 7th November Red Square parade, silence returned to the square. The four years of war for national survival had turned from near defeat as the first snows of winter fell on Moscow in November 1941 to Allied Victory in Europe followed by a decisively quick end to the war with Japan. There had been no German military parade in Moscow; however captured German soldiers had been paraded down Gorky Street and across the Krymsky Val bridge during the war. By May 1945, the most savage clash of land forces the world has ever seen had resulted in Red Army tanks being parked up alongside the Reichstag and the Brandenburg Gate, with Red Army tanks soon thereafter being paraded along Charlottenstrasse as part of the Allied Victory parade held in Berlin in September 1945. The return to peace in the Soviet Union, as with all the combatant nations, Allied and Axis, was far from instant. The estimated 27 million souls lost by the Soviet Union equated to some 15% of the entire population, and the numbers who returned with life-changing injuries were enormous. The disbalance in the ration of women to men in the Soviet Union in the post-war era would last for decades, and women would continue to work in industry in numbers that were significantly higher than other industrialised nations. As in Europe and even the United States, there were shortages of some

Lend-Lease Allis-Chalmers HD-10W tracked tractors towing 203mm B-4 tracked heavy howitzers through Red Square, 7th November 1945. (Mikhail Baryatinsky)

ZiS-12 truck with Z-15-4 searchlights led by Lend-Lease "Jeeps" marshalled on Manezhnaya Square before the 7th November 1945 military parade. (Mikhail Baryatinsky)

Ya-12 tracked tractors towing 122mm M-1931/37 (A-19) guns through Red Square for the 28th Anniversary of the "Great October Revolution", 7th November 1945. (Kinelovsky)

BA-64B armoured cars parked on Gorky Street awaiting the 7th November military parade. The date is confirmed by the "28th October" (28th Anniversary of the October Revolution) markings on the Central Telegraph building above the poster of Stalin in his military greatcoat. (RGAKFD)

basic foodstuffs and raw materials in the immediate post-war years, and the transition from war to consumer economy would be a long road for the Soviet Union.

At the end of the Second World War, the Red Army, its armoured forces and its "God of War" artillery defined the Soviet Union's presence in Europe. The role of the Red Army had been the defining element in ensuring the Allied victory against Fascism in Europe, and the Soviet Union had paid the highest price by far in terms of military and civilian losses during a war that was fought without reference to the niceties of the Geneva Convention.

As the world, and particularly Europe, readjusted to the realities of a return to peace after years of outright war, the alliances which had held the Allies together were reconsidered, and with no common enemy on which to focus, the Allied powers defaulted to each considering their own best options. The Soviet Union and the Red Army had been the Allies' greatest asset in the final months of World War Two. That same Red Army with its unparalleled armoured forces was now considered a potential threat in Europe. After a relatively short period of inaction by all the Allied powers, the inevitable realignment of post-war political and military alliances began. The Red Army de-facto held Berlin having paid the price in blood, while peace-time treaty obli-

THE RED ARMY ON PARADE 1917-45

T-34-85s of the Kantemirovskaya 4th Guards Tank Division move through Red Square, 7th November 1945. The oak leaves on the turret sides denote the division that has always historically provided the heavy armour used in Red Square military parades. The modifed turret with split-ventilators entered production in March 1945. A small number of such tanks were in combat in Czechoslovakia during the last days of the war in Europe. (Mikhail Baryatinsky)

A single surviving T-34 M-1941, (built at STZ in 1942) the tank "Kantemirovets" belonging to the Kantemirovskaya 4th Guards Tank Division, moves towards Red Square on 7th November 1945, commanded by General P.P. Poluboyarov. The only other time the early production T-34 M-1941 was seen on Red Square was 7th November 1941.

gations required that the city, and Germany, be divided into sectors among the Allies. The Berlin airlift, and the formation of new alliances under NATO and Warsaw Pact power blocs were in November 1945 all in the future. As the world celebrated peace in the final months of 1945, it was clear that the uneasy alliances of the wartime years could not be maintained, and the political map of Europe would change again dramatically in the years ahead. Within this context, the Soviet military parades would resume their pre-war role of demonstrating to the world that the armed forces of the Soviet Union were more than capable of defending the nation's interests. In the pre-war era, the Soviet Union, created from revolution in the early 20th Century, had found its place in the world alongside the old world European powers that had peaked in political and strategic status in the colonial era of the 19th Century, and were now, not least due to the result of two world wars fought on European soil, losing their political status in the world. The exponential growth in the strength of the post-war Soviet Union, politically and militarily, had been secured with the lives of an estimated 27 million of its citizens during the war. In the post-war years, there would be two "superpower" power blocks in the world, one entirely predominated by the United States and its NATO allies of variable quality and dependability, and the other being the Soviet Union and its equally diverse allies in the Warsaw Pact.

The T-34 M-1941 "Kantemirovets", which travelled from Belgorod to Prague during the war, was after the parade plinth mounted as a war memorial within the 4th Guards Kantemirovskaya Tank Division barracks at Naro-Fominsk, close to Kubinka west of Moscow. This contemporary photograph was taken in 1998. The tank has since been restored to running condition. (Andrey Aksenov)

# 7th November 1945 - Leningrad

Although Red Square in Moscow has always been the default location for Soviet parades, particularly from a foreign perspective (as it was the location to which foreign military attachés were primarily invited) the parades in Leningrad were always also substantial events. The 1945 parades, including the 7th November Leningrad parade seen here, were particularly interesting in that many of tanks were early war T-34 M-1942 and even T-34 M-1941 production models, few of which had survived by 1945. Presumably these tanks were from reserve Leningrad Military District (LVO) locations, having been damaged in battle, rebuilt but then kept locally due to having been replaced in production and front line service by the T-34-85. Leningrad was re-named St. Petersburg in 1991.

T-34 and T-34-85 tanks awaiting a parade on Dvortsovaya Ploshad (Palace Square), Leningrad, 7th November 1945. The early T-34 M-1942 tanks include one with a stamped ChKZ turret. Note the combat damage and repair on some tanks. Uritsky Square was renamed Palace Square in 1944.

THE RED ARMY ON PARADE 1917-45

T-34 tanks cross Palace Square, Leningrad, 7th November 1945. The T-34 M-1942 in the foreground has an early hull and glacis machine gun, with additional appliqué armour. In the background are a T-34 M-1943 and an early T-34 M-1941. (Mikhail Baryatinsky)

Lend-Lease Ford 2G8T trucks with 37mm M-1939 (61K) anti-aircraft guns on Palace Square, 7th November 1945. This view over the square is taken from the direction of the Hermitage, from the windows of which Tsar Nicholas II and his family looked out onto the square before revolution swept the country in 1917. (Mikhail Baryatinsky)

# 7th November 1945 - Kiev

As with Leningrad, the 1945 military parades held in Kiev, Kharkov and other cities in Ukraine also featured tanks and armoured vehicles that had seen combat. The parades also included some vehicles such as the rarely photographed ZiS-42 half-track that were never paraded on Moscow's Red Square. The ruined apartment blocks in the background of the Kiev parade were the result of the city having been lost to Axis forces, occupied and then re-taken by the Red Army during the war years.

Victory Parades and 7th November 1945 parades were held in most Soviet capitals and many other cities across the country. A T-34-85 and T-34 M-1943 on parade in Kreschatik, the main thoroughfare in Kiev, 7th November 1945.

Some military vehicles displayed in Soviet regional parades were never paraded on Moscow's Red Square. These ZiS-42M half-tracks are towing 85mm M-1939 (52K) anti-aircraft guns along Kreschatik, Kiev, 7th November 1945. (RGAKFD)

# 7th November 1945 – Other cities

While foreign attention has always primarily focused on the Red Square parades in Moscow, the Soviet Union staged annual military parades in many regional cities including the capital cities of all the Soviet republics. Some regional cities in the republics also staged annual military parades, often with significantly different military equipment to that paraded on Red Square. The Red Square parades have always been a window for foreign observers, but the military parades, during the Soviet era as now, have always been a nation-wide event.

Lend-Lease Allis-Chalmers HD-7 tracked tractors towing 152mm M-1937 (ML-20) heavy howitzers at a military parade in Riga, Latvia, 7th November 1945. (Mikhail Baryatinsky)

BA-64B armoured cars on parade in Kiev, 7th November 1945.

ISU-152s covered in a light dusting of snow on parade in Kazan, Tatarstan, 7th November 1945. The Wehrmacht had been as much unprepared for the Russian winter as they had for Soviet tenacity in the desperate winter of 1941.

THE RED ARMY ON PARADE 1917-45

# Red Army "Tekhnika" Displayed on Red Square, Moscow
# 1917-45

The Russians have a word, "tekhnika", which describes all manner of equipment of all types in a single word. In a military context, the word describes tanks, armoured cars, artillery, transport, engineering vehicles and all of the mechanised equipment used by military forces, which is clearly easier than describing all the individual types. A brief description of the main "tekhnika" displayed on Red Square in the years related in this volume is appended below.

After the Civil War the fledgling Red Army inherited 83 tanks of British and French origin, mainly British Mk. V "Rikardo" and Renault "FT-17" tanks, along with a varied collection of armoured cars of imported origin or built in Russia on imported chassis. At the end of the decade, in 1929, the Red Army had 65 tanks and 92 armoured cars in inventory. At the end of the next decade, as war embroiled Europe, the Red Army had 21,110 tanks and 2594 armoured cars in service. Two years later, as the Soviet Union was plunged into war, these numbers had risen to 23,367 tanks and 4345 armoured cars respectively. As such the Red Army in 1941 had one of the most powerful armoured forces in existence. Much of that technical and particularly numerical advantage was squandered in the early months of the war due to a lack of military leadership and tactical coordination, which was in part the result of the Red Army officer class having been decimated by Stalin's purges of the mid to late 1930s. The Red Army entered combat in 1941 with tanks, vehicles and artillery that were entirely fit for purpose, and in many cases more advanced than equivalent weapons developed by other countries. By 1945, the Red Army was equipped with tanks, armoured vehicles and transport that allowed it to deliver - together with Lend-Lease assistance that has always been acknowledged by the Soviet Union - a crushing defeat on the very German military machine that had subjugated most of Europe with little technical or tactical difficulty. The Red Army may not have been armed with equipment that had the engineering finesse of its German led Axis enemies, but in terms of producing fit for purpose military equipment designed for use with minimal training and suitable for mass production - in quantities that Germany simply could not match - it was in a league of its own. The military and industrial capability of the Soviet Union, with weapons being produced in manufacturing plants in Siberia to serve in combat in the heart of Europe, was proof if needed that the Soviet Union on the defensive was always a temporary situation, as valid in 1941 as in 1812 or immediately after 1917. In the pre-nuclear age, the armoured might of the Soviet Union was a war machine that had few rivals in the world. The armoured forces of the Red Army were the "armoured steamroller" that delivered the hammer blow to Germany's ambitions in the East, and that capability would define military thinking in the United States and Europe for decades to come.

The brief descriptions below are provided in chronological rather than numerical sequence, reflecting their service acceptance or parade debut dates.

# Armoured Cars

### BA-27

The first indigenous Soviet built armoured car was the B-27or BA-27 (BroneAvtomobil AMO M-1927 - Armoured Car Model 1927) which made its Red Square parade debut in 1929. Built at AMO on the strengthened AMO-F-15 Sp (spetsialnoe-special) chassis with armoured hull and turret sets provided by the Izhosky Plant, the BA-27 mounted the same turret as the MS-1 (T-18) light tank, armed with a 37mm PS-1 gun and a co-axial 6.5mm Fedorov or 7.62mm DT machine gun. The vehicle had an armour basis of 3-8mm and a combat weight of 4400kg. It was powered by a 35hp petrol engine which gave the vehicle a road speed of 45km/h.

The decision to accept the B-27 into service with the Red Army as the BA-27 was taken on 24th October 1927, with the first prototype BA-27 completed in January 1928 and tested for service in March 1928. The first production batch was built from January 1929 and subsequently series manufactured from October 1929 until the summer of 1931, with only between 195 and 215 BA-27 armoured cars being built in total according to conflicting sources. The BA-27 was displayed on Red Square from 7th November 1929 until replaced by FAI light and BAI medium armoured cars in 1934.

### D-8 and D-12

The D-8 (Dyrenkov-8) light armoured car was developed by the engineer N.I. Dyrenkov from 1931. The turretless reconnaissance vehicle had an armour basis of 3-7mm and was armed with a single 7.62mm DT machine gun. The vehicle was built in small numbers and displayed on Red Square in 1933-1934, together with the light FA-I and the medium BA-I armoured cars. The vehicle was not further developed, with its role being taken over by the Izhorsky plant developed FA-I. The D-12 version had a tourelle mounting for a single water cooled 7.62mm PM-1910 "Maxim" anti-aircraft machine gun. There were 45 D-12s in service with the Red Army on 1st June 1941.

### FA-I (FAI)

The first large scale production Soviet armoured cars were armoured at the Izhorsky plant, these being the FA-I light and BA-I medium armoured cars, both of which entered service at the beginning of the 1930s. The FA-I (Ford-Avtomobil Izhorsky) was the first truly series production light armoured car. The lightly armoured vehicle was built on the GAZ-A chassis and powered by a conventional 4 cylinder GAZ-AA automobile engine. Armament was a single turret mounted 7.62mm DT machine gun. The FA-I was later modernised on the GAZ-M1 chassis as the FAI-M before being replaced by the BA-20 series.

### FAI-M

The FAI-M replaced the short-lived FA-I in 1934. The modernized FAI-M mounted the original FAI hull and turret on the new GAZ-M1 chassis powered by an uprated GAZ-M engine. The GAZ-M1 had a longer chassis than the earlier GAZ-A, such that the rear of the FAI-M chassis was longer than the armoured body mounted on it, resulting in a distinctive "notch back" to the vehicle. The FAI and FAI-M were both replaced by the BA-20 series.

### BA-20 and BA-20M

The BA-20 was built at the Vyksunsky Plant on the MS-1 chassis supplied by GAZ. The original BA-20 was a modernisation of the FAI-M, based on the GAZ-M1 chassis and powered by a GAZ-M1 engine. It was armed with a turret mounted 7.62mm DT machine gun. The modernised BA-20M was introduced in 1938, with a conical turret and a whip aerial replacing the hull mounted frame aerial of the BA-20 in vehicles equipped with a 71-TK-3 radio. The BA-20 armoured car was the standard Red Army armoured car of the later 1930s and at the beginning of World War Two.

BA-27

D-12

FA-I (FAI)

BA-20M

BA-I

BAD-1 (ZhD)

BAD-2

BA-3

BA-6

BA-10A

### D-13

The D-13 (Dyrenkov-13) medium armoured car was developed from 1931 under the direction of lead engineer N.I. Dyrenkov at the Izhorsky Plant where it was also produced in small numbers. Similar to the rival BA-I, the D-13 was armed with a 37mm "Hotchkiss" (PS-1) tank gun and 7.62mm DT machine gun, and was powered by a GAZ-AA engine developing 40hp. It is one of the rarest of all Red Army armoured cars. It was paraded on Uritsky Square in Leningrad on 1st May 1933.

### BA-I (BAI)

The BA-I (BroneAvtombil-Izhorsky) was the first "series" production medium armoured car, developed by A.D. Kuzmin at the "Gudok Oktyabrya" plant near Gorky. The BA-I entered production at the Izhorsk Plant in 1932 on the Ford-Timken chassis, and was paraded in Red Square from 1933. The BA-I (also known as the BAI) was armed with a turret mounted 37mm PS-1 gun with a 34 round ammunition complement, and co-axial 7.62mm DT machine gun, with a second 7.62mm DT mounted in the hull rear. The BA-I had a crew of three, namely commander, loader and driver-mechanic. The BA-I was originally planned to be built in large numbers but due to assembly and scheduling difficulties, only 90 were completed in 1932-33 and a further 19 in 1934 (82 in total per other sources) as the Izhorsky plant moved to production of the BA-3 on a modified GAZ-AAA chassis. It should be noted the "I" was for "Izhorsk" not the numeral "1", though subsequent medium armoured cars were numerically designated BA-3, BA-6 and BA-10.

### BAD & BAD-2

Some of the most unique Red Army military vehicles were displayed in Leningrad before Moscow, and in some cases were displayed only in Leningrad. At the beginning of the 1930s, the Soviet Union began a programme to develop amphibious light tanks and armoured cars. The former entered service during the decade in the form of the T-37A, T-38 and the T-40 at the end of the decade. The latter began with development of the BAD (BAD-1) in 1931, and the later BAD-2 at OPGU from early 1932, both of which were paraded on Uritsky Square in Leningrad in 1933, but never shown in Moscow. The BAD amphibious armoured cars were followed later in the decade by the PB-4 and PB-7 which also did not enter series production.

### BA-3

The BA-3 replaced the BA-I in production at the Izhorsky plant in 1934, incorporating many changes, not least the use of a modified indigenous GAZ-AAA chassis. The BA-3 mounted the same turret and 45mm M-1932 (20K) tank gun armament as the concurrent T-26 M-1933 light tank. 180 BA-3 armoured cars were built at Izhorsky plant in 1934-35, before it was replaced in production by the BA-6.

### BA-6

The BA-6 replaced the BA-3 in production at the Izhorsky plant in 1935. The BA-6 featured a lengthened and modified hull, wider wheel track and other features such as "GK" bulletproof tyres. In addition to Red Square appearances, BA-6s of General Franco's army were paraded after the capture of Catalonia in Spain on 21st February 1939. A total of 386 BA-6 vehicles were produced from 1936-38.

### BA-10A and BA-10M

The BA-10 was a modernisation of the BA-6 developed at the Izhorsky plant KB via the BA-6M in 1936 in cooperation with GAZ. The GAZ-AAA derived GAZ-07 chassis was shortened 600mm, the hull modified accordingly, a new GAZ-M1 engine installed and the front suspension strengthened.

The new BA-10 retained the 45mm M-1934 (20K) and co-axial 7.62mm DT armament of its predecessor, with a 49 round ammunition complement. The BA-10 featured the all-welded hull of the BA-6M with a 3-10mm armour basis, mounting a new, conical welded turret also taken from the BA-6M, and armed with the 45mm M-1938 tank gun.

The BA-10 was accepted into service with the Red Army in 1938 and series produced until 1941 as the BA-10A. The BA-10A was modified as the BA-10M, which entered series production at the end of 1939. The BA-10M had detail changes, the most noticeable of which was the addition of reserve fuel tanks (containing 54.5 litres each) mounted the rear wheel guards, significantly extending overall range. The BA-10M was the final series production model of the BA medium armoured car series to be demonstrated on Red Square.

A total of 3311 BA-10A and BA-10M armoured cars were built in total at the Izhorsky plant in south eastern suburbs of Leningrad. Production ceased in September 1941 when the front line reached Kolpino where the Izhorsky plant was located.

### BA-64

The BA-64 armoured car was the only new Soviet armoured car design to enter production during the Second World War. The highly angular BA-64, based on the GAZ-64 chassis and the Izdeliye-64-125 prototype, was accepted for service with the Red Army in March 1942. Production was delayed due to various factors, not least that the GAZ plant was concentrating on the wartime production of everything from mortars to T-60 tanks, while the production of transport vehicles had been severely curtailed. The BA-64 was used by the Red Army during the last two years of the war in reconnaissance, command and communication roles. The two-man crew sat in tandem within the highly angulated hull. Standard turret armament was a 7.62mm DT machine gun, though other weapons were sometimes mounted. The original BA-64 was replaced in production by the BA-64B, mounted on the later GAZ-67B chassis, with a more powerful engine and increased track. The later and more numerous BA-64B was paraded at the Soviet Victory Parade on Red Square in June 1945.

BA-64

# Foreign Tanks

The Bolsheviks captured 83 foreign tanks of British and French origin during the civil war. Included within this total were 12 British Mk. A "Whippet" tanks (designated "Taylor" in Russian service from their engine nameplates) and a number of Mk.V tanks (designated "Rikardo" in Russian service). These tanks were used by the Red Army in the 1920s, with the Mk.A "Whippet" tanks being used until the beginning of the 1930s. The Red Army also captured a number of Renault FT-17 tanks during the Civil War, one of which was the first tank type to be paraded on Red Square and thereafter used as the prototype for the first Soviet indigenous tank, the KS.

# Light Tanks

### KS Infantry Tank

The KS (also known as the "Reno-Russky") was developed on the basis of a "Renault FT-17" tank captured near Odessa during the Russian Civil War and paraded on Red Square on 1st May 1919. The prototype Reno-Russky was completed at the Krasnoye-Sormovo Plant in Gorky (hence the designation KS) on 31st August 1920. The KS closely resembled the French prototype and in its time was a modern tank design. It was armed with a turret mounted 37mm gun and co-axial machine gun armament. The 16-18mm armour basis, 7000kg combat weight KS was powered by a petrol engine developing 33.5hp which provided the tank a maximum speed of around 9km/h, sufficient for infantry support which was the primary role of tanks at the time. A total of 15 KS tanks were built.

### T-18 (MS-1) Infantry Tank

The T-18 - also known as the MS-1 (Maly (tank) Soprovozhdeniya - small accompanying -1) tank was the first "series production" Soviet tank. Described as a manoeuvre tank, the MS-1 was armed with a 37mm PS-1 gun mounted together with a 6.5mm Fedorov (or later 7.62mm DT) machine gun in a small turret. The T-18 had an armour basis of 16-18mm and an initial combat weight of 5900kg. The engine developed 33.5hp, giving the tank a maximum speed of 8.5km/h, adequate for infantry support which was its intended role. The initial production model, sometimes designated MS-1 (T-18) M-1927, was series manufactured at the Bolshevik Plant in Leningrad from 1st February 1928 until 1930. A modified version, with a 37mm PS-1 tank gun, modified turret with turret bustle, uprated engine and maximum speed increased to 25km/h was introduced in 1930, sometimes designated MS-1 (T-18) M-1930. T-18 assembly continued until the end of 1931 when the tank was replaced in production by the mass production T-26. A total of 959 T-18s were built. The tank was the first Soviet developed and built tank to enter combat, in the autumn of 1929 in the region of Manchuria.

### T-26 Light Tank

The T-26 light tank was the default standard Red Army light tank of the 1930s and was the primary light tank type in service with the Red Army in 1941. The T-26 was developed in the Soviet Union as a indigenous modification of the British Vickers 6 ton light tank. On 28th May 1930, the Soviet government (specifically UMM RKKA, the Soviet mechanised forces command) signed a contract with Vickers to purchase 15 Vickers 6 ton light tanks with twin turrets and machine gun armament. The first tank was despatched on 22nd October 1930, the last on 4th July 1931. UMM RKKA meantime worked on modifying the design for series production in the Soviet Union via the UMM-1 and UMM-2 prototypes, with the "Vickers-26" being taken into service with the Red Army on 13th February 1931. 120 T-26 M-1931 tanks were built in 1931, and another 1410 in 1932. The original twin turreted, 7.62mm DT machine gun armed M-1931 was modified as the M-1932 with a 37mm PS-2 gun in one turret; and again in 1933 as the T-26 M-1933, with a single larger turret unified with the BT fast tank series, and initially armed with a 45mm M-1932 (20K) tank gun with a 136 round ammunition complement. The final variant of the T-26 was developed under the direction of S.A. Ginzberg at Plant №174 in Leningrad in 1936, and was to have been introduced in 1937; however there were delays in its implementation, some technical, others related to Stalin's purges, such that the final production model did not enter series production until 1938. The T-26 when fitted with a sloped turret but retaining the vertical hull side armour was often designated T-26 M-1938, with the final

*KS*

*T-18*

*T-26 M-1931*

*T-26 M-1933*

*T-26 M-1938-40.*

model with sloped hull armour and other modifications to communications and night fighting capability being designated T-26 M-1939, but the final production model T-26 was built in a myriad of variants, hence is sometimes designated T-26 M-1938-40. The T-26 was manufactured at Plant №174 in Leningrad, with 11,218 T-26 tanks being built in 1931-41 in three main variants and 53 modifications.

### T-27 Tankette

The diminutive T-27 tankette, derived from the British Carden-Loyd Mk VI tankette, was taken into service with the Red Army on 13th February 1931, with the tankette having its public debut on Red Square on 7th November 1932. The T-27 was used in large numbers by the Red Army in the early 1930s and although as with all tankettes it was not a particularly practical war machine, it gave thousands of tank crew vital training experience. The T-27 had a two man crew and was armed with a single 7.62mm DT machine gun. The armour basis was 4-10mm, with a combat weight of 2700kg. Power was provided by a GAZ-AA engine developing 40hp. A total of 3295 T-27 tankettes were produced, including specialist variants.

### T-37A Amphibious Reconnaissance Tank

The T-37 amphibious reconnaissance tank was a development of the British Vickers A4E11/A4E12 amphibious light tanks designed in 1930/31. The 7.62mm DT machine gun armed T-37 was tested alongside the alternative T-33 and T-41 tanks, and was accepted for service with the Red Army in 1933. The series production T-37A was produced from the summer of 1933. In total 2627 tanks were built, including 643 command and 75 KhT chemical tank versions.

### T-38 Amphibious Reconnaissance Tank

The T-37A was replaced in production by the N.A. Astrov designed T-38, the prototype of which was completed in June 1935. The T-38 had a wider, flatter hull providing improved buoyancy and stability in water, and a relocated turret. The T-38 retained the 7.62mm DT armament of the earlier tank, and performed the same reconnaissance roles as its predecessor. Power was again provided by a four cylinder GAZ-AA engine developing 40hp coupled to an automotive transmission. The T-38 entered series production in the spring of 1936, with 1382 built in total. The T-38 was replaced by the T-40, which was never displayed on Red Square.

### T-60 Small Tank

The wartime production T-60 was developed at Plant №37 but due to the outbreak of war and plant evacuation was produced at several plants including the GAZ automotive plant. The T-60 appeared only once on Red Square, on 7th November 1941, with the T-60s used during the parade subsequently used in the defence of Moscow. The T-60 tanks paraded included a small number fitted with the conical turret originally developed for the T-30. Some tanks, such as the wartime T-70 which replaced the T-60 in 1943, were never paraded on Red Square due to the timescale during which they served.

### PT-1 Amphibious Tank

The PT-1 amphibious tank was developed in 1930 by the later famous N.Astrov while he was at the OGPU design institute. The original PT-1 prototype was built at the "Krasny Proletarii" plant in Moscow in 1932 and was tested at the NIIBT polygon (today Kubinka). The large tank, fitted with the same turret at the T-26 M-1933, BT tanks and the BA-3 and BA-6 armoured cars, and armed with a 45mm tank gun, was demonstrated on Red Square only once, in May 1934. The original PT-1 was later modified as the PT-1A but the design was considered too heavy as a practical amphibious reconnaissance tank. The design specification would re-appear two decades later in the form of the PT-76 amphibious light tank.

T-27

T-37A

T-38

T-60

PT-1

# Fast and Medium Tanks

BT-2

BT-2

BT-5

BT-7 M-1935

BT-7 M-1937

### BT-2 Fast Tank

The BT "Bystry Tank" - fast tank) series was also developed as the result of a technology transfer arrangement, this time via the United States and the American tank designer Walter J. Christie, whose ideas fell on deaf ears in the US Ordnance department, but were to be widely used on "fast" or cruiser tanks in other countries, particularly Great Britain and the Soviet Union. A Soviet purchasing commission secured a contract with Christie's US Wheel Track Layer Corporation to purchase two M-1931 development tanks based on Christie's own M-1928 design, to be supplied without turrets or armament. These tanks arrived in the Soviet Union in 1931 and are sometimes referred to as the "BT-1". As with the T-26, a local redesign was undertaken in minimum time, modifying the Christie tank for local service specifics and production capabilities. The original BT-2 was series produced from 1932-33, armed with a 37mm M-1930 tank gun (208 built) or twin 7.62mm DT machine guns (412 built). The BT-2 was powered by a powerful but capricious M-5 aviation derived engine developing 400hp. Early BT series tanks could run on tracks at up to 52km/h or on wheels at up to 72km/h, for which the description "fast" is entirely appropriate for the early 1930s. The BT-2 was engaged in combat serving with the 11th Tank Brigade in the Khalkin Gol clashes with Japan long before the outbreak of World War Two in Europe.

### BT-5 Fast Tank

The BT-5 replaced the BT-2 in production in 1933. The BT-5 was a major modernisation of the original design, fitted with a new turret unified with the T-26 light tank, and similarly armed with the 45mm M-1932 tank gun and a co-axial 7.62mm DT machine gun, with a significant 115 round main ammunition complement. When fitted with a 71-TK-1 radio, the main ammunition complement was reduced to 72 rounds. The capricious M-5 engine of the BT-2 was retained while an alternative was being designed. The BT-5 could also run on tracks at 52km/h or on wheels at 75km/h, with road ranges of 150km and 220km respectively. A total of 2108 BT-5 tanks were built from 1933 to 1935, with the tank appearing on Red Square in parades in the mid 1930s. As with the BT-2, the BT-5 saw action in the Khalkin Gol region against Japan in 1939 well before the outbreak of World War Two on the Eastern Front.

### BT-7 Fast Tank

The BT-7 was a modernisation of the earlier BT-5, introduced in 1935 and built in three main production variants, the original BT-7 M-1935 (with cylindrical turret), later M-1937 (with conical turret) and the final V-2 diesel engined variant, the BT-7 M-1939 (BT-7M). The BT-7 was fitted with the modified 45mm M-1934 tank gun together with co-axial and secondary 7.62mm DT machine guns. The BT-7 M-1935 had an impressive ammunition complement of 172 rounds. The BT-7 M-1935 and later M-1937 were powered by the M-17T V-12 petrol engine developing 400hp and had similar performance, with a maximum road speed of 50km/h on tracks or 70km/h on wheels, with respective ranges of 230km and 350km. A total of 4965 BT-7 M-1935 and M-1937 tanks were built. The final production model BT-7 M-1939 (BT-7M) of which 790 were built, was developed from as early as 1936 at KhPZ (Plant №183) in Kharkov, but entered series production only in December 1939 due to disruption on the project caused by mass arrests at the plant at the time of Stalin's political purges. The tank was powered by a V-2 diesel engine developing 400hp and was used for particularly impressive high speed traverses of Red Square for the benefit of domestic and foreign camera crews. The BT-7 series was regularly paraded on Red Square from 1936-41.

### T-24 Medium Tank

The limited production T-24 was one of the earliest indigenous Soviet tank designs. In accordance with an UMM RKKA order dated 27th March 1930, an Establishment Lot of 15 tanks was built in late 1930 at KhPZ in Kharkov based on armour components provided by the Izhorsky Plant and using the same running gear and automotive components as later used for the Komintern artillery tractor. The "Establishment Lot" was completed by September 1930, with a total of 25 tanks built in Kharkov before production was curtailed.

The T-24 tank was armed with a turret mounted 45mm tank gun, powerful for its time, with an ammunition complement of 89 rounds, but was mechanically complex, such that mass series production was impractical. Production was terminated after, somewhat coincidentally, 24 tanks had been completed, together with a few additional hulls for firing trials. Though never paraded on Red Square, a T-24 tank participated in a parade held in Kharkov on 1st May 1932, together with T-26 M-1932 light tanks and BT fast tanks. The T-24 chassis and mechanical components formed the basis for the Komintern tracked artillery tractor, which was produced in relatively large numbers.

T-24

T-28

# Medium Tanks

### T-28 Medium Tank

The multi-turreted T-28 was the standard Red Army medium tank of the 1930s, complementing the BT series which was used in the fast tank or cavalry role. The T-28 was accepted for Red Army service in August 1933 and was produced at LKZ in Leningrad until 1940. The tank was assigned to the RVGK (strategic command reserve) for use as a breakthrough tank. The prototype, assembled in mild steel and armed with a 45mm M-1932 tank gun and three DT machine guns was completed in May 1932 and was paraded on Red Square only once in that year.

The first and second series production models, the T-28 M-1933 (41 built) and T-28 M-1934 (266 built) were armed with a 76.2mm KT-28 (PS-3) tank gun, with the later T-28 M-1938 (131 built in 1938-40) armed with the more powerful 76.2mm L-10 tank gun. As a result of combat feedback from the 1939-40 "Winter War" with Finland, the up-armoured T-28Э M-1940 was introduced into production (111 built), with the rarest version being the T-28 M-1940 fitted with a conical main turret, of which only 13 were built. T-28 tanks produced from 1935 as sometimes designated T-28A.

The T-28 with its main turret and two machine gun sub turrets was an impressive tank in its day, particularly for parade purposes. The tank was used in combat during the Russo-Finnish "Winter War" of 1939-40 and subsequently during the opening stages of "Operation Barbarossa" the German Axis invasion of the Soviet Union. The T-28 was however by the eve of World War Two an outdated design, a large target with significant areas of vertical armour plate, and combat losses were as might be expected for such an obsolete design.

### T-34 Medium Tank

Despite having been in series production for some time before the outbreak of war, the most famous of all Soviet tanks, the original 76.2mm armed T-34, did not appear on parade on Red Square until the 7th November 1941 parade. Many prototypes and pre-series tanks had been paraded through Red Square in the 1930s, but the T-34 medium and KV heavy tanks were noticeable by their absence in 1939 and 1940. The early T-34 M-1940 production model, armed with the 76.2mm L-11 gun, had entered production at KhPZ in Kharkov in 1940, with 115 built that

T-28

T-28Э (Eh) M-1940

T-34

T-34-85

T-34-85

T-34-85

year, and by June 1941 a further 1129 had been built, while the KV was in production at LKZ in Leningrad, so this was clearly a case of then Soviet Union maintaining secrecy with regard to their latest designs as war approached.

The original 76.2mm armed T-34 was demonstrated in M-1941 production model guise on Red Square only in November 1941, as the Battle for Moscow raged, being at its closest point only 16 kilometres away from Red Square. The T-34-76 M-1941s which were paraded through Red Square on 7th November were a few days later sent directly to the front.

Although later 76.2mm F-34 armed T-34 tanks, the T-34 M-1942, T-34 M-1943 and some early T-34 M-1941s were paraded in the Victory Parades in Leningrad in 1945 and even in Harbin, none were paraded in Moscow, as so few had survived on the "Western" front. The 1945 Victory Parade in Moscow featured T-34-85s (actually newly manufactured OT-34-85 flamethrower tanks); however, after the end of the war, on 7th November 1945, a single 1942 production T-34-76 M-1941, named "Kantemirovets" which had fought its way from Voronezh in Russia via Zhitomir and Lvov (today Lviv) in Ukraine to Krakow in Poland, then via Dresden in Germany to its final wartime operation at Prague in Czechoslovakia was paraded through Red square in front of columns of later T-34-85s.

It should be noted that the Soviets never designated the T-34-76 as such, rather it was known only as the T-34 followed by the production year, e.g. T-34 M-1941, while the later T-34-85 was designated as T-34 with 85mm gun, T-34-85.

### T-34-85 Medium Tank

The T-34-85 began to replace the T-34 in production from late 1943. The modified tank mounted a new, enlarged turret and was armed with a 85mm D-5T or later S-53 tank gun which provided parity with the armament of the latest Axis tanks. The T-34-85 had seen combat in the final assault on Berlin before it made its parade debut appearance on Moscow's Red Square on 1st May 1945. The T-34-85 was paraded on Red Square in the late 1940s before being replaced in service by the T-54. The T-34-85 is still used during commemorative Victory Day anniversary parades on Red Square. On 9th May 2017 a single T-34-85 led the 9th May Victory Parade on Red Square, followed by T-90A and T-14 "Armata" MBTs, 74 years after it entered service with the Red Army and 72 years after it was first demonstrated on Red Square.

# Heavy Tanks

### T-35 Heavy Tank
One of the great Soviet crowd-pleasers of all time was the T-35 heavy tank, the tracked land-battleship, which in the mid 1930s represented the epitome of Soviet heavy tank development. The first T-35 prototype, the T-35-1 was assembled at KhPZ in Kharkov from 1931 and made its public debut on Red Square on 7th November 1932. The T-35-1 was armed with a 76.2mm PS-3 (KT) tank gun and two 37mm PS-2 guns in auxiliary turrets, with another two subsidiary turrets with 7.62mm DT machine guns. Power was provided by an M6 petrol engine developing 300hp. The T-35-2 prototype featured changes to the construction, including a new turret unified with the T-28 design but retaining the 76.2mm PS-3 (KT) gun armament of the T-35-1. Power was provided by an M-17T engine developing 500hp. The T-35-1 and T-35-2 prototypes were displayed together on Red Square in November 1933.

The definitive production T-35A was developed in 1932-1933, concurrently with the T-35-2 prototype, retaining the 76.2mm PS-3 (KT) tank gun in the main turret but with 45mm M-1932 tank guns in the auxiliary turrets. It was approved for series production on 11th August 1933 and was assembled at KhPZ (Plant №183) in Kharkov from 1933 to 1939, the tank being a regular Red Square parade participant throughout the 1930's. The final production model, with conical turrets, was displayed on Red Square in 1939 and 1940 alongside the earlier standard T-35A production model. The Red Square parades were the T-35s finest moment. Less than 65 Only 61 of these amazing tanks were built, and all but one lost in the opening weeks of Operation Barabarossa, the only survivor being the trials evaluation tank kept at the Kubinka proving grounds, which was used in the defence of Moscow. The T-35s were for the most part not lost in combat, but rather were abandoned and destroyed by their crews, primarily after mechanical breakdown, lack of fuel or ammunition. While the obsolescent final production model T-35s were displayed on Red Square as late as May 1941, the prototype T-100, SMK and the "small turret KV" (the KV-1) – the latter then in series production - were conspicuous by their absence during the final pre-war parades of 1940 and 1941.

### KV-1 Heavy Tank
The KV-1 entered series production at the LKZ plant in Leningrad in 1940, and yet, like the T-34, it did not make an appearance on Red Square during the May or November 1940 parades, in stark contrast to the 1930s when many prototypes made their parade debut on Red Square before the type had been accepted for series production. The KV-1, like the early T-34, was paraded only once on Red Square, on 7th November 1941. The freshly built KV-1 tanks paraded on Red Square were built at ChTZ in Chelyabinsk in October 1941, armed with the 76.2mm ZiS-5 tank gun and with the cylindrical supplementary track fender fuel tanks common to the model. The tanks displayed on Red Square on 7th November 1941 belonged to the 89th Independent Tank Brigade of the 16th Army.

### IS-2 Heavy Tank
The IS-2 heavy entered service with the Red Army in 1944 and was used to great effect during the final two years of the Second World War. The IS-2 became highly symbolic of the Red Army "armoured steamroller" and victory in Europe when photographed outside the Reichstag in Germany. The IS-2 had its parade debut on Red Square on 1st May 1945 as the war was in its final days, at which time the IS-2 was also in evidence for the world to see parked up in front of the Reichstag and the Brandenburg Gate in Berlin.

T-35

T-35

KV-1

KV-1Э (Eh)

IS-2

### IS-3 Heavy Tank

The IS-3 heavy tank was unveiled at the Allied Victory Parade in Berlin in September 1945, much to the surprise of the Allied commanders present. The IS-3 retained the venerable 122mm D-25T tank gun of the IS-2, but the IS-3 was a sleek, low profile design with steeply angled hull armour, including a "schuka" pike nose plate, and a particularly low profile and apparently ballistically perfect turret. The IS-3 was without doubt an advanced tank, but had been rushed into production, and as such was capricious and particularly high-maintenance in service. The IS-3 was latterly rebuilt in tank repair plants as the IS-3M, after which it was immediately placed in strategic storage. An earlier and less extensive upgrade was exported to the Middle East with these exported tanks participating in the Arab Israeli wars of 1967 and 1973.

IS-3

SU-1-12

SU-76M

SU-100

ISU-122

# Self-Propelled Artillery

### SU-12 (SU-1-12)

The first wheeled Red Army SPG was the SU-12 (SU-1-12). The vehicle consisted of the 76.2mm M-1927 Regimental Gun with an armoured shield, turntable mounted on the chassis of the GAZ-AAA (SU-12-1) and imported American Moreland (SU-12) chassis at the Krasny Putilovets plant in Leningrad from 1933 to 1935. The SU-12 and SU-12-1 had their combined parade debut on 1st May 1933. It was first displayed in Leningrad and latterly in Moscow, with 51 being built on the GAZ-AAA chassis and 48 on the Moreland chassis.

### SU-76M

The SU-76 SPG was a dual purpose self propelled artillery and close support weapon, mounting the 76.2mm ZiS-3 dual-purpose gun on a chassis heavily modified from the T-70 light tank. The SU-76M was extensively used in the latter half of the Second World War on the Eastern Front, and was second only to the T-34 in terms of production output. The SU-76M had its public debut on Red Square in 1945.

### SU-100

The SU-100 entered service in 1944, based heavily on the earlier SU-85. The SU-100 mounted the highly effective 100mm D-10S gun, derived from a naval weapon, which, later modified as the 100mm D-10T would become in the post-war era standard armament on the T-44, T-54 and T-55. The SU-100 was a highly potent tank killer, and was used in the final year of the Second World War. It was paraded on Red Square in 1945 and for several years thereafter. The SU-100 was also assembled postwar in Czechoslovakia and was widely exported.

### ISU-122

The ISU-122 heavy assault gun was built on the chassis of the IS-2 heavy tank and mounted the 122mm A-19 gun as used on the 122mm M-1931 (A-19) towed "Corps Duplex" artillery piece. The later ISU-122 entered service in March 1944. Though defined as an "SAU" or self propelled gun, it was almost exclusively used in the overwatch tank killer role. The ISU-122 was displayed on Red Square from 1945 until the early 1950s. The ISU-122S, which was distinguished by its ball mount mantlet, was also displayed on Red Square in small numbers in the immediate post-war parades.

### ISU-152

The ISU-152 entered service in 1944 alongside the ISU-122. Armed with the 152mm M-1937

(ML-20S) howitzer, the weapon, which was also technically designated "SAU" or self propelled gun (howitzer) was a highly effective tank destroyer, used to great effect in the final stages of World War Two. It was paraded through Red Square from 1945 until the end of the 1940s.

There followed a gap of more than two decades between the wartime generation of self-propelled artillery vehicles, which were primarily close support weapons, and the introduction of the GRAU index "2S" self-propelled artillery family from the early 1970s. An entire generation of self propelled guns was developed in the intervening years, but none entered service, the Soviet Union continuing to rely on towed artillery systems long after other countries had mechanised their artillery.

ISU-152

# Towed Artillery

### 45mm M-1932/1937/1942 Anti-Tank Gun
Development of the 45mm M-1932 anti-tank gun began in 1930, with the first series production version of the weapon being accepted for service with the Red Army in 1932. The 45mm M-1932 was superseded in production by the 45mm M-1937 (53K), which featured a monoblock breech and other manufacturing and operational improvements. The final production model was the wartime 45mm M-1942 (M-42) which was recognisable by its a significantly longer barrel. The weapons were manufactured at Plants №8, №172 and №235. The later and more powerful 45mm M-1942 could penetrate 51mm of vertical armour at 1000m, or up to 61mm at 500m.

### 57mm M-1941/1943 (ZiS-2) Anti-Tank Gun
The 57mm ZiS-2 anti-tank gun was a highly effective weapon developed immediately prior to the outbreak of World War Two, with a tank gun variant, the ZiS-4, installed in a small number of T-34-57 tanks.

Production of the original 57mm M-1941 was stopped prematurely in favour of the dual-purpose 76.2mm ZiS-3 despite its effectiveness as an anti-tank weapon, with production later re-started at Plant №92 as the 57mm M-1943, again primarily for its better anti-tank capability. The 57mm ZiS-2 was used throughout the Second World War and was displayed on Red Square in the immediate post-war years, with production continuing post war at Plant №235. The weapon looked very similar to the 76.2mm ZiS-3 dual purpose gun, with an almost identical gun carriage, but had a smooth barrel with no muzzle brake.

### 76.2mm M-1927 Regimental Gun
The 76.2mm M-1927 Regimental Gun was a common infantry support weapon which entered service with the Red Army in 1928. It was displayed on Red Square during the 1930s towed behind a variety of vehicles, and was widely used albeit in decreasing numbers throughout the Second World War.

### 76.2mm M-1936 (F-22) Divisional Gun
The 76.2mm M-1936 divisional gun was accepted for service with the Red Army in 1936. The weapon was designed as a dual purpose universal gun, but proved difficult to manufacture with some inherent design faults. Production ceased in 1939, a relatively short production run, the weapon being replaced by the 76.2mm M-1939 (USV). The weapon was used in combat against Japan in the Battles of Lake Khasan and Khalkin Gol and in the Russo-Finnish Winter War before the outbreak of war with Germany in 1941.

57mm M-1941/43 (ZiS-2)

76.2mm M-1927 Regimental Gun

76.2mm M-1936 (F-22) Divisional Gun

On 1st June the Red Army had 2844 76.2mm M-1936 (F-22) guns in service, of which some survived late into the war.

### 76.2mm M-1939 (USV) Divisional Gun

The 76.2mm M-1939 divisional gun was developed from 1937 as a service replacement for the 76mm M-1902/30 divisional gun and also the 76.2mm M-1936 (F-22) divisional gun which was considered not sufficiently modernised for long term application and also had awkwardly placed sights for use in a dual-purpose or anti-tank role. The 76.2mm M-1939 was adopted for service with the Red Army in 1939. It is also known as the F-22 and the USV. The weapon was series manufactured from 1939-41, there being 1070 "USV" weapons in service on 1st June 1941. The weapon was replaced in service by the 76.2mm M-1941/42 ZiS-3.

### 76.2mm M-1941/42 (ZiS-3) Dual Purpose Gun

The dual-purpose 76.2mm M-1942 (ZiS-3) divisional gun was used during World War Two as a field gun and also in the anti-tank role, in which it was highly effective. It was displayed on Red Square in the immediate post-war years, towed by ZiS-5 and Studebaker US6 trucks, and later even the BTR-152. The weapon was also mounted in the SU-76 self propelled gun which was second only to the T-34 in terms of production output during World War Two.

### 100mm M-1944 (BS-3) Dual Purpose Gun

The 100mm M-1944 (BS-3) anti-tank gun entered service with the Red Army in 1944 and was used both as an anti-tank weapon and as an artillery piece. The weapon was closely related to the 100mm D-10S mounted in the SU-100 SAU and fired the same ammunition types. Although used in relatively small numbers, the weapon was a powerful tank destroyer. Firing the BR-412 armour-piercing round the BS-3 could penetrate 150-170mm of vertical armour at a range of 1000m and 190mm if the distance was closed to 500m.

### 122mm M-1910/30 Divisional Howitzer

The 122mm M-1910 divisional howitzer was used during the First World War and the Russian Civil War, and modified as the M-1910/30 was used against the Japanese during the Battles of the Khalkin Gol and in the early stages of World War Two. The weapon fired a 21.76kg HE-Frag shell to a maximum range of 8940m, with a rate of fire of 5-6 rounds/minute. The original 122mm M-1910 was updated as the M-1910/30 with some simplifications, new sights, a strengthened gun carriage with modified wheels and suspension, and new limbers, allowing the (originally horse drawn) howitzer to be towed at higher road speeds behind motorized transport. 3395 M-1910/30 howitzers were built in Perm in the years 1937-41, and 762 M-1910 howitzers were rebuilt to M-1910/30 standard.

### 122mm M-1938 (M-30) Howitzer

The 122mm M-1938 (M-30) Howitzer was a standard Red Army towed howitzer used throughout the Second World War and modernised thereafter.

### 122mm M-1931/37 Corps Gun

The 122mm M-1931/37 was a modification of the earlier 122mm M-1931 "Corps Duplex" heavy artillery field gun, with various modifications including the use of stamped disc wheels with an element of suspension in the tyres, replacing the spoked pattern, solid rubber rims of the earlier variant. The 122mm M-1931/37 (and its earlier variant) were a common sight during Red Square parades in the 1930s and in the immediate post-war era. The weapon was mounted in the ISU-122 self propelled gun where it was a particularly potent tank killer.

### 152mm M-1937 (ML-20) Corps Howitzer

The 152mm M-1937 (ML-20) "Corps Duplex" heavy artillery field howitzer was used in a similar role to the 122mm M-1931/37 field gun. The weapon was used throughout the Second World War and was particularly effective in destroying hard points and bunkers, and also enemy tanks

*76.2mm M-1939 (USV) Divisional Gun*

*76.2mm M-1942 (ZiS-3) Dual Purpose Gun*

*100mm M-1944 (B-3) Dual Purpose Gun*

*100mm M-1944 (BS-3) Dual Purpose Gun*

when required to do so due to the sheer weight of projectile rather than its terminal velocity. The 152mm M-1937 (ML-20) was mounted in the SU-152 and later ISU-152 self propelled guns and was a potent killer of German medium and heavy tanks, hence the description "Zvereboi" or animal hunter for the self-propelled version.

### 152mm M-1935 (Br-2) Tracked Gun

The 152mm M-1935 (Br-2) tracked gun-howitzer was developed at Plant №232, the "Bolshevik" plant, with series production undertaken at Plant №221, the "Barrikady" plant using the same tracked gun carriage as the 203mm M-1931 B-4 howitzer. The weapon was primarily used in the Red Army for destroying reinforced emplacements and other hard targets and had a range of up to 25,750m depending on ammunition type, with a rate of fire of 1 round per minute. With a firing weight of 18,200kg and a transport weight of 19,500kg, the weapon required a tracked artillery tractor to move it. The 152mm (152.4mm) M-1935 (Br-2) was mounted in the SU-14-2 self propelled gun.

The tracked 152mm Br-2 gun-howitzer was displayed on Red Square during the 1930s. Similar in appearance to the 203mm B-4 tracked howitzer, the 152mm Br-2 had a distinctively longer gun barrel.

### 203mm M-1931 (B-4) Tracked Howitzer

The 203mm B-4 tracked howitzer was developed from 1927 by the Artillery Committee GAU under the direction of F.F. Lender. With a firing weight of 17,700kg, the tracked weapon was a particularly heavy but stable firing platform. The weapon fired 100kg high-explosive fragmentation and specialised concrete piercing rounds, with a maximum range of 18,000m, with a rate of fire of one round every 1-2 minutes. A total of 889 were produced over a particularly long production period. A favourite "bunker buster", the weapon was highly effective in built up areas during the last months of the war, bringing down entire buildings where snipers were present. The weapon was usually transported over long distances in two loads, barrel and gun carriage at a maximum speed of 15km/h. The 203mm B-4 was modified post-war as the B-4M, now mounted on a wheeled gun carriage and maintained in service for several years despite its obsolescence, primarily on the basis that it could fire the 203mm 3BV2 nuclear round.

### 210mm M-1939 (Br-17) Gun and 305mm M-1939 (Br-18) Howitzer (RVGK)

The similar looking 210mm Br-17 gun and 305mm Br-18 howitzer were large calibre weapons developed immediately before World War Two on the basis of a licence production agreement with the Czechoslovakian company Skoda signed in 1938. Both weapons were accepted into service in 1939, but at the outbreak of war on 22nd June 1941, a total of only nine 210mm Br-17 guns and three 305mm Br-18 howitzers had been built at Plant №221, the "Barrikady" plant. The gun carriages for these exotic weapons were nearly identical. The 210mm Br-17 fired a 135kg HE-Frag and 154kg anti-concrete rounds with a maximum range of 29,400m depending on ammunition type, with a rate of fire of 1 round every 2 minutes. The 305mm Br-18 howitzer fired the same ammunition types but with the rounds being 330kg and 465kg respectively, with a range of up to 16,580m depending on ammunition type. Although being a heavy howitzer the range was far less, the 305mm anti-concrete round was capable of destroying reinforced concrete up to 2.1m thick. The Br-18 had a rate of fire of 1 round every 3 minutes. Both weapons had a transport weight of approximately 54,000kg, with the barrel of the 305mm Br-18 having a weight of 12,400kg , hence the barrel was removed from the carriage for transport. These exotic systems were accordingly displayed on Red Square broken down into carriage and barrel sections and towed behind tracked tractors.

152mm M-1937 (ML-20) Howitzer

152mm M-1937 ML-20 Howitzer

152mm Br-2 Gun

203mm B-4 Howitzer

210mm Br-17 Gun

25mm 94KM Anti-Aircraft Gun

76.2mm M 1915 Anti-Aircraft Gun

Z-15-4 Searchlight

ZT-5 Sound Locator

### 25mm 94KM (72K) Anti-Aircraft System
The 25mm 94KM anti-aircraft gun system was introduced to service with Red Army in late 1939. It is sometimes designated the 25mm M-1940 anti-aircraft gun. The weapon, which had a practical 70rpm rate-of-fire provided short-range anti-aircraft support with a firing altitude of 2000m and 6000m range. It was displayed on Red Square immediately before and after World War Two.

### 76.2mm M-1915 (ZU-25) and M-1915/28 (ZU-29) Anti-Aircraft System
The World War One era 76mm M-1915 (ZU-25) anti-aircraft gun was displayed on Red Square during the 1920s, towed by Bolshevik and latterly Kommunar artillery tractors. The weapon was mounted on a twin axle carriage with spoked wheels and fold down sections forming a circular base for the gun crew. The gun carriage, specifically the suspension and wheels and tyres, were modernised in the late 1920s, the latter variant sometimes being designated 76mm M-1915/28.

### 85mm M-1939 and M-1944 Anti-Aircraft Guns
The 85mm M-1939 anti-aircraft gun entered service with the Red Army in 1939. It was primarily used as an anti-aircraft weapon, but was also supplied with 53-UBr-365 and 365K anti-tank rounds. In the anti-aircraft mode the weapon had a firing altitude of 10,230m and a horizontal range of 15,650m.

### Z-15-4B Searchlight
The Z-15-B searchlight was commonly paraded on Red Square in the pre-war 1930s and was also paraded during the June 1945 Victory Parade in Moscow. It was produced from 1937 until 1942, at the Moscow "Kaganovich" projector plant and at Plant №686 in Novosibirsk, with 15,529 manufactured in total. The 1.5m diameter 650 million candle power searchlight could light up targets at a maximum range of 7-9km. It was mounted on the ZiS-12 truck and was used in conjunction with the ZT-5 sound locator.

### ZT-2, ZT-4, ZT-5 Sound Locators
The curious looking but effective ZT series "zvukoulavlivatel" or sound locators were used to locate aircraft by amplifying their approaching engine noise. They were used in conjunction with mobile searchlight systems.

The ZT-2 was an early trailer mounted which was displayed on Red Square towed behind a ZiS-5. The later ZT-4 and ZT-5 systems were usually mounted directly on GAZ-AAA and ZiS-6 truck chassis. The ZT-5 was manufactured from 1937 at the Moscow "Kaganovich" projector plant.

### Multiple Rocket Systems
The BM-8, BM-13 and BM-31 multiple rocket launchers all entered service after the outbreak of World War Two, and were therefore displayed on Red Square only in 1945, all mounted on the Lend-Lease Studebaker US6 chassis.

# Military Transport

### AM-600 Motorcycle

The AM-600 military motorcycle was assembled at the Taganrog Instrument Plant (hence sometimes designated TIZ AM-600) from 1935 to 1941. The motorcycle was a Soviet development of a British BSA design, powered by a 595cm$^3$ sidevalve 4 stroke engine developing 18hp, coupled to a 4 speed gearbox, giving a maximum speed of 95km/h. The AM-600, which was built in mono and sidecar combination configurations, was a common participant in Red Square parades in the late 1930s. It was also produced at the Tyumen Motozavod.

### M-72 Motorcycle

The M-72 military motorcycle was a development of the BMW R-71 design. It featured a 2 cylinder 746cm$^3$ 4 stroke engine developing 22hp, coupled to a 4 speed gearbox which gave a maximum road speed of 110km/h. It was built in Moscow from 1941, with manufacturing after plant evacuation being re-established at Irbit in the Urals and the Gorky Motozavod. The first M-72 was despatched to the Red Army on 26th February 1942, with 6000 being built in the war years 1941-45. The M-72 remained in production post-war until 1960 in various guises. The M-72 was built in mono and sidecar combination configurations, the latter having a capacity of three people plus 100kg of cargo.

### Russo-Balt "Prombron-1"

The Russo-Baltisky Vagonny Zavod (RBVZ) plant in Riga began series production of light passenger cars in 1909, with the best known vehicles being the S-24 series. The plant also began to build armoured cars in small numbers. After the Russian Revolution, the plant was nationalised and became the first Russian state armour plant (BTAZ №1), specialising in the assembly and re-build of armoured cars. In 1922, the plant built its first vehicle designed specifically for military use, based on the Russo-Balt S-24-40, and designated "Prombron-1", which was demonstrated to the political and military leadership of the country in 1922.

### AMO-F-15 4x2 Truck

The AMO-F-15 was the first Soviet indigenous design to be series manufactured. Based on the FIAT F-15ter design, which was assembled at AMO in Moscow from 1917-1919 and also displayed on Red Square, the 1.5 tonne payload 4x2 AMO-F-15 was used in general service and specialist roles including anti-aircraft, sound locator and searchlight vehicle. The first prototype AMO-F-15 was completed on 1st November 1924, with ten completed by 6th November, all of which had their public debut on Moscow's Red Square the following day. The AMO F-15 was paraded on Red Square in general service, anti-aircraft gun, searchlight and ZT-4 sound locator configurations. The relatively short-lived AMO-F-15 was replaced by the mass production GAZ-AA in the early 1930s. The strengthened AMO-F-15Sp chassis was used for the BA-27 armoured car.

### GAZ-A 4x2 Light Vehicle

The GAZ-A passenger car was produced at GAZ as a licence production version of the American Ford-A, modified for Soviet road conditions. The 4 seat 4x2 GAZ-A was powered by a GAZ-A engine developing 40hp, which gave the vehicle a maximum road speed of 95km/h. It was series produced from 1932-36 and was used by the Red Army as an officer transport and liaison vehicle. The base variant was paraded on Red Square in the early 1930s, later followed by specialist versions such as the 5AK radio station. The Red Army had 2757 GAZ-A vehicles in service on 1st May 1941.

### GAZ-4 Pikap

The GAZ-4 was a 4x2 pick-up (hence "pikap") 500kg capacity load carrier version of the GAZ-A, which was produced from 1933 to 1937. The vehicle, with its 40hp GAZ-A engine, could transport a 500kg load at road speeds of up to 90km/h. It was used in the Red Army in a variety of roles including communications and even as a light anti-aircraft mount. The Red Army had 545 GAZ-4 "Pikap" vehicles in service on 1st May 1941. They were occasionally paraded on Red Square in the mid 1930s but were more common in parades in other cities.

GAZ-AA

### GAZ-67 Light Vehicle

The GAZ-67 entered production at GAZ in 1942 as a Soviet version of the American "Jeep", based on the earlier limited series production GAZ-64. The GAZ-67 was powered by a petrol engine developing 54hp, which provided the command and reconnaissance vehicle with a 450kg load capacity and a 90km/h maximum road speed. The GAZ-67 was produced from May 1942, with sporadic production at GAZ due to other priorities at the plant. 2500 were nevertheless delivered to the Red Army during the war years, and the GAZ-67 appeared on Red square in 1945. The BA-64 armoured car series was based on the GAZ-67 (and later on the modernized GAZ-67B) chassis.

GAZ-MM

GAZ-AA with 25mm M-1940 (94KM)

### GAZ-AA 4x2 Truck

The GAZ-AA was the first 4x2 truck to be series produced in the Soviet Union using mass production techniques. The GAZ-AA was a 1.5 tonne load carrier version of the Ford-AA modified and strengthened for operation on Russian roads. The first Establishment Lot was built at the end of January 1932, with the GAZ-AA being produced in huge numbers and serving with the Red Army in load carrier and numerous specialized roles. The GAZ-MM was introduced in 1938, with an uprated engine and other modifications. The wartime production GAZ-MM-V featured numerous simplifications including the use of angular welded rather than stamped rounded wheel fenders, wooden and latterly wooden and canvas cab construction, reduced lighting and braking. The GAZ-AA in all variants was by far the most common vehicle in service with the Red Army before

ZiS-5

ZiS-5

and during the Second World War. The Red Army had 102,462 GAZ-AA/MMs in service on 1st January 1941, with a further 78,000 delivered to the Red Army during the war years.

### GAZ-MM 4x2 Truck

The GAZ-MM (Molotov Modernization) was a militarised version of the original GAZ-AA, introduced into service in 1938. The vehicle was almost identical in appearance to the earlier GAZ-AA, but had a strengthened chassis, was fitted with an uprated GAZ-M engine developing 50hp, and featured a new cylindrical fuel cylindrical tank on the right side of the vehicle. The GAZ-MM was, like the GAZ-AA, used in large numbers by the Red Army. The wartime versions of the GAZ-MM, designated GAZ-MM-V (voenniy - military) had various levels of simplification, including the use of fabricated angular front mudguards, part wooden and even part canvas cabs.

### GAZ-AAA 6x4 Truck

The GAZ-AAA was developed as a 6x4 version of the GAZ-AA, which was series produced at GAZ from 1935 to 1943 and used by the Red Army in large numbers, primarily in specialised rather than general service versions. The Red Army had 3585 GAZ-AAA trucks in service on 1st January 1941, with 3150 delivered to the Red Army in the years 1941-43 before production ceased. Specialised variants, of which there were many, included the Tokarev designed 4M quadruple 7.62mm Maxim machine gun mounting and the SU-1-12 self propelled guns of which 51 were built on the GAZ-AAA chassis.

### ZiS-5, ZiS-5V, UlZiS-5V, UralZiS-5V 4x2 Truck

The ZiS-5 4x2 truck was developed at the AMO (ZiS) plant in Moscow based on the AMO-3 4x2 2.5 tonne truck (produced 1931-33), which was in turn based on the AMO-2, a locally produced version of the American Autocar SA truck design. The ZiS-5 was produced at ZiS from June 1933 until the ZiS plant was evacuated in the autumn of 1941, and during the war at Ulyanovsk (as the

UlZiS-5, produced 1942-44) and Miass (as the UralZiS-5, produced 1944-47). The ZiS-5 was powered by a 6 cylinder engine developing 73hp. It was the default heavy general service truck used by the Red Army during the 1941-45 war, later supplemented by Lend-Lease supplied vehicles. The ZiS-5 base model was simplified for wartime production with welded angular wheel fenders and wooden cabs as with the GAZ-MM-V. The wartime simplified production models are often designated ZiS-5V and UralZiS-5V. The Red Army had 59,829 ZiS-5 trucks in service on 1st January 1941, with a further 67,000 or so produced during the war years. In total, 571,199 ZiS-5 vehicles of all variants were manufactured, with many civilian vehicles being requisitioned during the war for military use.

## ZiS-12 4x2 Truck

The ZiS-12 was a specialised long wheelbase version of the ZiS-5 with a lowered cargo area modified for use with weapons such as the 25mm 94KM anti-aircraft gun system (produced 1934-40) and the 1.5 metre diameter, 650 million candle power Z-15-4B searchlight, built at the Moscow "Projector" plant, which had a range of approximately 10km. The vehicle was modified from the earlier AMO-4 which served a similar role. The ZiS-12 was produced at ZiS in Moscow from 1934-41. The ZiS-14, produced from 1936-41 looked near identical to the ZiS-12 but had larger wheels taken from the ZiS-16 bus.

## ZiS-6 6x4 Truck

The ZiS-6 was a 6x4 version of the 4x2 ZiS-5, produced at ZiS in Moscow from 26th June 1933 until the autumn of 1941. The 3 axle "4 tonne" (2.5 tonne all terrain) ZiS-6 was powered by a ZiS-5 engine developing 73hp, providing a maximum road speed of 38km/h. The vehicle was used as a general service cargo vehicle, for mounting special workshop bodies, as a fuel bowser and most famously for mounting the BM-13 "Katyusha" rocket system. The Red Army had 1673 ZiS-6 load carrier vehicles in service on 1st January 1941.

## Ya-5 4x2 Truck

The Ya-5 4x2 was the first Yaroslavl truck to be formally accepted into service with the Red Army. The 5 tonne capacity Ya-5 was powered by a 7.022 litre Hercules engine developing 93.5hp, giving a very reasonable road speed of 50km/h. The Ya-5 was used as a load carrier and for transporting the 122mm M-1910 howitzer mounted on the rear cargo body together with ammunition complement and crew. The vehicle was displayed on Red Square in 1931. A total of 2273 Ya-5 trucks were built.

## YaG-10 6x4 Truck

The 6x4 YaG-10 was used in small numbers by the Red Army. The only variant displayed on Red Square was an anti-aircraft version mounting the 76.2mm M-1931 (29K) in the rear cargo body, which had its parade debut on Red Square on 1st May 1934. Only 61 of these specialised YaG-10 based anti-aircraft vehicles were produced. The YaG-10 was produced in small numbers from 1931 to 1940.

## Bolshevik Artillery Tractor

The diminutive Bolshevik tracked artillery tractor was the first tracked artillery tractor to be adopted by the Red Army. It was displayed on Red Square during the 1920s towing medium artillery and AAGs. It was replaced at the very beginning of the 1930s by new generations of Soviet designed light and medium tracked tractors.

## Kommunar 3-90 Artillery Tractor

The Kommunar 3-90 universal tracked tractor was developed at the "Komintern" steam locomotive plant in Kharkov (KhPZ) and was in series production there from 1924-35. The tractor was powered by a petrol engine developing 90hp which gave the 4200kg towing capacity tractor a 12km/h maximum road speed. The Kommunar 3-90 was used by the Red Army for towing medium and heavy artillery. It was the earliest series production heavy artillery tractor to be adopted by the Red Army, with 1488 remaining in service with the Red Army on 1st January 1941.

ZiS-12

ZiS-6 BM-13

ZiS-6 Searchlight

YaG-10

Bolshevik

Stalinets-60 (S-60)

Stalinets-65 (S-65)

Pioner

T-20 Komsomolets

T-26T

### Stalinets-60 (S-60) Artillery Tractor

The Stalinets-60 (S-60) tracked tractor entered production at the Chelyabinsk Tractor Plant (ChTZ) on 1st June 1933. The S-60 was used for various agricultural and engineering applications, and in large quantity by the Red Army as an artillery tractor. The engine ran on kerosene and developed 60hp (hence S-60) which coupled with a 3F 1R gearbox gave the tractor the ability to tow any Soviet artillery piece up to a tow load of 5500kg at a sedate towing speed of 6-7km/h, with a range of 300km. The S-60 had an open cab with no weather protection and can be distinguished from the later S-65 by the prominent horizontal cylindrical fuel tank. The S-60 remained in production until 31st March 1937, with 69,100 being built in total. On 1st January 1941, the Red Army had 5559 S-60 artillery tractors in service, but was able to commandeer many more civil tractors after the outbreak of war.

### Stalinets-65 (S-65) Artillery Tractor

The Stalinets-65 (S-65) was a modernised version of the S-60, which replaced the earlier tractor in production at ChTZ from 1937, remaining in production until 1941 when the production capacity was released for additional tank output at ChTZ. The S-65 was powered by an M-17 diesel engine developing 65hp. Performance for the 42001kg tow capacity S-65 was similar to the S-60. The S-65 was used in large numbers by the Red Army throughout the Second World War, and towed heavy artillery such as the 203mm M-1931 B4 tracked howitzer at a sedate 3-7km/h across Europe to Berlin in 1945. A total of 10,630 S-65 tractors were in service with the Red Army on 1st January 1941; however commandeering of civil tractors added significantly to this total after 1941.

### Pioner Artillery Tractor

The Pioner was developed from 1935 at NATI under the direction of A.S. Sheglov as a light artillery tractor for towing light artillery such as the 45mm M-1932 anti-tank gun and 76.2mm M-1927 regimental gun. The Pioner was based on the mechanical components and running gear of the T-37A amphibious light tank. The first production batch of 50 Pioner tractors was built in 1936 at Plant №37 in Moscow, with the tractor making its Red Square parade debut on 7th November 1936. The lack of armour was problematical, and the Pioner was replaced in production by the armoured Komsomolets light artillery tractor.

### Komsomolets (T-20) Artillery Tractor

The Komsomolets armoured light artillery tractor was developed for towing light artillery such as the 45mm M-1932 anti-tank gun and 76.2mm regimental gun. It was a direct replacement for the limited series production Pioner, developed by N.A. Astrov at Plant №37 in Moscow under the plant index "020". Designed to tow 45mm anti-tank guns, mortars and other light artillery, the Komsomolets provided armoured 7-10mm armour protection for the vehicle crew, but the six man gun crew were seated on back to back seats and open to the elements. The vehicle was powered by a 4 cylinder GAZ-M engine coupled to a 3 speed automotive gearbox. The Komsomolets was manufactured at Plant №37 from 1937 until July 1941 when production ceased in favour of the T-60 light tank. A total of 7780 Komsomolets tractors were built, of which only 1662 remained in service on 1st September 1942. The T-20 Komsomolyets was a regular participant in Red Square parades in Moscow, and also in other cities from Kharkov to Khabarovsk.

### T-26T Artillery Tractor

The T-26T was a tracked artillery tractor derivative of the T-26 light tank. The majority (173 of the 183 built) had an unarmoured upper structure with a canvas tilt for weather protection, with a small number with fully enclosed armour being built which were paraded on Red Square. A single T-26T made its public debut on 7th November 1933, with the number increasing to six on parade by 1st May 1937. The T-26T was developed to tow light and medium wheeled artillery but was not accepted for full series production as the tank chassis was considered too valuable in all senses of the word to be used for such mundane secondary roles for which unarmoured tracked artillery tractors were available. Most of the tractors were built in 1933.

## Komintern Artillery Tractor

The Komintern tracked artillery tractor was developed at built at "Komintern" steam locomotive plant in Kharkov (KhPZ) based on the chassis and mechanicals of the limited series production T-24 tank. The Komintern, which entered production in 1934 and remained in production until 1940, was used for towing heavy artillery such as the 203mm B-4 tracked howitzer. The Komintern featured a central cab and rear cargo area that could accommodate the gun crew and ammunition complement. It had a towing capacity of 8800kg and a cargo load capacity of 2000kg of ammunition and gun crew. The 130hp petrol engined Komintern could provided a sustained towing speed of 15km/h when towing a tracked artillery piece, and a maximum speed of 30km/h unladen. On 1st January 1941 the Red Army had 1581 Komintern artillery tractors in service, with 1798 produced in total. Most were lost in the initial months of the "Great Patriotic War".

## Voroshilovets Artillery Tractor

The Voroshilovets tracked artillery tractor was also developed at KhPZ (Plant №183) from 1935 based on a combined GAU and GABTU requirement for a heavy artillery tractor capable of towing a 22 tonne load at a speed of at least 30km/h. The Voroshilovets was powered by a V-2V diesel engine derived from that later used in the T-34 medium tank, providing a 10,000kg towing capacity and a cargo load of 3000kg or 16 gun crew at up to 35km/h. The Voroshilovets was produced from late 1939 until September 1941. On 1st January 1941 the Red Army had 706 Voroshilovets artillery tractors in service.

## STZ-5 Artillery Tractor

The forward control cab STZ-5 was developed as a universal artillery tractor which could tow artillery to a maximum towed load of 2450kg, with a cargo capacity of 1500kg for ammunition and the gun crew. The STZ-5 was produced at the Stalingrad Tractor Plant (STZ) from 1937 to 1942, latterly alongside the T-34 medium tank. The STZ-5 was based on the STZ-3 agricultural tractor, but with a forward control cab and rear cargo area with stake body. It was powered by a four cylinder kerosene fuelled engine which gave the STZ-5 a maximum road speed of 32km/h. The Red Army had 4121 STZ-5 tractors in service on 1st May 1941. The STZ-5 was displayed on Red Square from 1937 to 1941.

## Ya-12 Artillery Tractor

The Ya-12 (Yaroslavl-12) artillery tractor was developed during World War Two and was initially expected to enter series production in April 1943; however production was delayed due to Luftwaffe bombing of the GAZ engine plant. Production commenced in August 1943, with 285 built in the first year of production. The Ya-12 was fitted with a GMC-4-71 diesel engine developing 110hp and providing a maximum 38km/h road speed; the externally near identical Ya-13 being fitted with the ZiS-5M engine developing 77hp and providing a maximum 20km/h road speed. The Ya-12 (Ya-13) had a towing capacity of 8000kg, with a cargo capacity of 2000kg for ammunition and the gun crew.

The Ya-12 participated in the 24th June 1945 Victory Parade on Red Square. Post-war it was replaced in production by the M2 artillery tractor, though the Ya-12 served with the Soviet Army into the 1950s.

## Allis-Chalmers HD-7W and HD-10W

The Lend-Lease Allis-Chalmers HD-7W, with an 8000kg towing capacity and the more powerful HD-10W, with a 14,000kg towing capacity, were used in Soviet parades in 1945, towing 152mm Br2 and 203mm B-4 tracked heavy artillery pieces. 2106 HD-7W and 413 HD-10W tracked artillery tractors were delivered to the Red Army in 1942-44.

Komitern

Komitern

Voroshilovets

Voroshilovets

Ya-12

# "Tekhnika" Paraded on Red Square 1917-45

The data tables below provide a guide to the parade debut and subsequent parade appearances of each type of tank, armoured car, transport vehicle and artillery piece or system displayed on Red Square. The guide is far from definitive and there are inevitable gaps in the available data, but the tables provide a general reference as to what was displayed on Red Square and when.

## 1918-1929

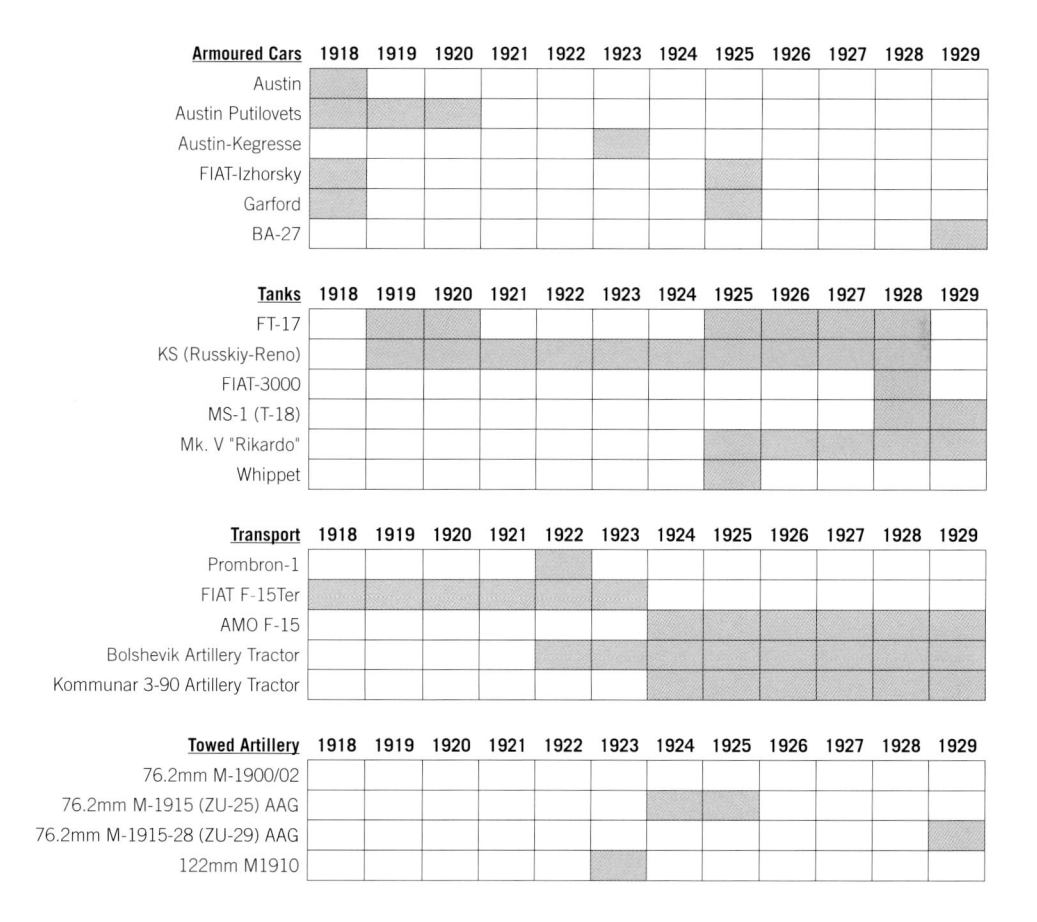

| Armoured Cars | 1918 | 1919 | 1920 | 1921 | 1922 | 1923 | 1924 | 1925 | 1926 | 1927 | 1928 | 1929 |
|---|---|---|---|---|---|---|---|---|---|---|---|---|
| Austin | ■ | | | | | | | | | | | |
| Austin Putilovets | ■ | ■ | ■ | | | | | | | | | |
| Austin-Kegresse | | | | | | ■ | | | | | | |
| FIAT-Izhorsky | ■ | | | | | | | ■ | | | | |
| Garford | ■ | ■ | | | | | | | | | | |
| BA-27 | | | | | | | | | | | ■ | |

| Tanks | 1918 | 1919 | 1920 | 1921 | 1922 | 1923 | 1924 | 1925 | 1926 | 1927 | 1928 | 1929 |
|---|---|---|---|---|---|---|---|---|---|---|---|---|
| FT-17 | | ■ | ■ | | | | | ■ | | | | |
| KS (Russkiy-Reno) | | ■ | ■ | ■ | ■ | ■ | ■ | ■ | ■ | ■ | ■ | ■ |
| FIAT-3000 | | | | | | | | | | | ■ | |
| MS-1 (T-18) | | | | | | | | | | | ■ | ■ |
| Mk. V "Rikardo" | | | | | | | ■ | ■ | ■ | ■ | ■ | ■ |
| Whippet | | | | | | | ■ | | | | | |

| Transport | 1918 | 1919 | 1920 | 1921 | 1922 | 1923 | 1924 | 1925 | 1926 | 1927 | 1928 | 1929 |
|---|---|---|---|---|---|---|---|---|---|---|---|---|
| Prombron-1 | | | | | ■ | | | | | | | |
| FIAT F-15Ter | ■ | ■ | ■ | ■ | ■ | ■ | | | | | | |
| AMO F-15 | | | | | | | ■ | ■ | ■ | ■ | ■ | ■ |
| Bolshevik Artillery Tractor | | | | | ■ | ■ | ■ | ■ | ■ | ■ | ■ | ■ |
| Kommunar 3-90 Artillery Tractor | | | | | | | ■ | ■ | ■ | ■ | ■ | ■ |

| Towed Artillery | 1918 | 1919 | 1920 | 1921 | 1922 | 1923 | 1924 | 1925 | 1926 | 1927 | 1928 | 1929 |
|---|---|---|---|---|---|---|---|---|---|---|---|---|
| 76.2mm M-1900/02 | | | | | | | | | | | | |
| 76.2mm M-1915 (ZU-25) AAG | | | | | | | | ■ | | | | |
| 76.2mm M-1915-28 (ZU-29) AAG | | | | | | | | | | | | ■ |
| 122mm M1910 | | | | | ■ | | | | | | | |

## 1930-1939

| Armoured Cars | 1930 | 1931 | 1932 | 1933 | 1934 | 1935 | 1936 | 1937 | 1938 | 1939 |
|---|---|---|---|---|---|---|---|---|---|---|
| BA-27 | ■ | ■ | ■ | | | | | | | |
| D-8 | | | | ■ | ■ | | | | | |
| D-12 | | | | ■ | ■ | | | | | |
| FAI | | | | | ■ | ■ | ■ | ■ | | |
| BA-I | | | ■ | ■ | ■ | | | | | |
| BA-3 | | | | | ■ | ■ | | | | |
| BA-6 | | | | | | ■ | ■ | ■ | ■ | |
| BA-10 | | | | | | | | | | |
| BAD-1 | | | | P | | | | | | |
| BAD-2 | | | | P | | | | | | |
| BA-20 | | | | | | | | ■ | ■ | ■ |
| BA-20M | | | | | | | | ■ | ■ | ■ |

| Tanks | 1930 | 1931 | 1932 | 1933 | 1934 | 1935 | 1936 | 1937 | 1938 | 1939 |
|---|---|---|---|---|---|---|---|---|---|---|
| Vickers Medium Mk. II | | | ■ | | | | | | | |
| T-18 (MS-1) | ■ | ■ | ■ | | | | | | | |
| T-26 M-1931 | | ■ | ■ | ■ | ■ | ■ | | | | |
| T-26 M-1932 | | | ■ | ■ | ■ | | | | | |
| T-26 M-1933 | | | | ■ | ■ | ■ | ■ | ■ | ■ | |
| T-26 M-1938 & M-1939 | | | | | | | | | | ■ |
| T-27 Tankette | | | ■ | ■ | | | | | | |
| PT-1 | | | | P | | | | | | |
| T-37A | | | | ■ | ■ | | | | | |
| T-41 | | | | P | | | | | | |
| T-38 | | | | | | | | | ■ | ■ |
| BT-2 | | ■ | ■ | ■ | ■ | | | | | |
| BT-5 | | | | ■ | ■ | ■ | ■ | | | |
| BT-7 M-1935 | | | | | | ■ | | | | |
| BT-7 M-1937 | | | | | | | | | ■ | ■ |
| BT-7 M-1939 (BT-7M) | | | | | | | | | | |
| T-28 1st Prototype (T-28-1) | | | | P | | | | | | |
| T-28 | | | | | ■ | ■ | ■ | ■ | ■ | ■ |
| T-35 1st Prototype (T-35-1) | | | | P | | | | | | |
| T-35 2nd Prototype (T-35-2) | | | | P | P | | | | | |
| T-35A | | | | | | ■ | ■ | ■ | | |
| T-35 Final | | | | | | | | | | |

| Transport | 1930 | 1931 | 1932 | 1933 | 1934 | 1935 | 1936 | 1937 | 1938 | 1939 |
|---|---|---|---|---|---|---|---|---|---|---|
| TIZ-AM-600 motorcycle | | | | | | | ■ | ■ | ■ | ■ |
| GAZ-A | | ■ | ■ | ■ | ■ | | | | | |
| AMO F-15 | ■ | ■ | | | | | | | | |
| AMO F-15 Searchlight | | ■ | | | | | | | | |
| AMO F-15 7.62mm PM-1910 AA | | | | | | | | | | |
| AMO-4 | | | ■ | ■ | ■ | ■ | | | | |
| AMO-4 w/searchlight | | | ■ | ■ | ■ | ■ | | | | |
| GAZ-AA | | | | | | | | | | |
| GAZ-AAA | | | | ■ | ■ | ■ | ■ | ■ | ■ | ■ |
| GAZ-AAA 4M | | | | ■ | ■ | ■ | ■ | ■ | ■ | ■ |
| GAZ-AAA SU-1-12 | | | | ■ | ■ | ■ | | | | |
| Autocar SA | | | | ■ | ■ | | | | | |

P - Prototype

# 1930-1939

| Transport (continued) | 1930 | 1931 | 1932 | 1933 | 1934 | 1935 | 1936 | 1937 | 1938 | 1939 |
|---|---|---|---|---|---|---|---|---|---|---|
| Moreland SU-12 | | | | ■ | ■ | | | | | |
| ZiS-5 | | | | ■ | | | | | | |
| ZiS-12 | | | | ■ | | | | | | |
| ZiS-12 w/Z-15-4 searchlight | | | | | | ■ | | | | |
| ZiS-12 (ZiS-14) w/25mm 94KM AAG | | | | | | | | | ■ | |
| ZiS-6 w/searchlight | | | | | | | | | ■ | |
| ZiS-6 w/ST sound locator | | | | | | | | | ■ | |
| Ya-4 (YaG-4) | ■ | | | | | | | | | |
| YaG-5 w/122mm M-10 | ■ | ■ | | | | | | | | |
| YaG-10 w/76.2mm M1931 (29K) AAG | | | | ■ | ■ | ■ | ■ | | | |
| Bolshevik w/76.2mm M-1915 (ZU-25) | ■ | | | | | | | | | |
| Kommunar w/76.2mm M-1915 | | | | | ■ | | | | | |
| Kommunar w/203mm B4 | | | | | | ■ | | | | |
| Komintern | | | | | | | ■ | ■ | ■ | ■ |
| Komintern with 76.2mm M-1915 | | | | | | | ■ | ■ | ■ | ■ |
| Komintern w/122mm M-1931 | | | | | | | | ■ | ■ | ■ |
| Komintern w/152mm Br-5 | | | | | | | | ■ | ■ | ■ |
| Pioner w/45mm ATG | | | | | | | | ■ | ■ | |
| Komsomolets with 45mm ATG | | | | | | | | | ■ | ■ |
| Komsomolets w/76.2mm M-1927 | | | | | ■ | ■ | ■ | ■ | ■ | ■ |
| T-26T | | | | | | | | | | |
| T-26T w/76.2mm M-1927 | | | | | | ■ | ■ | | | |

| Towed Artillery | 1930 | 1931 | 1932 | 1933 | 1934 | 1935 | 1936 | 1937 | 1938 | 1939 |
|---|---|---|---|---|---|---|---|---|---|---|
| 45mm M-1932/37 ATG | | | | | | | | ■ | ■ | ■ |
| 76.2mm M-1915/28 (ZU-29) AAG | ■ | | | | | | | | | |
| 76.2mm M-1936 (F-22) | | | | | | | ■ | ■ | | |
| 76.2mm M-1927 Infantry Gun | | | | ■ | ■ | ■ | ■ | | | |
| 122mm M-1910 | ■ | | | | | | | | | |
| 122mm M-1931 | | | | | | | | | | |
| 122mm M-1931/37 (A-19) | | | | | | | | ■ | ■ | ■ |
| 152mm M-1937 (ML-20) | | | | | | | | | | |
| 152mm Br-5 | | | | | | | ■ | | | |
| 203mm B-4 | | | | | ■ | ■ | ■ | ■ | ■ | ■ |
| 210mm Br-17 | | | | | | | | | | |
| 305mm Br-18 | | | | | | | | | | |

| Self Propelled Artillery | 1930 | 1931 | 1932 | 1933 | 1934 | 1935 | 1936 | 1937 | 1938 | 1939 |
|---|---|---|---|---|---|---|---|---|---|---|
| SU-1-12 (SU-12) | | | | ■ | ■ | ■ | ■ | | | |

# 1940-1945

| Armoured Cars | 1940 | 1941 | 1942 | 1943 | 1944 | 1945 |
|---|---|---|---|---|---|---|
| BA-20M | ■ | ■ | | | | |
| BA-10 | ■ | | | | | |
| BA-10A | ■ | | | | | |
| BA-64 | | | | | | ■ |

| Wheeled APC | 1940 | 1941 | 1942 | 1943 | 1944 | 1945 |
|---|---|---|---|---|---|---|
| M3A1 White | | | | | | ■ |

| Tanks | 1940 | 1941 | 1942 | 1943 | 1944 | 1945 |
|---|---|---|---|---|---|---|
| T-38 | ■ | | | | | |
| T-60 | | ■ | | | | |
| BT-7 M-1937 | ■ | | | | | |
| BT-7 M-1939 | ■ | ■ | | | | |
| T-28 M-1940 | ■ | | | | | |
| T-34 M-1941 | | ■ | | | | |
| T-34-85 | | | | | | ■ |
| OT-34-85 | | | | | | ■ |
| T-35A | ■ | ■ | | | | |
| T-35 conical turret | ■ | ■ | | | | |
| KV-1 (ChKZ M-1941) | | ■ | | | | |
| IS-2 | | | | | | ■ |
| IS-3 | | | | | | |

| SPG | 1940 | 1941 | 1942 | 1943 | 1944 | 1945 |
|---|---|---|---|---|---|---|
| SU-76 | | | | | | ■ |
| SU-100 | | | | | | ■ |
| ISU-122 | | | | | | ■ |
| ISU-122S | | | | | | ■ |
| ISU-152 | | | | | | ■ |

| Transport | 1940 | 1941 | 1942 | 1943 | 1944 | 1945 |
|---|---|---|---|---|---|---|
| AM-600 Motorcycle | ■ | | | | | |
| M-72 Motorcycle | | | | | | ■ |
| GAZ-67B | | | | | | |
| GAZ-AA (MM) | ■ | ■ | | | | ■ |
| GAZ-AA 4M AAMG | | ■ | | | | |
| GAZ-AA w/45mm M-1937 ATG | ■ | | | | | ■ |
| ZiS-5 | ■ | ■ | | | | ■ |
| ZiS-5V | | | | | | |
| ZiS-5 w/37mm M-1939 AAG | | | | | | |
| ZiS-5 w/85mm M-1939 AAG | | | | | | |
| ZiS-5V w/ 160mm M-1943 mortar | | | | | | ■ |
| ZiS-5V w/122mm M-1938 (M-30) | | | | | | ■ |
| UralZiS-5V | | | | | | |
| ZiS-12 w/25mm 94KM AAG | | | | | | |
| ZiS-12 w/ Searchlight | | ■ | | | | |
| GAZ-AAA | ■ | ■ | | | | |
| GAZ-AAA w/76.2mm ZiS-3 | | | | | | ■ |
| GAZ-AAA w/76.2mm F-22 | | ■ | | | | |
| GAZ-AAA w/76.2mm M-1927 | | ■ | | | | |

# 1940-1945

| Transport (continued) | 1940 | 1941 | 1942 | 1943 | 1944 | 1945 |
|---|---|---|---|---|---|---|
| ZiS-6 w/76.2mm F-39 | | ▓ | | | | |
| ZiS-6 with ZT Sound Locator | | | | | | ▓ |
| YaG-10 w/76.2mm M-1931 (29K) AAG | ▓ | ▓ | | | | |
| Dodge 3/4 Tonne | | | | | | ▓ |
| Studebaker US6 | | | | | | ▓ |
| Studebaker US6 w/100mm BS-3 ATG | | | | | | ▓ |
| Studebaker US6 w/85mm M-1939 AAG | | | | | | ▓ |
| T-20 Komsomolets | ▓ | | | | | |
| STZ-5 Tractor | ▓ | | | | | |
| Komintern w/152mm M-1937 | ▓ | | | | | |
| Voroshilovets w/122mm M-1931 (A-19) | | | | | | ▓ |
| Voroshilovets w/152mm Br-5 | | ▓ | | | | |
| Voroshilovets w/203mm B4 | | ▓ | | | | |
| Voroshilovets w/305mm Br-18 carriage & barrel | | | | | | ▓ |
| Ya-12 w/122mm M-1931 (A-19) | | | | | | ▓ |
| Ya-12 w/122mm M-1931/37 (A-19) | | | | | | ▓ |
| Ya-12 w/152mm M-1937 (ML-20) | | | | | | ▓ |
| Allis Chalmers HD-10W w/152mm Br-5 | | | | | | ▓ |
| Allis Chalmers HD-10W w/203mm B-4 | | | | | | ▓ |

| Towed Artillery | 1940 | 1941 | 1942 | 1943 | 1944 | 1945 |
|---|---|---|---|---|---|---|
| 25mm M-1940 (94KM) | | | | | | ▓ |
| 37mm M-1939 AAG | | | | | | ▓ |
| 57mm ZiS-2 | | | | | | ▓ |
| 76.2mm M-1900/02 | | ▓ | | | | |
| 76.2mm ZiS-3 | | | | | | ▓ |
| 76.2mm M-1939 (USV) | ▓ | | | | | |
| 76.2mm M-1915/28 AAG | | ▓ | | | | |
| 85mm M-1939 AAG | | | | | | ▓ |
| 100mm M-1944 | | | | | | ▓ |
| 122mm M-1938 (M-30) | | | | | | ▓ |
| 122mm M-1931/37 (A-19) | ▓ | | | | | |
| 152mm M-1910 | | | | | | ▓ |
| 152mm M-1937 (ML-20) | ▓ | | | | | ▓ |
| 152mm Br-2 | | | | | | ▓ |
| 160mm M-1943 mortar | | | | | | ▓ |
| 203mm B-4 | ▓ | ▓ | | | | ▓ |
| 305mm Br-18 (barrel and gun carriage sections) | | | | | | ▓ |
| BM-8-72 (Studebaker US6) | | | | | | ▓ |
| BM-13N (Studebaker US6) | | | | | | ▓ |
| BM-31 (Studebaker US6) | | | | | | ▓ |

| SPADS | 1940 | 1941 | 1942 | 1943 | 1944 | 1945 |
|---|---|---|---|---|---|---|
| 4M (GAZ-AA/AAA) | ▓ | ▓ | | | | |

# Bibliography

## Books

Voennye Parady Na Krasnoy Ploshadi. Multiple authors. Voennoye Izdatelstvo MoD USSR, Moscow 1980
Baryatinsky, Mikhail, Kolomiets, Maksim. Broneavtomobili Russkoy Armii 1906-1917. Tekhnika-Molodezhy, Moscow, 2000.
Baryatinsky, Mikhail. Parady Stali i Motorov. Zheleznodorozhnoe Delo, Moscow, 2003.
Baryatinsky, Mikhail. T-54 i T-55. Yauza, Eksmo, Moscow, 2015.
Baryatinsky, Mikhail. Tank XXI Veka. Yauza, Eksmo, Moscow, 2012.
Baryatinsky, Mikhail and Kinnear, Jim. The Russian T-28 Medium Tank. Barbarossa, Tiptree, Great Britain, 2000.
Baryatinsky, Mikhail. Tyazhely Tank IS. Yauza, Eksmo, Moscow, 2006.
Chubachin, Aleksander. SU-76. Yauza, BTV-Kniga, Moscow, 2009.
Chuprin, K.V. Vooruzhenye Sily Stran SNG i Baltii. Sovremennaya Shkola, Moscow, 2009.
Dashko, Dmitry. Transport Krasnoy Armii Velikoy Otechestvennoy Voiny. Avtomobilnogo Arkhivnogo Fonda, Moscow, 2015.
Drozdov, Georgy, Ryabko, Evgenny. Parad Pobedy. Planeta Publishing House, Moscow, 1985.
Dupouy, Alain. Les Dossiers Des Vehicules Sovietiques (multiple titles). Grenoble, France.
Evtifeev, M.D. Iz Istorii Sozdaniya Zenitno-Raketnogo Schita Rossii. Vyzovskaya Kniga, Moscow, 2000.
FM 30-40 Handbook on Soviet Ground Forces HQ Department of the (US) Army. 30.06.75.
Frankopan, Peter. The Silk Roads. Bloomsbury, London, 2015.
Kinnear, James. Russian Army on Parade. Tankograd. Erlangen, 2009.
Kirindas, Aleksander. Artilleriysky Tyagach "Komintern". Yauza, Moscow, 2017.
Kochnev, Evgeny. Avtomobili Krasnoy Armii 1918-1945. Yauza, Eksmo, Moscow, 2009.
Kochnev, Evgeny. Avtomobili Sovietskoy Armii 1946-1991. Yauza, Eksmo, Moscow, 2011.
Kochnev, Evgeny. Avtomobili Velikoy Otechestvennoy. Yauza, Eksmo, Moscow, 2010.
Kochnev, Evgeny. Entsiklopedia Voennykh Avtomobiley 1769-2006. Za Roulem, Moscow, 2008.
Kochnev, Evgeny. Sekretnye Avtomobili Sovietskoy Armii. Voina Motorov, Yauza, Moscow, 2011.
Kolomiets, Maksim and Kinnear, Jim. The Russian T-35 Heavy Tank. Barbarossa, Tiptree, Great Britain. 2000.
Kolomiets, Maksim. Bronya Na Kolesakh. Yauza, Eksmo, Moscow, 2007.
Kolomiets, Maksim. Legkye Tanki BT. Yauza, Eksmo, Moscow, 2007.
Kolomiets, Maksim, Moshchansky, Ilya. Mnogobashennye Tanki RKKA. Frontovaya Illustratsiya, Moscow, 1999.
Kolomiets, Maksim. Russkie Broneviki v Boyu. Yauza, Eksmo, Moscow, 2013.
Kolomiets, Maksim. Sredny Tank T-28. Yauza, Eksmo, Moscow, 2007.
Kolomiets, Maksim. Sukhoputnye Linkory Stalina. Yauza, Eksmo, Moscow, 2009.
Kolomiets, Maksim. T-35 "Sukhoputnye Linkory" Stalina. Yauza, Eksmo, Moscow, 2014.
Kolomiets, Maksim, Fedoseev, Semeon. Tank №1 Reno-FT. Yauza, Eksmo, Moscow, 2010.
Kolomiets, Maksim. Legkye Tanki BT. Yauza, Eksmo, Moscow, 2007.
Kostenko, Yury P. Nekotorye Voprosy Razvitiya Otechestvennoy Bronetekhniki v 1967-1987. Uniar-Print, Moscow, 2000
Luzhkov, Yury (Head of Council). Parad Paradov. Atlantida - XXI Vek, Moskovskie Uchebniki, Moscow, 2000.
Milsom, John. Russian Tanks 1900-1970, Arms & Armour Press, London, 1970.
Shirkorad, Aleksander V. Atomny Schit Rossii. OOO Veche, Moscow, 2017.
Shirkorad, Aleksander V. Entsiklopediya Otechestvennoi Artillerii. Harvest, Minsk, 2000.
Shunkov, Viktor N. Polnaya Entsiklopedia Sovremennogo Vooruzheniya Rossii. AST. Moscow, 2017.
Shunkov, V.N. Polnaya Entsiklopediya Vooruzheniy SSSR 1939-45. Harvest, Minsk, 2010.
Simakov, V.G. Sovremennoye Voennoye Oruzhie Rossii. Eksmo. Moscow, 2014.

Soviet Military Power (US DoD). Various years and editions.
Suvorov, Sergey. Russky Tigr. Yauza, Eksmo, Moscow, 2016.
Svirin, Mikhail. Samokhodki Stalina. Yauza, Eksmo, Moscow, 2008.
Svirin, Mikhail. Stalnoy Kulak Stalina. Yauza, Eksmo, Moscow, 2006.
Voennye Parady Na Krasnoy Ploshadi. Multiple authors. Voennoye Izdatelstvo Soviet MoD Moscow 1980.
Zheleznyakov, Aleksander. 100 Luchshikh Raket SSSR & Rossii. Yauza. Moscow, 2016.
Pavlov, I.V, Pavlov, M.V, Solyankin, A.G, Zheltov, I. G. Otechestvennye Bronirovannye Mashiny XX Vek. Volume 1 1905-1941. Eksprint, Moscow, 2002.
Pavlov, I.V, Pavlov, M.V, Solyankin, A.G, Zheltov, I. G. Otechestvenniye Bronirovannye Mashiny XX Vek. Volume 2 1941-1945. Eksprint, Moscow, 2005.

## Soviet & Russian Television and Newsreel Sources

RIA Novosti
RT (Russia Today)
Moskovskoye VOKU imeni Verkhovnogo Soveta RSFSR - Uchilis-che Na Parade - parade documentaries, various years
Zvezda (Telekanal Zvedza)

## Digital Sources

Istoriya Voennykh Paradov na Krasnoy Ploshadi. Krilya Rossii Moscow 2013
Parad na Krasnoy Ploshchadi 1941-45 (DVD) Voenkino Rossii, Moscow, 2003

## Websites

Club.foto.ru
Defence.ru
Kolesa.ru
Kommersant.ru
Oruzhie.ru
Photosight.ru

Coldwar.org
Gruzovikpress.ru
Kollektsiya.ru
Lifeisphoto.ru
News.rambler.ru
Sputnik.by

## Journals, Magazines, Newspapers

Aerokosmichesky Vestnik
Armies & Weapons
Bastion
Frontovaya Illustratsiya
Izvestia
Jane's Defence Weekly
Jane's Soviet Intelligence Review
Joint Services Recognition Journal (UK MoD)
Kommersant
Military History Monthly
Moskovsky Komsomolets
Nauka i Tekhnika
Nevsky Bastion
Ogonyok
Oruzhie
Poligon
Soviet Military Review
Tekhnika-Molodezhi
Tekhnika i Vooruzhenie
Voenny Parad
WPT (Poland)

## Photographic Archives

| | |
|---|---|
| RGAEh (РГАЭ) | Russian State Economic Archives |
| RGAKFD (РГАКФД) | Russian State Archive of Cinematic-Photographic Documents |
| RGASPI (РГАСПИ) | Russian State Archive of Social-Political History |
| TsAMO RF (ЦАМО РФ) | Central Archives of the Ministry of Defence of the Russian Federation |

## Glossary (Russian Terms)

| | |
|---|---|
| ABTU (АБТУ) | Avtobronetankovoye Upravlenie (Auto-Tank Directorate) |
| AMO (АМО) | Avtomobilnoye Moskovskoye Obshchestvo - Moscow Automobile Society - later ZiS, ZiL |
| ANIOP (АНИОП) | ANIOP Artillery Proving Grounds (Gorokhovets) |
| ArtKom (АртКом ГАУ КА) | Artillery Committee Main Artillery Directorate of the Red Army |
| BMD (БМД) | Boevaya Mashina Desanta - Airborne Combat Vehicle |
| BMP (БМП) | Boevaya Mashina Pekhoty - Infantry combat vehicle |
| BRDM (БРДМ) | Bronirovannaya Razvedyvatelnaya Mashina - Armoured Reconnaissance Vehicle |
| BTR (БТР) | Bronetransporter - Armoured Personnel Carrier |
| ChTZ (ЧТЗ) | Chelyabinsky Tractorny Zavod (Chelyabinsk Tractor - and from 1941-1958 Tank - Plant) |
| GABTU KA (ГАБТУ КА) | Glavnoye AvtoBronetankovoye Upravlenye KA - Main Auto-Tank Directorate of the Red Army. From 7th December 1942 renamed GBTU KA (ГБТУ КА) |
| GBTU KA (ГБТУ КА) | Glavnoye Bronetankovoye Upravlenye KA - Main Armoured Directorate of the Red Army. |
| GAU (ГАУ) | Glavnoye Artilleriiskoye Upravleniye - Main Artillery Directorate |
| GAZ (ГАЗ) | Gorky Avtomobilny Zavod - GAZ plant (named after Molotov) |
| GKO (ГКО) | Gosudarstnenny Komitet Oborony - State Defence Committee of the USSR |
| GRAU (ГРАУ) | Glavnoye Raketno-Artilleriyskoye Upravleniye - Main Rocket-Artillery Directorate |
| GRU (ГРУ) | Glavnoye Razvedovatelnoye Upravleniye - Main Reconnaissance Directorate |
| GVKhU (ГВХУ КА) | Glavnoe Voenno-Khimicheskoe Upravleniye Krasnoi Armii - Main Military - Chemical Forces Directorate (of the Red Army) |
| KA (КА) | Krasnaya Armya - Red Army (also known as RKKA) |
| KB (КБ) | Konstruktorskoye Bureau - Design Bureau |
| KhPZ (ХПЗ) | Kharkovsky Paravozstroitelny Zavod (Kharkov Steam Locomotive Plant) - Later Plant №183 |
| LKZ (ЛКЗ) | Leningradsky Kirovsky Zavod (Leningrad Kirov plant) |
| LVO (ЛВО) | Leningradsky Voenny Okrug (Leningrad Military District) |
| MO (МО) | Ministerstvo-Oborony - Soviet (latterly Russian) Defence Ministry |
| MBR (МБР) | Mezhkontinentalnaya Ballisticheskaya Raketa (ICBM) |
| MVD (МВД) | Ministerstvo Vnutrennikh Del - Ministry of Internal Affairs (1946-) |
| MVO (МВО) | Moskovsky Voenny Okrug - Moscow Military District |
| NATI (НАТИ) | Nauchny Avto-Traktorny Institut (Scientific Auto-Tractor Institute) |
| NIBT (НИБТ) | Nauchno-Ispytatelny Bronetankovy (Scientific Tank Testing Institute). Kubinka, near Moscow. Evacuated to Kazan in autumn 1941, relocated back to Kubinka in the autumn-winter of 1942. |
| NKAP (НКАП) | Narkomat Aviatsionnoy Promyshlennosti - Minsitry of Aviation Industry |
| NKO (НКО) | Narodny Kommisariat Oborony - State Defence Committee (Narkomat as person - Kommissar) |
| NKO (НКО) | Narkomat Oborony (Soviet/Russian Ministry of Defence) |
| NKV (НКВ) | Narodny Kommisariat Voorzheniya - People's Kommissariat of Armaments |
| NKVD (НКВД) | Narodny Kommissariat Vnutrennikh Del (People's Commissariat for Internal Affairs) 1934-46 |
| OGPU (ОГПУ) | Obiedenennoye Gosudarstvennoye Politicheskoye Upravlenye (United State Political Directorate) |
| OKB (ОКБ) | Otdelnoye Konstruktorskoye Bureau - Independent Design Bureau |
| OTR (ОТР) | Operativno Takticheskaya Raketa (tactical rocket) |
| OTRK (ОТРК) | Operativno-Takticheskiy Raketny Kompleks (Ground-Ground Tactical Rocket) |
| PU (РУ) | Puskovoya Ustanovka (launch vehicle) |
| PVO (ПВО) | Protivovozdushnaya Oborona - Air Defence |
| RGK (РГК) | Reserv Glavnogo Komandovaniya (high command reserve) |

| | |
|---|---|
| RKKA (РККА) | Raboche-Krestyanskaya Krasnaya Armiya Workers and Peasants Red Army (Red Army) |
| RKKVF (РККВФ) | Raboche-Krestyansky Krasny Vozdushny Flot (Workers and Peasants Red Air Fleet) |
| RPU (РПУ) | Reaktivnaya Puskovaya Ustanovka (rocket launcher system) |
| RSFSR (РСФСР) | Russian Soviet Federative Socialist Republic (RSFSR) |
| RSZO (РСЗО) | Reaktivnaya Systema Zalpovnogo Ognya - Multiple Rocket Launcher System |
| RVGK (РВГК) | Reserv Verkhovnogo Glavnogo Komandovaniya (Supreme High Command Reserve) |
| RVS (РВС) | Revvoensovet - Revolutsionny Voenny Soviet (Revolutionary Military Council) - formed 1918 |
| RVSN (РВСН) | Raketnye Voyska Strategicheskogo Naznacheniya - Strategic Rocket Forces |
| RYaN (РЯН) | Raketno Yadernoye Napadeniye - Nuclear Rocket Attack |
| SAU (САУ) | Samokhodnaya Artilleryskaya Ustanovka - Self Propelled Artillery Unit (SAU or SU) |
| SKB (СКБ) | Spetsialnoye Konstruktorskoe Bureau - Special Design Bureau |
| SM SSSR (СМ СССР) | Soviet Ministrov SSSR - Council of Ministers of the USSR |
| SNK (СНК СССР) | Soviet Narodnykh Kommissarov - Council of People's Commissars |
| SPU (СПУ) | Samokhodnaya Puskovaya Ustanovka (Self Propelled Launch Vehicle) |
| SSR (ССР) | Soviet Socialist Republic |
| STZ (СТЗ) | Stalingradsky Traktorny Zavod - Stalingrad Tractor Plant (later VTZ, VgTZ) |
| TsAGI (ЦАГИ) | Tsentralny Aerogidrodinamichesky Institut - Central Aerodynamic Institute (TsAGI) |
| TsAMO RF (ЦАМО РФ) | Tsentralny Arkhiv Ministerstva Oborony Rossiskoy Federatsii - Central Archives of the Ministry of Defence of the Russian Federation |
| TsIK (ЦIК) | Tsentrany Ispolnitelny Komitet - Central Executive Committee (of the USSR) |
| TsK KPSS i SM SSSR | Central Committee of the Communist Party and Council of Ministers of the Soviet Union |
| TsVKP(b) (ЦК ВКП(б) | Central Committee of the CPSU(b) - Communist Party (Bolshevik) of the USSR |
| TBr (ТБр) | Tankovaya Brigada - Tank Brigade |
| TIZ (ТIЗ) | Taganrog Instrumentalny Zavod (TIZ AM-600 motorcycle) |
| TOS (ТОС) | Tyazhelaya Ognemetnaya Systema - heavy flamethrower system |
| TPK (ТПК) | Transportno-Puskovoy Konteyner (Transport-Launch Container) |
| TTT (ТТТ) | Taktiko-Tekhnicheskye Trebovaniya - Tactical Technical Requirements |
| TU (ТУ) | Transportno-Ustanovochny Agregat - Transporter-Installation Vehicle |
| TZM (ТЗМ) | Transportno-Zaryazhayuschaya Mashina (transport-reload vehicle) |
| UMM RKKA (УММ РККА) | Upravleniye Mekhanizatsii i Motorizatsii - Mechanisation and Motorisation Directorate of the Red Army |
| VAMM (ВАММ) | Voennaya Akademya Mekhanizatsii i Motorizatsii (Military Academy of Mechanisation and Motorisation) |
| VgTZ (ВгТЗ) | Volgograd (Stalingrad) Tractor Plant - formerly STZ |
| Voenizdat | State Military Publisher NKO SSSR |
| VDV (ВДВ) | Vozdushno Desantnye Voiska - Airborne Forces |
| VKP (b) (ВКП(б)) | The Communist Party of the Soviet Union (Bolshevik) |
| VKS (ВКС) | Vozdushno-Kosmicheskye Sily - Air Space Forces (formed 01.08.15) |
| VMF (ВМФ) | Voenno-Morskoy Flot (Soviet Navy) |
| VMS (ВМС) | Voenno-Morskye Sily - Naval Forces (Soviet Navy) |
| VTZ (ВТЗ) | Volgograd Tractor Plant (later VgTZ) |
| VVS KA (ВВС КА) | Voenno-Vozdushnye Sily Krasnoy Armii - Red Army Air Force |
| ZRK (ЗРК) | Zenitno-Raketny Kompleks - Air Defence Rocket Complex |
| ZRPK (ЗРПК) | Zenitno-Raketno-Pushechny Kompleks - Air Defence Rocket-Gun Complex |
| ZRS (ЗРС) | Zenitno-Raketnaya Systema - Air Defence Rocket System |
| ZSU (ЗСУ) | Zenitnaya Samokhodnaya Ustanovka - Self Propelled Ant-Aircraft Gun |

## General Glossary

| | |
|---|---|
| AAG | Anti-Aircraft Gun |
| AAMG | Anti-Aircraft Machine Gun |
| APFSDS | Armour Piercing Fin Stabilised Discarding Sabot |
| ATGM | Anti-Tank Guided Missile |
| CEP | Circular Error Probability (rocket accuracy) |
| DEFCON | Defence of the Continent (U.S. Government Alert status) |
| GS | General Service |
| ICBM | Inter-Continental Ballistic Missile |
| MoD | Ministry of Defence |
| MRS | Multiple Rocket System |
| MRBM | Medium Range Ballistic Missile |
| MRD | Motorised Rifle Division |
| MRS | Multiple Rocket System |
| NBC | Nuclear, Biological, Chemical warfare |
| RAP | Rocket Assisted Projectile |
| SAM | Surface to Air Missile System |
| SPAAG | Self Propelled Anti-Aircraft Gun |
| SPADS | Self Propelled Air Defence System |
| SPG | Self Propelled Gun |
| SPH | Self Propelled Howitzer |
| SRBM | Short Range Ballistic Missile |
| SSM | Surface to Surface Missile |
| TEL | Transporter Erector Launcher |

## Soviet Ministries

Soviet ministries were abbreviated to NK (Narodny Kommissariat - People's Commissariat) followed by the responsibility, e.g. NKV (Vooruzhenie - armaments), NKSM (Srednie Mashinostroeniye - medium machine building (actually tank production)) etc. The minister was known as the Narkom (Kommissar). Commissariat can be interpreted as Ministry, and Commissar as Minister

| | |
|---|---|
| NKAP | People's Commissariat of Aviation Industry |
| NKGK | People's Commissariat of State Control |
| NKO | People's Commissariat of Defence |
| NKS | People's Commissariat of Machine Tool Building |
| NKSM | People's Commissariat of Medium Machine Building |
| NKSP | People's Commissariat of Steel Production |
| NKTM | People's Commissariat of Heavy Engineering |
| NKTP | People's Commissariat of Heavy Production |
| NKTP | People's Commissariat of Tank Production |
| NKV | People's Commissariat of Armaments |
| NKVD | People's Commissariat of Internal Affairs |

## Soviet Ministries - As written in the original Russian:

НКАП Наркомат Авиационной промышленности - People's Commissariat of Aviation Industry - NKAP
НКГК Народный Комиссариат Государственного Контроля - People's Commissariat of State Control - NKGK
НКС Народный Комиссариат Станкостроения - People's Commissariat of Machine Tool Building - NKS
НКСМ Наркомат Среднего Машиностроения - People's Commissariat of Medium Machine Building - NKSM
НКТП Народный Комиссариат Танковой Промышленности - People's Commissariat of Tank Industry - NKTP
НКВ Народный Комиссариат Вооружения - People's Commissariat of Armaments - NKV
НКТМ Наркомат Тяжелого Машиностроения - People's Commissariat of Heavy Machine Building - NKTM
Наркомат (Ministry...)
Народный (People's....)

## Russian Terms (in original language)

| | |
|---|---|
| АБТУ | Автобронетанковое управление (Auto and Armour Directorate) |
| АНИОП | Артиллерийский научно-исследовательский опытный полигон - Artillery Scientific Experimental Test Range |
| БТР | Бронетранспортер (armoured personnel carrier) |
| БТУ | Bronetankovoe Upravlenie - Tank Directorate |
| ГАБТУ | Главное автобронетанковое управление (Main Armoured Directorate) |
| ГАУ | Главное артиллерийское управление (Main Artillery Directorate) |
| ГКО | Государственный Комитет Обороны (State Defence Committee) |
| ГКОТ | Государственный комитет по оборонной технике (State Committee for Defence Equipment) |
| ГРАУ | Главное ракетно-артиллерийское управление (Main Rocket-Artillery Directorate) |
| ЗСУ | Зенитная самоходная установка (Self Propelled Anti-Aircraft System) |
| КА | Красная Армия, Краснознаменная армия (Red Army) |
| КБМ | Конструкторское бюро машиностроения (Machine Building Design Bureau) |
| ЛВО | Ленинградский военный округ (Leningrad Military District - LVO) |
| МВО | Московский военный округ (Moscow Military District - MVO) |
| МИТ | Московский институт теплотехники (Moscow Institute of Heating Technology) (i.e. rockets) |
| МО | Министерство обороны (Ministry of Defence) |
| НКВД | Народный комиссариат внутренних дел (NKVD and other internal security forces) |
| НКО | Народный комиссариат Обороны (State Defence Committee) |
| ПВО | Противовоздушная оборона (Air Defence Forces) |
| ПТУР | Противотанковая управляемая ракета (Anti-Tank Guided Rocket) |
| ПУ | Пусковая установка (Launch System) |
| РГК | Резерв Главного Командования (Main Command Reserve) |
| РВГК | Резерв Верховного Главного Командования (Main Higher Command Reserve) |
| РВСН | Ракетные войска стратегического назначения (Strategic Rocket Forces) |
| RKKA | Рабоче-крестьянская Красная Армия (Workers and Peasants Red Army) |
| РККВФ | Рабоче-крестьянский красный воздушный флот) (Workers & Peasants Red Air Fleet) |
| РСЗО | Реактивная система залпового огня (Reactive Rocket System - MRS) |
| САУ | Самоходная артиллерийская установка (Self Propelled Artillery Unit) |
| СВГК | Ставка Верховного Главного Командования (High Command) |
| СКБ | Специальное конструкторское бюро (Special Design Bureau) |
| СПУ | Самоходная пусковая установка (Self Propelled Launch System) |
| СТЗ | Сталинградский тракторный завод (Stalingrad Tractor Plant) |
| ТЗМ | Транспортно-заряжающая машина (Transport-Reload Vehicle) |
| ТТТ | Тактико-технические требования (Tactical Technical Requirements) |
| ТТХ | Тактико-технические характеристики (Tactical Technical Characteristics) |
| УММ | Управление механизации и моторизации РККА (Mechanisation and Motorisation Directorate |
| УТТХ | Улучшенные тактико-технические характеристики (Improved Tactical-Technical Characteristics) |

# Acknowledgements

The author would like to thank Andrey Aksenov, Mikhail Baryatinsky, Aleksandr Koshavtsev, Viktor Kulikov, Vladimir Nikitin, Yuri Pasholok, Nikolai Polikarpov, Sergei Popsuevich, Mikhail Svirin, Steven J. Zaloga and Igor Zheltov for their assistance in compiling the material used in this book, and for the myriad corrections made relating to the Soviet and modern designations. The material was collected over a period of many years, and as is always the case with such publications, the enthusiasm of individuals willing to help is remembered long after the material has been located or the obscure question answered. The photographic material collected for these volumes has also led to many friendships along the way that have proven to be enduring. In particular the author would like to pay his respects to the tank historian Mikhail Svirin, who sadly died recently. Many years ago, Mikhail insisted that he and Mikhail Kolomiets escort me to my apartment entrance through the streets of his home city of Moscow rather than letting a foreigner find his own way home late at night - a typical act of kindness that epitomises the Russian soul. The author would also like to thank the Russian Ministry of Defence for assisting with photographic material, which has made the book series far more complete than it could otherwise have possibly been. My thanks also go to the Kremlin Commandant Service and the Federal Security Service (FSB) that were also more helpful than could have ever been imagined in arranging my personal attendance at recent Red Square parades - a very different experience to watching the Soviet era parades on television so many years ago.

The author is indebted to the patience and assistance of his family with regard to his esoteric interests, in particular Elizabeth for her proof reading and editing assistance. It is a mark of the passage of time touched with pride when a daughter, having been taught to spell and play chess by her father, then surpasses the grumpy old one rather too easily in both.

### Note on Russian State Archive records

The historical context for this book has been taken entirely from original Soviet and current Russian documentation. Photographs have also come primarily from Soviet era sources, private collections and the author's own photograph archives taken at some of the post-Soviet era parades. There are some conflations in information between some Soviet era and Russian modern sources, in particular relating to the hierarchy present at parades rather than the vehicles and weapons displayed.

Similarly, the dates indicated in captions are where known as quoted in the original archive records; however these original records are not always entirely accurate as to the date, or location. In some cases photographs were archived years after they were taken (as indicated in the archive notes) and as a result the exact year given for a particular event is on occasion out of sequence by a year or so. In some cases the date of the archive being raised is conflated with the date the photograph was taken. Many original data cards were also removed from the archives during the 1990s and the original text accompanying negative archives lost.

Some regional city locations are conflated in original archive material. Some archive records for-instance locate armoured vehicles as being in Khabarovsk, when they are clearly in Minsk, as that city has a particularly austere and distinctive government building complex which forms the background to many period parade photographs, which can be verified today.

Where sufficient other material has not been available to absolutely identify the location, or exact date, the most logical has been quoted. Some mistakes are inevitable considering the primary source material, for which the author bears entire responsibility.

## About the Author

James Kinnear was born in Aberdeen in Great Britain in 1959 and graduated from Aberdeen University with an MA (Hons) in History in 1982. He has researched the topic of Soviet and Russian military hardware since his first visit to the enigmatic and mysterious Soviet Union as a young teenager in 1973. James subsequently lived and worked in the post-Soviet Russian Federation and the other states of the former Soviet Union throughout the entire period of post-Soviet "stability" - the decades between the Soviet Union being considered a military threat and the Russian Federation finding itself again categorised as such for political purposes in recent history.

James has written hundreds of articles on Soviet and Russian military technology after having taken a more long-term interest than most in the subject matter of the blurry British and American sourced images of Soviet military equipment used for training purposes during British military service.

This series of books on Russian, Soviet, and now again Russian military parades on Moscow's Red Square is the culmination of many years of collecting material on a subject which, despite it being a primary source for foreign intelligence, and a relatively public one at that, has never been covered in depth as a dedicated subject either in the Russian Federation or abroad.

It is hoped that the reader will find the content both an interesting and enlightening window on what is not only the 100 year anniversary of military parades being held on Moscow's Red Square; but is also by association a window on 100 years of the military history of a state which always had at its centre what is today the Russian Federation.

James has published books on Soviet military technology with Barbarossa, Canfora, Darlington, Osprey and Tankograd. He is also a formal contributor to IHS Jane's defence yearbooks.

*"Those who cannot remember the past are condemned to repeat it."*

Spanish Philosopher George Santayana (Jorge Agustín Nicolás Ruiz de Santayana y Borrás) 1905*

* Quote often misattributed to Winston Churchill